FOUR
VIEWS
ON
HELL

Books in the Counterpoints Series

Church Life

Bible and Theology

FOUR
VIEWS
ON **HELL**

SECOND EDITION

Denny Burk

John G. Stackhouse Jr.

Robin A. Parry

Jerry L. Walls

Preston Sprinkle, general editor
Stanley N. Gundry, series editor

ZONDERVAN

Four Views on Hell
Copyright © 2016 by Preston Sprinkle, Denny Burk, John Stackhouse Jr., Robin Perry, and Jerry Walls

This title is also available as a Zondervan ebook. Visit www.zondervan.com/ebooks.

Requests for information should be addressed to:
Zondervan, 3900 Sparks Drive SE, Grand Rapids, Michigan 49546

Library of Congress Cataloging-in-Publication Data

    Four views on hell / Denny Burk, John G. Stackhouse Jr., Robin A. Parry, Jerry
L. Walls; Preston M. Sprinkle, general editor. — Second Edition.
       p. cm.
    Includes bibliographical references and index.
    ISBN 978-0-310-51646-0 (softcover)
    1. Hell—Christianity. I. Sprinkle, Preston M., 1976—editor.
BT836.3.F68 2016   2015030118

Cover design: Tammy Johnson
Cover photography: 2happy/Masterfile
Interior design: Matthew Van Zomeren

Printed in the United States of America

HB 05.21.2024

CONTENTS

BIBLE VERSIONS

All Scripture quotations in the first essay, unless otherwise indicated, are taken from *New American Standard Bible®*. Copyright © 1960, 1962, 1963, 1968, 1971, 1972, 1973, 1975, 1977, 1995 by The Lockman Foundation. Used by permission. (www.Lockman.org).

All Scripture quotations in the second essay, unless otherwise indicated, are taken from *New Revised Standard Version Bible®*. Copyright © 1989 National Council of the Churches of Christ in the United States of America. Used by permission. All rights reserved.

All Scripture quotations in the third and fourth essays, unless otherwise indicated, are taken from The Holy Bible, New International Version®, NIV®. Copyright © 1973, 1978, 1984, 2011 by Biblica, Inc.® Used by permission of Zondervan. All rights reserved worldwide. www.Zondervan.com. The "NIV" and "New International Version" are trademarks registered in the United States Patent and Trademark office by Biblica, Inc.®

Scripture quotations marked ESV® Bible (The Holy Bible, English Standard Version®). Copyright © 2001 by Crossway, a publishing ministry of Good News Publishers. Used by permission. All rights reserved.

INTRODUCTION

PRESTON M. SPRINKLE

The doctrine of hell has always been part of Christian theology. Unfortunately, hell has had a bit of a checkered past. From the *Apocalypse of Peter's* gruesome depictions of women hanging over boiling mire, to skin curling images of hell in Dante's *Inferno*, to Jonathan Edwards's blistering sermon *Sinners in the Hands of an Angry God*, to twentieth-century Bible-belt preachers barking with anger about the wrath to come, hell has been used—and some would say abused—to scare people into obedience or increase their tithe.

Now, however, Christians are more than ever questioning a traditional view of hell. In the last one hundred years, towering Christian thinkers have described hell in nontraditional terms. Theologians and writers such as Karl Barth, C. S. Lewis, John Stott, and N. T. Wright all believe in hell, but their depictions don't match what many Christians have believed. More recently, the discussion has intensified as an increasing number of proponents of both traditional and nontraditional views of hell have looked to the Scriptures as the basis for their views.

This new Counterpoints book contributes to this rapidly growing debate about the nature of hell. It serves to replace the previous edition of the Counterpoints book on hell, which was published in 1996. This new volume brings in a new set of authors who will espouse fresh insights that build on the flurry of recent books and discussions about the nature of hell.

At the time the previous Counterpoints book came out, the famed evangelical leader John Stott had published his leanings toward annihilation.[1] Evangelicalism as a whole was perplexed and unpersuaded. I remember hearing about Stott's shift and thinking, "I thought John Stott was a Christian!" There's nothing in the Bible or the early church creeds that view annihilation as unchristian and heretical. Yet this was a

---

1. John Stott and David Edwards, *Evangelical Essentials: A Liberal-Evangelical Dialogue* (Downers Grove, IL: Intervarsity Press, 1989).

9

common knee-jerk reaction people had—and some still have—toward anyone who doesn't believe that hell consists of everlasting conscious torment. But things are different today. Evangelicals are reexamining some cherished doctrines, and the nature of hell is on the table.

There have been three main developments over the last twenty years that have cultivated a need for this new Counterpoints book.

First, the annihilation view of hell has grown in popularity among evangelicals. Many theologians, pastors, and Christian laypeople today are leaning toward or embracing an annihilation view of hell. In the past, it was primarily those who couldn't stomach the traditional view who opted for this "softer" view of God's judgment. But now many evangelicals are arriving at this view in light of a fresh look at the biblical text.

Second, Christian universalism is gaining ground as well. While some proponents of universalism—the belief that everyone will eventually be rescued out of hell—base their view on sentimentality, others are digging it out of the biblical narrative. As you will see in the following pages, there are some powerful biblical arguments that Christians need to wrestle with. No longer can evangelicals scoff at this view as the byproduct of too many hours of Oprah.

Third, an ecumenical spirit is growing among evangelicals. Some Protestants and Catholics have always been able to dialogue, but that number is on the rise, especially among younger believers who find it much harder to write off the faith of their Catholic brothers and sisters. This desire to dialogue has cultivated theological cross-pollination. With regard to hell and the afterlife, Protestants are exploring views that are traditionally considered Catholic, and vice-versa. Purgatory, as we will see in this book, is becoming a theological option among evangelicals, and it needs to be evaluated based on its exegetical and theological strength. It can't be dismissed as being simply un-Protestant (or unchristian).

As history has shown, doctrines often become stronger when they are tested. The last twenty years have witnessed many robust defenses of the traditional view of hell in response to these three developments. Rather than assuming the traditional view to be correct, fresh voices have reexamined the traditional view and have found it to be correct. Some have maintained a traditional view after they have weeded out some of its unbiblical baggage.[2] It's difficult to find a book defending a traditional view of hell that doesn't also respond to the aforementioned developments.

This is why this new Counterpoints book is so needed. It sits at the cusp of an ongoing discussion. It brings the three developments into dialogue with the traditional view of hell. Now more than ever, Christians want to know what the Bible really says about hell.

The Existence of Hell

The reader must note that none of the contributors in this volume deny the *existence* of hell. The question they are raising is not "Is there a hell?" but "What is hell like?" Every view espoused in this book is built on the fact that the Bible clearly talks about hell.

The primary Greek word for hell is *Gehenna*, which is used twelve times in the New Testament. The word is derived from Old Testament prophetic passages that talk about God's future judgment of the wicked in the Valley of Hinnom, or *Gehenna* (Jer. 7:29–34; 19:6–9; 32:35). Jews living around the time of Jesus coined the term *Gehenna* ("hell") as the place where the wicked would be punished, though they didn't always maintain that the Valley of Hinnom would be the specific place of punishment. Other images such as fire, destruction, darkness, and weeping were used to describe this place of punishment, whether or not the word *Gehenna* was used.

When we come to the New Testament, we must interpret it in light of the Jewish thought-world that surrounds it. When we do, we find that Jesus and the New Testament writers adopted both the word *Gehenna* and other hellish images to describe the fate of the wicked, such as everlasting fire, weeping, death, destruction, outer darkness, and a fiery lake. Like their Jewish brothers, New Testament writers believed that hell was a terrible place of punishment for the wicked.

The Bible clearly talks about hell. And all of the contributors to this volume agree with this. They agree that hell exists, but they differ on what this hell is like.

---

2. See, for instance, Joshua Ryan Butler's *The Skeletons in God's Closet: The Mercy of Hell, the Surprise of Judgment, and the Hope of Holy War* (Nashville: Thomas Nelson, 2014).

The Nature of Hell

The Bible is arguably less clear on the nature of hell than on the existence of hell. This is why Bible-believing Christians disagree about how the Bible answers our question, "What is hell like?" Some passages seem to support the traditional view. Matthew 25:46, for instance, says that the wicked "will go away to eternal punishment" and contrasts this fate with the righteous, who will inherit "eternal life." The contrast between "eternal punishment" and "eternal life" suggests that the punishment of the wicked is indeed everlasting (see also Dan. 12:2; Rev. 14:9–11).

But other passages talk about the fate of the wicked in terms of death and destruction—terms that suggest finality and not an ongoing act of punishing. Jesus says that we should "not be afraid of those who kill the body but cannot kill the soul. Rather, be afraid of the One who can destroy both soul and body in hell" (Matt. 10:28). The parallel between "kill" and "destroy" seems to say that the punishment of the wicked will be death, the termination of life, and not an ongoing conscious existence.

Still other passages suggest that everyone will be reconciled to God in the end. Paul says that Adam's sin "resulted in condemnation *for all people*"—and in the context this most probably means every single human and not just every type of person. But then he says, " ... so also one righteous act resulted in justification and life *for all people*" (Rom. 5:18). Could the first reference to "all people" mean *everyone* while the second reference means *just Christians?* Christian universalists say no. "All people" means everyone in both instances.

Then there are some passages that seem to talk about some sort of postmortem cleansing of believers in Christ (1 Cor. 3:10–15). Almost every Protestant rejects the idea of such purgatory on the grounds that it's an affront to the finished work of Christ. But what if purgatory had to do with sanctification, in which believers participate, and not God's finished work of atonement? Would this conflict with the Protestant view of justification by faith? Or more importantly: Is it biblical?

These are some of the questions that you will wrestle with in this book. We have enlisted a remarkable team of Christian scholars to articulate and defend different views of the nature of hell.

Introduction to the Authors

Denny Burk will begin the discussion by arguing for a traditional view of hell—namely, that hell is a place where the wicked will experience everlasting conscious torment. Burk is a Professor of Biblical Studies and the director of the Center for Gospel and Culture at Boyce College. As a biblical scholar, Burk uses extensive scriptural argumentation, rather than relying on tradition, to articulate his view. He also integrates theological reasoning to show that the traditional view of hell makes the most sense of what the Bible says about the character of God and the magnitude of sin.

John Stackhouse will argue for what he calls "terminal punishment," otherwise known as "conditionalism" or "annihilationism." Stackhouse is the Samuel J. Mikolaski Professor of Religious Studies and Dean of Faculty Development at Crandall University in Moncton, New Brunswick, and has authored several books and more than 600 essays and book chapters on theology, ethics, and history. He used to embrace a traditional view of hell, but now believes that unbelievers will indeed be punished in hell, yet that punishment will consist of death and destruction. Unbelievers will *not* live forever in a state of conscious torment, for their life will be terminated after judgment day. Stackhouse tethers biblical exegesis of relevant texts with theological argumentation to present a provocative case for a nontraditional view of hell.

Robin Parry has a PhD from the University of Gloucestershire (UK) and serves as the commissioning editor for Wipf and Stock Publishers. He is also the author of several books, including *The Evangelical Universalist*.[3] Parry argues for what has been called "Christian universalism" or "ultimate reconciliation"—a view that was not entertained in the previous Counterpoints volume on hell.

Parry's view must be distinguished from pluralistic universalism, which says—in popular jargon—"all roads lead to heaven." He argues that only one road leads to heaven (or the new creation): the way of Christ. Yet all creation, through the atoning work of Christ, will ultimately be reconciled to its Creator. While some Christians embrace universalism out of sentiment and an unwillingness to believe in a God

---

3. Subtitle: *The Biblical Hope that God's Love Will Save Us All* (London: SPCK, 2008).

who could send people to hell, Parry argues extensively from Scripture that the Bible itself teaches that the future judgment will be followed by reconciliation.

The final essay is written by Jerry Walls, Professor of Philosophy at Houston Baptist University. Walls has written three volumes on the afterlife in Christian theology, including *Purgatory: The Logic of Total Transformation*,[4] a book that articulates more extensively the view he will advocate in this volume.

Walls assumes a traditional view of hell, but argues that the righteous in Christ will undergo a time of sanctification between their death and resurrection. Walls does *not* believe that purgatory will consist in *satisfaction* (or atonement) of sin but in *sanctification* (growth toward holiness). The believer's sins are fully paid for by the blood of Christ; this is a cardinal truth for any Protestant. However, all Protestants believe that the Christian must also pursue sanctification. Walls argues that believers who aren't fully sanctified in this life will finish the process of sanctification after death.

Challenge to the Reader

Again, none of the authors in this volume deny the existence of hell. All of the authors are committed Christians who believe in the full inspiration and authority of the Bible. The discussion they will have does not surround the *existence* of hell—for the Bible clearly says there is a hell—but the *nature* of hell. Each will articulate his position and argue against the opposing views by using scriptural and theological arguments. They will not rely on emotional or sentimental arguments, nor will they base their views on experience. All of the authors will derive and articulate their different views based on Scripture and theological reasoning.

Most readers will already have a view firmly fixed in their mind. I would encourage you, the reader, to hold onto this view loosely as you consider the arguments in this book. If you hold onto your view too tightly, unwilling to reexamine it in light of Scripture, then you are placing your traditions and presuppositions on a higher pedestal than Scripture itself. If the view you have always believed is indeed

---

4. (Oxford: Oxford University Press, 2011).

Scriptural, then there's nothing to fear by considering and wrestling with other views. If Scripture is clear, then such clarity will be manifest. But there's a chance that the view you currently hold to is not a biblical one. And we all, therefore, need to be open to having our preconceived views corrected by Scripture.

The post-Reformation scholars used to say, *ecclesia semper reformanda est*, or "the church is (reformed and) always reforming." The reformers returned to Scripture and celebrated its ultimate authority over all belief and practice. They were not just *reformed* (that is, Protestant), but always eager to be constantly *reforming* in light of Scripture. But this should be an ongoing posture and not a one-time event. The (Protestant) church should constantly drag traditionally held doctrines back to the text of Scripture and eagerly demand reexamination.

It's common, perhaps likely, that unexamined beliefs become detached from their scriptural roots over time and through repetition. We become convinced of certain truths, but don't know why. We believe particular doctrines, but can't always defend them biblically. Yet this is unacceptable for anyone who claims to believe in God's inspired word as the ultimate and final authority of truth. We should be reformed and always reforming.

I, therefore, encourage you to evaluate each of the following essays on the basis of its biblical and theological evidence. If you simply presuppose that the view you hold is the right one and then read these essays in light of this presupposition, there's a good chance that you will not fairly evaluate the biblical strengths of each essay or your own view of hell. But this is not an *ecclesia semper reformanda est* posture. As Christians, we should seek to understand before we refute, and if we refute, we must do so based on compelling biblical evidence and not out of fear or presupposition. You, of course, will probably agree with only one of the following essays and disagree with the other three. But keep in mind: disagreement is not refutation. We must be able to refute the evidence of the views that we disagree with and then provide more compelling biblical evidence for the view that we uphold. As Christians, we must stand on God's inspired word, even if this leads us to conclusions that are different from what we have previously believed.

CHAPTER ONE

ETERNAL CONSCIOUS TORMENT

DENNY BURK

John Stott has summed up perhaps for all time the visceral reaction many people have to the traditional doctrine of hell. He writes, "I find the concept intolerable and do not understand how people can live with it without either cauterizing their feelings or cracking under the strain."[1] Stott's revulsion against "eternal conscious torment" is certainly not an outlier. One can hardly contemplate the horror of an eternal hell without shuddering at the thought of anyone having to bear such a fate. Yet I agree with Stott that the decisive factor in determining the matter cannot be an emotional response that precludes serious consideration of the traditional view. Rather, the text of Scripture must be the ultimate arbiter of the debate. But it is precisely here that an emotional reflex against the traditional view forearms many readers against certain interpretations of Scripture.[2] People can hardly comprehend how the traditional view can be reconciled with the ways of a just and loving God.

Some oppose the traditional view on exegetical grounds; others express objections that are more theological in nature. Herman Bavinck says, "The grounds on which people argue against the eternity of hellish punishment always remain the same."[3] Of the five reasons he lists, the first three are based less on specific Scripture passages than they

---

1. David L. Edwards and John R. W. Stott, *Evangelical Essentials: A Liberal-Evangelical Dialogue* (Downers Grove, IL: InterVarsity, 1988), 314–15.

2. So John G. Stackhouse Jr., "Foreword," in *Rethinking Hell: Readings in Evangelical Conditionalism*, ed. Christopher M. Date, Gregory G. Stump, and Joshua W. Anderson (Eugene, OR: Cascade Books, 2014), ix–xiv.

3. Herman Bavinck, *Reformed Dogmatics*, ed. John Bolt, trans. John Vriend, vol. 4, Holy Spirit, Church, and New Creation (Grand Rapids: Baker, 2008), 704.

are on human estimations of the way God ought to behave: (1) Eternal punishment contradicts the goodness, love, and compassion of God and makes him a tyrant; (2) Eternal punishment contradicts the justice of God because it is in no way proportionate to the sin in question; and (3) Eternal punishment that is purely punitive and not remedial has no apparent value.[4] Indeed it is such questions that Augustine dealt with extensively in his defense of eternal conscious punishment over 1,500 years ago.[5] Such objections have indeed been long-standing and can provoke an emotional response that precludes certain readings of the text. The objections provoke questions that some people think have no good answers under the traditional view. What kind of a God would preside over a place of eternal conscious torment? Can the loving God of the Bible possibly be responsible for punishing the unrepentant in this way?

The burden of this essay will be to explain what the relevant texts of Scripture actually teach. But to see what the Bible says, perhaps it would be beneficial to begin with a challenge to the theological presuppositions that often predispose readers against the traditional view. To that end, I begin with a kind of parable in which you, the reader, are the main character.[6]

A Parable on Punishment and Justice

Imagine that you are walking along a sidewalk and come upon a stranger sitting on a bench. As you walk by, you notice that he has something in his hands. You cannot quite make out what it is, but as you look a little closer, you discover that he has a grasshopper in his hands and that he is pulling the legs off the grasshopper. How would you respond? You might think it strange and perhaps a little bizarre to see a grown man dismembering an insect. You might walk past the man a little faster than you otherwise would have. But you are unlikely to initiate a confrontation over the life of a grasshopper.

Rewind the scene. Imagine that you happen upon the stranger to

---

4. Ibid.

5. In particular, see Book XXI in Augustine, "The City of God," in *Augustine: City of God, Christian Doctrine*, ed. Philip Schaff, trans. Marcus Dods, Nicene and Post-Nicene Fathers 2 (Peabody, MA: Hendrickson, 2004).

6. I first heard this illustration about twenty years ago in a sermon delivered by a dear friend and mentor, Joe Blankenship, who currently serves as pastor of Springs of Grace Bible Church in Tulsa, Oklahoma (http://springsofgracebiblechurch.org).

find him pulling the legs off a frog. How would you respond then? It would be a little bit more disturbing than the grasshopper, but would you intervene? Rewind the scene again. What if you come upon the stranger and he were pulling the legs off a bird? How would you respond then? Perhaps you might at least say something in protest to the man. Would you call authorities? Rewind the scene again. What if the stranger were attempting to tear the legs off a puppy? Now that certainly crosses a line. Would you not intervene in some way if it were a puppy? You might not risk your own person to intervene, but you would at least contact authorities. Rewind the scene one last time. What if the stranger was holding a human baby in his hands and was attempting to tear the legs off a human baby? There is no question what you would do in that scenario. If you witnessed an attempt to assault a baby, you would move heaven and earth to save that baby. You would do something risky to rescue that baby. Justice would require you to intervene on behalf of that baby, and so you would.

What is the difference in each of these scenarios? Why would you react with virtual indifference to the dismembering of a grasshopper but with heroic intervention to the dismembering of a baby? Why would your reaction be different? In each of the scenarios above, the "sin" is the same—pulling the legs off. The only difference in each of these scenarios is the one sinned against. And that is why you move heaven and earth to save the baby and do nothing to save the grasshopper. You react differently because the seriousness of the sin is not measured merely by the sin itself (pulling off the legs) but *by the value and the worth of the one being sinned against.* The more noble and valuable the creature, the more heinous and reprehensible it is to assault the creature. And there is a world of difference between a grasshopper and a baby.

This is the underlying theological principle of the essay that you are about to read. The seriousness of sin—and thus of the punishment due to sin—is not measured merely by the sin itself but by the value and the worth of the one sinned against.[7] If God were a grasshopper, then to sin against him would be of no great moral consequence. Eternal conscious torment would be an unjust overreaction if God were a grasshopper. It

---

7. So Bavinck, *Reformed Dogmatics*, 4:711. Also see Augustine, "The City of God," XXI.11.

would be an overreaction if God were exactly like you and me. But God is not a grasshopper. And he is not exactly like you and me. God is holy and infinite. He is compassionate and gracious. He is the definition of beauty. He is infinitely more precious than the tiniest baby. He is infinitely nobler than the best person. He is the first and best of beings. His glory and worth are boundless. Thus to sin against an infinitely glorious being is an infinitely heinous offense that is worthy of an infinitely heinous punishment.

Our emotional reflex against the traditional doctrine of hell reveals what we really believe about God. We tend to have a diminished view of sin — and thus of the judgment due to sin — because we have a diminished view of God. The god of our imagination sometimes falls short of the God of Scripture. We fail to take sin and judgment as seriously as we ought because we fail to take God as seriously as we ought. And so we are often tempted to view the penalty of hell — eternal conscious suffering under the wrath of God — as an overreaction on God's part. My contention is that if we knew God better, we would not think like that. And we would not begin our reading of Scripture predisposed against the traditional view. We would begin on an entirely different footing.

So the question of eternal conscious torment really does come down to who God is. Is God the kind of God for whom this kind of punishment for sin would be necessary? Or is he not? What does the Bible say about God and the judgments that issue forth from him? The aim of this essay will be to answer these questions and to argue that the Bible teaches eternal conscious torment in a place called *hell* as the lot of every person who dies in an unrepentant state. All those who fail to experience saving faith in Jesus while they are alive in this age will be resurrected and condemned when Christ returns. They will then be cast into hell where they will suffer never-ending punishment. This view of God's judgment is not a cause for embarrassment for Christians, but will ultimately become a source of joy and praise for the saints as they witness the infinite goodness and justice of God (Rev. 18:20; 19:3).

Scriptural Teaching on Hell

At the end of the day, the case for the traditional understanding of hell must not be based on theological conjecture but on biblical truth. It is necessary, therefore, to establish the biblical foundations for hell as a place of eternal conscious torment for the unrepentant. Robert Peterson has argued that there are at least ten texts of Scripture that deal explicitly with hell and with the final state of the wicked: Isaiah 66:22–24; Daniel 12:2–3; Matthew 18:6–9; 25:31–46; Mark 9:42–48; 2 Thessalonians 1:6–10; Jude 7, 13; Revelation 14:9–11; 20:10, 14–15.[8] As we focus on each of them, we find that the final state of the damned has at least three characteristics: (1) final separation, (2) unending experience, and (3) just retribution. *Final separation* occurs at the last judgment and consists in the irrevocable separation of the wicked from the righteous and from the presence of God's mercy. *Unending experience* indicates that the punishments of hell will be consciously experienced forever and will not abate with the annihilation or eventual salvation of the damned. *Just retribution* indicates that the terrors of the damned are a recompense for evil, not a means of redemption or renewal. It is a punitive judgment intended to magnify the justice of God. These three characteristics of hell emerge from the ten foundational texts of Scripture. They also by definition rule out the annihilationist position (which denies that the torments of hell are everlasting), the universalist position (which holds that all people will eventually be saved), and the notion of purgatory (which views the flames of final judgment as a potential gateway to eternal life).

Foundation #1: Isaiah 66:22 - 24

Isaiah 66:22–24 is the first of two Old Testament texts that offer explicit support for the traditional view. This passage of Scripture is foundational because Jesus himself alludes to it to describe the final state of the wicked. Key images commonly associated with hell—the undying worm and the unquenchable fire—derive from this text.

Final Separation

Verse 22 identifies "the new heavens and the new earth" as the context for these statements, indicating that Isaiah is looking far beyond the immediate events of his own day to the eschatological renewal of heaven

---

8. Robert A. Peterson, "The Foundation of the House: Scripture," in *Two Views of Hell: A Biblical & Theological Dialogue*, by Edward William Fudge and Robert A. Peterson, Spectrum Multiview Books (Downers Grove, IL: InterVarsity, 2000), 129–69.

and earth.[9] God promises to create "new heavens and a new earth" after the last judgment (Isa. 65:17). This new place will be a domain in which there is no more weeping (65:19), no more untimely death (65:20), no more want (65:21–22), no more bloody conflict or evil (65:25). It is a place of God's presence and comfort for all of God's people. "All nations and tongues" will eventually see God's glory and declare it (66:18–19).

But the wicked will not share in the joy of this new creation. In fact, the worshipers inhabiting the new heavens and the new earth will be able to see that the lot of those who "rebelled" against God is very different from their own. As the worshipers leave the temple, they see the corpses of the Lord's enemies strewn about what is most likely the Valley of Hinnom.[10] Hinnom is the very place where Ahaz and Manasseh burned human sacrifices to the false god Molech (2 Kings 16:3; 21:6), and it would explain why this place became associated with fire. These enemies will be separated from the joys of the "new heavens and the new earth" and will instead undergo the judgment of fire and worm (Isa. 66:24). The worm pictures the disgrace of decaying bodies left exposed after their defeat. Gary Smith suggests that the image may be growing out of the scene in Isaiah 37:36, where "the decomposing carcasses of the 185,000 Assyrian troops that were left to rot in the fields around Jerusalem when God defeated the army of Sennacherib."[11] Isaiah elsewhere invokes fire as an image of God's holy presence (e.g., Isa. 33:14), and the fire may appear here as a just recompense for those who caused innocents to pass through the fire of Molech. In any case, both the worm and the fire are vivid images of the horror that is to come for the damned.[12]

This judgment does not take place in the holy city, for the worshipers must "go forth" (66:24) from the city to look on the corpses of those under judgment. In spite of a popular and long-running

---

9. Daniel I. Block, "The Old Testament on Hell," in *Hell Under Fire: Modern Scholarship Reinvents Eternal Punishment*, ed. Christopher W. Morgan and Robert A. Peterson (Grand Rapids: Zondervan, 2004), 60.

10. A comparison with Jeremiah 7:32–8:3 suggests that this area is the Valley of Hinnom. So Peterson, *Hell on Trial: The Case for Eternal Punishment*, (Harmony Twp., NJ: P&R Publishing, 1995), 31.

11. Gary V. Smith, *Isaiah 40–66*, New American Commentary 15B (Nashville: B&H, 2009), 752–53.

12. C. F. Keil and F. Delitzsch, *Commentary on the Old Testament*, trans. James Martin, vol. 7, Isaiah (Peabody, MA: Hendrickson, 2011), 640–41.

misunderstanding, there is no evidence that the Valley of Hinnom was ever used as a garbage dump.[13] Hinnom was not infamous as a flaming heap of garbage. Rather, it was most likely known for abominable idolatry outside the city where God's judgment would eventually fall on his enemies. At the very least, it pictures a separation between the righteous and the wicked. The wicked are consigned to a place of judgment outside and away from the worshipers of Yahweh.[14] The imagery pictures what John Watts calls "complete separation" of God's enemies from his worshipers.[15]

Unending Experience

Notice that in verse 22, the worshipers of Yahweh will "endure" in a state of blessedness for as long as the "new heavens and the new earth" endure. That means that the final state of the worshipers will be permanent worship and blessedness. In short, it is an unending experience of worship and joy in the presence of the Lord. Likewise, the final state of the wicked will also be permanent. The "dead bodies of those who rebelled" against God are in a perpetual state of dishonor (v. 24 NIV). Under normal circumstances, fire and worm would consume a corpse until there was nothing left. But in the eschatological age, the circumstances are not normal. The devouring worm "will not die" and the consuming fire "will not be quenched" (v. 24). This means that the bodily degradation of the wicked never ends but partakes of the same longevity as the new heavens and the new earth. What kind of body could withstand fire and worm such that their work would go on forever? Though not mentioned specifically in this text, this scene seems to assume that God's enemies have been given a body fit for an unending punishment. This implies the coming of a special resurrection of the

---

13. Lloyd R. Bailey, "Gehenna: The Topography of Hell," *Biblical Archaeologist* 49, no. 3 (1986): 189. So also G. R. Beasley-Murray, *Jesus and the Kingdom of God* (Grand Rapids: Eerdmans, 1986), 376–77, n. 92; Peter M. Head, "The Duration of Divine Judgment in the New Testament," in *Eschatology in Bible & Theology: Evangelical Essays at the Dawn of a New Millennium*, ed. K. E. Brower and M. W. Elliott (Leicester: Apollos, 1997), 223; Francis Chan and Preston M. Sprinkle, *Erasing Hell: What God Said about Eternity and the Things We Made Up* (Colorado Springs: David C Cook, 2011), 59–61.

14. So Brevard S. Childs, *Isaiah*, The Old Testament Library (Louisville, KY: Westminster John Knox, 2001), 542.

15. John D. W. Watts, *Isaiah 34–66*, Revised, Word Biblical Commentary 25 (Waco, TX: Thomas Nelson, 2000), 941.

damned—one anticipated in Isaiah 26:19 but revealed most clearly later by Daniel 12:1–2.[16] This resurrection implies that their experience will involve consciousness of their unending punishment.

Just Retribution

There is no future redemption for the ones condemned to unending punishment. Isaiah 66:24 is the last verse in the book, and the implication is that the final word corresponds to their final state which is unending. This means that the punishment of the wicked is not *disciplinary* or *restorative*. Rather, it is a *punitive* measure to recompense the wicked for rebelling against God. The "continual burning" of the "consuming fire" (Isa. 33:14) of God does not purge evil but punishes evil.

Foundation #2: Daniel 12:2–3

N. T. Wright argues that the main source for the ideas and images in Daniel 12:2–3 is Isaiah. The "most obvious passage" is Isaiah 26:19, which "few doubt" to be the background of this pivotal text.[17] This means that Daniel did not innovate the idea of resurrection after death. His prophecy is consistent with what came before in Isaiah.[18]

Final Separation

Daniel 12:2–3 predicts a dual destiny for those who "sleep" in death: "Multitudes who sleep in the dust of the earth will awake: some to everlasting life, others to shame and everlasting contempt" (Dan. 12:2 NIV). Some try to limit Daniel 12's resurrection to a specific group of people and not to all of humanity.[19] Nevertheless, Jesus clearly alludes to Daniel's prophecy to describe the final resurrection of all people in John 5:28–29: "Do not marvel at this; for an hour is coming, in which all who are in the tombs shall hear His voice, and will come forth; those who

---

16. Block, "The Old Testament on Hell," 59.

17. N. T. Wright, *The Resurrection of the Son of God*, Christian Origins and the Question of God 3 (Minneapolis: Fortress, 2003), 115–16. See also Daniel P. Bailey, "The Intertextual Relationship of Daniel 12:2 and Isaiah 26:19: Evidence from Qumran and the Greek Versions," *Tyndale Bulletin* 51, no. 2 (2000): 305–8.

18. Mitch Chase shows that resurrection hope has precursors not only in Isaiah, but also elsewhere in the Law, the Prophets, and the Writings. See Mitchell Lloyd Chase, "Resurrection Hope in Daniel 12:2: An Exercise in Biblical Theology" (PhD diss., The Southern Baptist Theological Seminary, 2013), 77–161.

19. E.g., Wright, *The Resurrection of the Son of God*, 110.

did the good deeds to a resurrection of life, those who committed the evil deeds to a resurrection of judgment."[20] So either by original sense or by implication, Daniel 12:2–3 describes what ultimately happens to all people at the final judgment after they die. There is a double resurrection. Not only do the righteous anticipate resurrection after death, but so do the unrighteous. The clear implication is that all of humanity will ultimately be resurrected to "everlasting life" or to "disgrace and everlasting contempt" (v. 2). As Bruce Milne has commented on this text, "The most impressive implication to be drawn is *the clear either/or* which is reflected here. There are no third categories or third options as far as human destiny is concerned."[21] Ultimately, the destinies of these two groups are separate.

Unending Experience

This final separation is permanent. The state of those resurrected to life is "everlasting" or "eternal." The Hebrew term translated as "everlasting" in the NASB is ʿôlām, which often has the connotation of time extending into the distant past *and* into the future indefinitely. For the righteous, their life in the future is unending.[22] Likewise for the unrighteous, their "disgrace and everlasting contempt" are also unending. Because the same term ("everlasting" / Heb. ʿôlām) describes the duration of both the righteous and the wicked, it is obvious that their destinies are equally extended.[23]

The Hebrew term translated in the NASB as "contempt" *(dērāʾôn)* appears only one other time in the Old Testament, and that is in Isaiah 66:24 where it refers to unburied corpses who have fallen under the judgment of God. The term evokes the same imagery in Daniel, suggesting that those resurrected to "contempt" are awakened for judgment and punishment. The awakening implies consciousness, but it is

---

20. Chase lists five reasons for understanding John 5:28–29 as an allusion to Daniel 12:2–3. See Chase, "Resurrection Hope in Daniel 12:2: An Exercise in Biblical Theology," 203. See also Andreas J. Köstenberger, "John," in *Commentary on the New Testament Use of the Old Testament*, ed. G. K. Beale and D. A. Carson (Grand Rapids: Baker, 2007), 442.

21. Bruce Milne, *The Message of Heaven and Hell: Grace and Destiny*, The Bible Speaks Today (Leicester, England; Downers Grove, IL: InterVarsity, 2002), 104.

22. E. Jenni, "עוֹלָם ʿôlām Eternity," in *Theological Lexicon of the Old Testament*, ed. Ernst Jenni and Claus Westermann, trans. Mark E. Biddle, vol. 2 (Peabody, MA: Hendrickson, 1997), 852–62, see 860.

23. Milne, *The Message of Heaven and Hell*, 104.

a consciousness of judgment and eschatological "contempt" that does not end.

Just Retribution

Because it does not end, the purpose of this eschatological judgment cannot be redemptive or transformative in any sense. It is a recompense for unrepentant sin, not a purging of sin. This leads to the conclusion that the final state of the damned is retributive. As Tremper Longman comments on this text, "The problem of retribution is a huge one in the Bible, particularly in the Old Testament ... Daniel 12, however, makes it clear that the wicked will ultimately get what they deserve—destruction and shame."[24]

Foundation #3: Matthew 18:6-9

No one speaks more clearly and frequently about hell in Scripture than Jesus. Nevertheless, his words about hell remain some of the most contested in all of Scripture. To be sure, the exegesis of key biblical texts continues to be a matter of debate, even among some who identify themselves as evangelical.

In Matthew 18:6–9, Jesus recycles an image that appears earlier in this Gospel (5:29–30).[25] In both texts, Jesus exhorts his listeners to take drastic measures to avoid the penalty of hell. Both texts speak of perishing in a place called *Gehenna*, but Matthew 18:8–9 adds notions of double resurrection, fire, and eternality that are not mentioned in 5:29–30.

Final Separation

Verses 6–7 warn of placing "stumbling blocks" in the way of disciples. Such obstacles cause the complete falling away of the "little ones," defined not merely as children but as those who have believed in Jesus (v. 6). That is why Jesus delivers the double woe in verse 7. It is no less woeful when a disciple places stumbling blocks in his own way (vv. 8–9). Such obstacles can lead to complete destruction in "eternal fire" (v. 8) and "fiery hell" (v. 9).

---

24. Tremper Longman III, *Daniel*, NIV Application Commentary (Grand Rapids: Zondervan, 1999), 304.

25. Peterson, "The Foundation of the House: Scripture," 138.

The term rendered as "hell" or transliterated as *Gehenna* (v. 9) is the Greek term *geenna*, which derives from the Hebrew *gê hinnōm*, which means "Valley of Hinnom." As mentioned above, this valley was the site of child sacrifices to the idol Molech during the era of the kings (2 Kings 16:3; 21:6). The practice so provoked the Lord to anger that Jeremiah prophesied God would destroy these idolaters in the Valley of Hinnom and would leave their corpses to rot. There would be so many corpses that there would be no room to bury them all and that the valley would be renamed "Valley of Slaughter" (Jer. 7:31–34 NIV). This valley's association with fire and judgment is the background for its use in intertestamental literature and for its appropriation in the New Testament, where it became an image for the place of final judgment.[26]

These verses indicate that hell is but one of two possible destinies in the afterlife. The other alternative is for people to "enter life" (vv. 8–9). Every other instance of "life" in Matthew refers to eschatological life or "eternal" life (Matt. 7:14; 19:16, 17, 29; 25:46), and that is how it is used here. It is the "life" of the age to come.[27] There are only two destinies. Those who are disciples enter into eternal "life," and those who are not disciples enter into "the eternal fire" or "the fiery hell." The contrast could not be starker. Those who enter life enter into blessing. Those who enter into the eternal fiery hell receive judgment because through them come the "stumbling blocks" (v. 7) and because they "despise one of these little ones" — that is, the disciples (v. 10). Their destinies are parallel but separate and extend equally into eternity future. This passage is based on the same supposition of double resurrection that appears in Daniel 12:2. Thus the wicked are resurrected to consciousness for a place that is separate from that of the righteous and from the presence of God's mercy.

Unending Experience

"Eternal fire" and "fiery hell" (vv. 8–9) are set in parallel, a connection that explicitly renders hell an everlasting reality. The term translated as "eternal" *(aiōnios)* means "a long period of time" in a handful of New

---

26. Joachim Jeremias, "γέεννα," in *Theological Dictionary of the New Testament*, ed. Gerhard Kittel, trans. Geoffrey W. Bromiley, vol. 1 (Grand Rapids: Eerdmans, 1964), 657–58.

27. Leon Morris, *The Gospel According to Matthew*, Pillar New Testament Commentary (Grand Rapids: Eerdmans, 1992), 463.

Testament texts. But its use in Matthew's Gospel routinely means a "period of unending duration" or a time "without end."[28] It is best not to take the eternal fire as literal but as a metaphorical expression that is drawn from Old Testament antecedents (e.g., Isa. 66:24) and that expresses the pain that must be endured by those in hell.[29] Leon Morris writes, "Jesus leaves his hearers in no doubt as to the seriousness of the eternal state of sinners."[30] The experience of fire will be unending in its duration.

Just Retribution

Jesus pronounces "woe" on the world because of its many enticements to sin (v. 7). Without question, this was a common prophetic response to rebellion against God and his law (e.g., Isa. 3:11; 5:8, 11, 18, 20, 21, 22). He also indicates that those who stumble over their own fleshly enticements to sin will be met with painful punishments in hell (Matt. 18:7–8). Every indication is that the *woes* and hell are recompense for sin—the just deserts of those who stumble or cause stumbling. In short, the punishments are presented as strictly retributive without any mention of renewal or restoration. Rather, the punishments extend infinitely into the future.

Foundation #4: Matthew 25:31–46

Matthew 25:31–46 gives one of the starkest depictions of final judgment in all of Scripture. It pictures the Son of Man coming in his glory to judge the nations. As the "Son of Man," Jesus appears as the Davidic fulfillment of Daniel's vision in Daniel 7:13–14.[31] This Son of Man rules over the nations as the world's true king, and he will render justice to every individual who has ever lived.

---

28. BDAG, s.v. αἰώνιος, 3.

29. On the different approaches to literal and metaphorical depictions of hell, see Andrew David Naselli, "Hellfire and Brimstone: Interpreting the New Testament's Descriptions of Hell," *9Marks eJournal* 7, no. 4 (Sept.–Oct. 2010): 16–19. It is difficult to be dogmatic on this point, but I generally take the metaphorical approach and recognize that the realities symbolized by the metaphors are no less dreadful for their being depicted symbolically. See also Chan and Sprinkle, *Erasing Hell*, 153–55.

30. Morris, *The Gospel According to Matthew*, 463.

31. James M. Hamilton, *With the Clouds of Heaven: The Book of Daniel in Biblical Theology*, New Studies in Biblical Theology 32 (Downers Grove, IL: InterVarsity, 2014), 134–54, 185–90.

Final Separation

The first scene of the Son of Man's judgment involves a final separation of the sheep from the goats—an image depicting the final division of all humanity into two groups. The Son of Man separates them from one another because he intends to treat them differently based on what they are. The sheep are Jesus' faithful followers who have heard the shepherd's voice, have trusted in him, and are allied to him. The goats are those who have not listened to the shepherd's voice, do not trust him, and are not allied to him. Those on his right are "blessed of [the] Father" and will "inherit the kingdom prepared for [them] from the foundation of the world" (v. 34). Those on his left are "accursed" and are heading to "eternal fire" (v. 41). The first act of the final judgment will be a separation. And in that moment, the horrifying realization will begin to descend on the goats. They will know that it is the last time they will ever see the sheep again, and they will know that what is about to happen to them will be irrevocable.

Unending Experience

The goats will experience a destiny far removed from that of the sheep. Far from being blessed and inheriting the kingdom (v. 34), the goats are cursed and forced into eternal fire (v. 41) and eternal punishment (v. 46). When God curses someone, it means that he has called down harm or misfortune upon that person.[32] The nature of the misfortune is summed up in the phrases "eternal fire" and "eternal punishment." As mentioned above, the fire refers to the painful experience that must be endured for time "without end."[33] Likewise, the "punishment" is unending *(aiônios)* as well. Annihilationists argue that the punishment is eternal only in the sense of an ongoing fire of judgment. The fire keeps burning, but the ones tossed into it are ultimately destroyed. It only keeps going as more people are put into it.[34] But this misses the point of the double resurrection alluded to earlier in Matthew 18:8–9 (see above). The

---

32. Friedrich Büchsel, "κατάρα," in *Theological Dictionary of the New Testament*, ed. Gerhard Kittel, trans. Geoffrey W. Bromiley, vol. 1 (Grand Rapids: Eerdmans, 1964), 449.

33. *Aiônios* is an adjective that means "pertaining to an age." But in this context, the age in question is the age to come. And that age is "without end." See Morris, *The Gospel According to Matthew*, 641, n. 79. Contra R. T. France, *The Gospel of Matthew*, NICNT (Grand Rapids: Eerdmans, 2007), 966–67.

34. So France, *The Gospel of Matthew*, 967.

bodies that are cast into the fire have properties that make them fit for an eternal destiny. Thus the punishment is in fact everlasting for every individual that enters the fire.

Just Retribution

The word translated as "punishment" *(kolasis)* in the NASB appears only twice in the New Testament (Matt. 25:46; 1 John 4:18). Some have questioned the traditional gloss "punishment" in favor of "correction." Rob Bell, for example, makes the following argument in his popular work *Love Wins:*

> The word *kolazo* is a term from horticulture. It refers to the pruning and trimming of the branches of a plant so it can flourish.
>
> An *aion* of *kolazo*. Depending how you translate *aion* and *kolazo*, then, the phrase can mean "a period of pruning" or "a time of trimming," or an intense experience of correction.
>
> In a good number of English translations of the Bible, the phrase *"aion* of *kolazo"* gets translated as "eternal punishment," which many read to mean "punishment forever," as in never going to end. But "forever" is not really a category the biblical writers used.[35]

In this way, Jesus' words are fit into a universalist's paradigm, where hell becomes a temporary place of correction until the sinner becomes rehabilitated and fit for heaven. It makes hell into a place where there might "be endless opportunities in an endless amount of time for people to say yes to God" and be saved.[36]

This argument is completely undermined by the fact that *kolasis* never means "correction" or "pruning" anywhere else in the New Testament or related literature.[37] The term is used one other time in the New Testament, in 1 John 4:18 where it clearly means punishment.

---

35. Rob Bell, *Love Wins: A Book about Heaven, Hell, and the Fate of Every Person Who Ever Lived* (New York: HarperOne, 2011), 91–92.

36. Ibid., 106–107. See Chan and Sprinkle's excellent counterargument to this view in Chan and Sprinkle, *Erasing Hell*, 84–86.

37. The meanings "checking the growth of trees" and "chastisement, correction" appear in Liddell, Scott, and Jones's Greek Lexicon. See LSJ, s.v. κόλ-ασις, 1 and 2. Still, LSJ only lists those meanings in literature prior to the period of the New Testament. In its use in the New Testament, LSJ translates κόλασις as "divine retribution." The entries for κόλασις in *Theological Dictionary of the New Testament* (vol. 3) and *New International Dictionary of New Testament Theology and Exegesis* (vol. 2) also have no reference to "correction." Koine usage appears to know nothing of this early meaning of κόλασις.

Also, the verb form *kolazō* appears twice in the New Testament (Acts 4:21; 2 Peter 2:9). Both of these uses refer to punishment as well.[38] The standard lexicon of New Testament Greek does not list "correction" or "pruning" as possible meanings. Rather, the semantic range is limited to either divine or human punishment. It defines *kolasis* in Matthew 25:46 as "transcendent retribution."[39] This meaning is in line with its use in intertestamental literature, where it often refers to the penalty imposed for wrongdoing (2 Macc. 4:38; 3 Macc. 1:3; 7:10; 4 Macc. 8:9), but never to "correction."

Another reason we know that it does not mean "correction" is that "eternal punishment" in verse 46 is the same place as "eternal fire which has been prepared for the devil and his angels" in verse 41.[40] Interpreters tend to agree that hell is a permanent place of punishment for demonic creatures. Indeed Revelation 20:10 confirms that the devil and his minions will be cast into the lake of fire and "tormented day and night forever and ever." It is not a place of correction for them. If unbelievers are cast into the same place as the demons, that suggests that the duration is the same for both groups. There are no grounds in this text for saying that hell is corrective for the one and not for the other. If it is retributive for demonic creatures, then it is also for those unbelievers who share their fate in the judgment.

For these reasons, we can be confident that *kolasis* is a punishment for sin that is unending. It is retributive in nature with no notion of rehabilitation or restoration in view.

Foundation #5: Mark 9:42–48

This passage makes its own contribution in the wider context of Mark's Gospel, but for our purposes we note the overlaps with the parallel text that we have already seen in Matthew 18:7–10. Both passages deal with those who cause the "little ones" to stumble (v. 42), with those who stumble over themselves (vv. 43–47), and with a place called *Gehenna* (mentioned three times in this passage).

---

38. BDAG, s.v. κολάζω.
39. BDAG, s.v. κόλασις, 2.
40. In this line of response, I am following Chan and Sprinkle, *Erasing Hell*, 84–86.

Final Separation

As in Matthew, Mark's use of the term "life" refers exclusively to eschatological life or "eternal" life (Mark 10:17, 30). So the term's appearance in 9:43 and 9:45 must also be interpreted as life in the age to come. This eschatological interpretation is confirmed by the fact that "life" in verses 43 and 45 is parallel to "kingdom of God" in verse 47.[41] And in Mark's Gospel, the kingdom is both "already" and "not yet," with an emphasis on the "not yet" in verse 49. Jesus' point is that the believer's experience of the consummated reign of Christ will be marked by eternal life in the age to come.

Those who do not enter life will be put into "hell" (vv. 43, 45, 47). It is the same term used in Matthew and likewise accesses the image of the valley outside of Jerusalem that became associated with the fire of God's judgment and subsequently with the place of God's final judgment.[42] Hell is not the literal valley but the place of God's final judgment. It is a fate separate from those who enter life and separate from the presence of God's mercy.

Unending Experience

Our observations on Matthew apply as well to Mark 9:43 and 47, which define "hell" as a place of "unquenchable fire" (v. 43) "where their worm does not die, and their fire is not quenched" (v. 48).[43] Both of these statements are allusions to the judgment scene outside Jerusalem from Isaiah 66:24. It is the place where God's enemies are cast down to suffer under the devouring worm (that never finishes devouring) and the burning fire (that never finishes burning). It presupposes a double resurrection in which the wicked are given bodies fit for an everlasting punishment. It is an experience of judgment that has no end.[44]

---

41. Adela Yarbro Collins, *Mark: A Commentary*, ed. Harold W. Attridge, Hermeneia (Minneapolis: Fortress, 2007), 454.

42. James R. Edwards, *The Gospel According to Mark*, Pillar New Testament Commentary (Grand Rapids: Eerdmans, 2002), 294.

43. Contrary to some English versions, the second appearance of "hell" in this text has no modifying statement. Verses 44 and 46 are not original to Mark's Gospel. The earliest and best manuscripts do not contain them. They were likely added later out of a wish to conform to verse 48, which does appear in the earliest and best witnesses. So Bruce M. Metzger, *A Textual Commentary on the Greek New Testament*, 2nd ed. (Stuttgart: United Bible Societies, 2002), 86–87.

44. So Robert H. Stein, *Mark*, Baker Exegetical Commentary on the New Testament (Grand Rapids: Baker, 2008), 449.

Just Retribution

Verse 41 says, "Whoever gives you a cup of water to drink because of your name as followers of Christ, truly I say to you, he shall not lose his reward." The term "reward" *(misthos)* is defined as "recompense." *Misthos* refers to a reward in verse 41, but the term appears elsewhere as a reference to punishment (2 Macc. 8:33; cf. Isa. 40:10 [LXX]; Rev. 22:12). It is "recognition (mostly by God) for the moral quality of an action"—in this case for receiving Christ's messengers favorably.[45] That reward is a payment of what is owed. Even though the term is not used in verse 42, the concept is implied by verse 41 so that drowning should be viewed as the recompense for anyone who causes the little ones to stumble. This concept of recompense in verses 41–42 informs the interpretation of eternal destinies in verses 43–48. The recompense for faithfulness is entering into life and the kingdom of God. Likewise, the recompense for stumbling is hell. Thus, Jesus depicts hell as the just and punitive response to unrepentant sin.

Foundation #6: 2 Thessalonians 1:6 - 10

Paul's second letter to the Thessalonians begins with one of the most fearsome predictions of judgment in the entire Bible. It does not mention hell *per se*, but it does evoke descriptions of final judgment that are commensurate with the passages that do. In short, Paul assures his readers that their current affliction has not gone unnoticed by God. Yes, they may have to suffer now as a result of their faith in Christ, but God will one day "repay with affliction" their tormentors (v. 6). That day will come when Jesus Christ is "revealed from heaven" (v. 7) to rescue his people and to punish his enemies. This event is a *parousia* (1 Thess. 3:13), even though it is here called an *apokalypsis* (cf. 1 Cor. 1:7; 1 Peter 1:7, 13), which means that it is a "revelation" of someone who is currently concealed.[46] Thus, the scene is unambiguously eschatological—a reference to the judgment that unfolds at the second coming of Christ.

---

45. BDAG, s.v. μισθός, 2.
46. Leon Morris, *1 and 2 Thessalonians: An Introduction and Commentary*, 2nd ed., Tyndale New Testament Commentaries (Grand Rapids: Eerdmans, 1984), 120.

Final Separation

Paul tells his readers that their present distress is not their future destiny. On the contrary, their present affliction will give way to relief when Jesus returns. As their affliction ends, their persecutors' affliction will begin (vv. 6–7). The ones inflicting suffering on the Thessalonian believers will suffer divine retribution at the hands of Jesus when he is revealed from heaven. These tormentors will be numbered among those "who do not know God" and "do not obey the gospel" (v. 8). In other words, the tormentors will be swept up into the final disposition of all those who have rebelled against God and who have refused to believe the gospel.

The damned will have to suffer "eternal destruction, away from the presence of the Lord and from the glory of His power" (2 Thess. 1:9).[47] Thus, a key feature of eternal destruction is alienation from the presence of the Lord. But it is not a generic alienation, but a specific alienation from the "presence of his power." The Greek term translated as "power" is the noun *ischus*. It often appears with *dunamis* and related words as an attribute of God.[48] This usage might lead one to understand *ischus* here as a generic reference to God's power, but elsewhere the term is used specifically of God's ability to raise from the dead. For example, Ephesians 1:19–20 reads, "The surpassing greatness of His power *[dunamis]* toward us who believe. These are in accordance with the working of the strength of His might *[ischus]* which He brought about in Christ, when He raised Him from the dead."[49] This interpretation of God's strength makes sense in the context of 2 Thessalonians 1:9–10, where Paul makes two references to glorification — "the *glory* of His power" (v. 9) and "*glorified* in His saints on that day" (v. 10). "Eternal destruction" (v. 9), then, is separation from the resurrection to blessedness that the Lord Jesus will give to his people on the last day.

If this connection is correct, then Paul is not saying that unbelievers will be separated from God in every respect. He is saying that they will

---

47. The parallel with Isaiah 2:10 (LXX) shows that the preposition apo indicates the location of the unbeliever "away from" the presence of Christ, not the location "from" which the judgment comes. So Gordon D. Fee, *The First and Second Letters to the Thessalonians*, New International Commentary on the New Testament (Grand Rapids: Eerdmans, 2009), 259. This is the way it is interpreted in most of the modern English translations (e.g., NASB, NIV, ESV, RSV, NRSV, NET, NAB, NJB; contra HCSB; KJV).

48. See BDAG, s.v. ἰσχύς.

49. Cf. Rom. 1:4; 1 Cor. 6:14; 15:43; 2 Cor. 4:7; 13:4; Phil. 3:10.

be separated from the mercy of resurrection life to be revealed on the last day. They will in fact be in the presence of God's wrath in their eternal destruction, for it is God himself who will "afflict" them (v. 6) and the Lord Jesus who will give them "retribution" (v. 8). But their separation from the mercy of Christ and from those who experience that mercy will be horrifying and irrevocable.

Unending Experience

Annihilationists deny that conscious torment is unending and argue that "destruction" (v. 9) means that the damned will at some point cease to exist. Thus "eternal destruction" means that their annihilation will be permanent. Their suffering will eventually come to an end.[50] But this is a misunderstanding of Paul's language. "Destruction" *(oletheros)* does not mean "cease to exist." If I were to say that my car was destroyed in a crash last week, no one hears that to mean that the car ceases to exist. They understand it to mean that the car was completely ruined and lost to me as a result of the accident. That is the sense in which the Greek term *oletheros* is used here. Indeed, Paul is the only New Testament author to use this term, and in none of its other uses does it mean "cease to exist" (cf. 1 Cor. 5:5; 1 Thess. 5:3; 1 Tim. 6:9). Its primary sense is something more along the lines of ruin or loss, not annihilation.[51] It refers to what Gordon Fee calls "the ultimate desolation" and the "absolute loss of ... glory."[52] So "eternal destruction" refers to everlasting[53] ruin or loss, not annihilation.

Just Retribution

The passage begins with a reference to God's justice: "It is only just for God to repay with affliction those who afflict you" (2 Thess. 1:6). The term translated "repay" *(antapodidōmi)* is the language of retribution.[54] The term appears twice in the New Testament, each time within a verse that quotes Deuteronomy 32:35:

---

50. E.g., Edward Fudge, *The Fire That Consumes: A Biblical and Historical Study of the Doctrine of Final Punishment* (Eugene, OR: Cascade Books, 2011), 197–98.

51. So Douglas J. Moo, "Paul on Hell," in *Hell Under Fire: Modern Scholarship Reinvents Eternal Punishment*, ed. Christopher W. Morgan and Robert A. Peterson (Grand Rapids: Zondervan, 2004), 104–5.

52. Fee, *The First and Second Letters to the Thessalonians*, 259, 260.

53. See comments above on αἰώνιος. Also, BDAG, s.v. αἰώνιος, 3.

54. BDAG, s.v. ἀνταποδίδωμι, 2: "to exact retribution."

Romans 12:19 Never take your own revenge, beloved, but leave room for the wrath of God, for it is written, "Vengeance is Mine, I will repay *[antapodidōmi]*," says the Lord.

Hebrews 10:30 For we know Him who said, "Vengeance is Mine, I will repay *[antapodidōmi]*." And again, "The Lord will judge His people."

This idea of God's righteous judgment expressed in vengeance is certainly what is in view in 2 Thessalonians 1:6. In fact, verse 8 says that the Lord Jesus will give out "retribution" or vengeance *(ekdikēsis)*— the very same term from Deuteronomy 32:35 and from the other two New Testament texts that quote it. Gordon Fee says the combination of the term *antapodidōmi* with a reference to God's justice calls to mind the *lex talionis* of the Old Testament—an eye for an eye (Ex. 21:24; Lev. 24:20).[55] Only in this case it is "affliction for affliction." In other words, it is God upholding his own justice by repaying evil doers what their deeds deserve. There is no hint of restoration, only of pure retribution according to the righteousness of God.

It is worth noting that the ones who receive retribution are those "who do not know God" and "do not obey the gospel" (2 Thess. 1:8). Many commentators understand these two phrases to refer to two different kinds of unbelievers. Those who do not know God are pagans who should have acknowledged God on the basis of natural revelation, for that which is known about God has been clearly seen through what has been made (Rom. 1:19–20). Those who do not obey the gospel are those who have rejected the gospel explicitly. Both groups of people—those who have heard the gospel and those who have not—are consigned to the same judgment.[56] In other words, everyone who fails to respond in faith to God's revelation before death will face eternal destruction.

Foundation #7: Jude 7

Jude writes his letter to exhort his readers to contend for the faith once for all delivered to the saints (v. 3). The situation was urgent because "certain persons" had crept into the congregation and were undermining the faith

---

55. Fee, *The First and Second Letters to the Thessalonians*, 255.
56. So Morris, *1 and 2 Thessalonians*, 121. Contra Fee, *The First and Second Letters to the Thessalonians*, 258.

by turning the grace of God into a pretext for sin (v. 4). God had marked out such men for condemnation. To show that God knows how to judge the ungodly, Jude gives three examples of God's judgment from the Old Testament. The second example is in verse 7, and it alludes to the fiery judgment that God poured out on Sodom and Gomorrah in Genesis 19.

Final Separation

Jude cites God's judgment on Sodom and Gomorrah as an example of the judgment that is to come upon "certain persons." As Tom Schreiner has argued: "The destruction of Sodom and Gomorrah is not merely a historical curiosity; it functions typologically as a prophecy of what is in store for the rebellious."[57] Therefore, the destruction of Sodom and Gomorrah does not imply some kind of eschatological annihilation of the wicked in hell. Rather, the fire that rained down on the infamous cities was an example of "eternal fire," or "fire of the age to come," invading the present age. The fire that was revealed in part in the destruction of Sodom and Gomorrah will be revealed in full at the final judgment in the age to come. The destiny of the wicked, therefore, is separate from the destiny of the Christians reading Jude's letter. Jude's readers anticipate not "eternal fire" (v. 7), but "eternal life" (v. 21).

Unending Experience

The word "eternal" used to describe "life" in verse 21 is the same one used to describe "fire" in verse 7. That suggests that the fire of judgment is of the same duration as life in the age to come. Just as life in the age to come is everlasting, so also is the fiery punishment in the age to come. Sodom and Gomorrah are a temporal example of a fire that will not abate in the age to come. Thus the damned experience everlasting fire in the age to come.

Just Retribution

Jude 7 says that the people of Sodom and Gomorrah underwent the "punishment of eternal fire"[58] The word translated as "punishment"

---

57. Thomas R. Schreiner, *1, 2 Peter, Jude*, New American Commentary 37 (Nashville: Broadman & Holman, 2003), 453.

58. "Eternal fire" could possible modify "example," but it is more likely that it appears in connection with "punishment." So Richard Bauckham, *Jude, 2 Peter*, Word Biblical Commentary 50 (Waco, TX: Word, 1983), 55.

(*dikē*) evokes the idea of justice. It refers specifically to "punishment meted out as legal penalty."[59] Thus, the eternal fire is retributive in nature, not restorative. In this way, Jude depicts this fire as the just deserts of the damned.

Foundation #8: Jude 13

Jude 12–13 describes the false teachers with a series of metaphors, the last of which is the most relevant for our concern: "wandering stars, for whom the black darkness has been reserved forever" (v. 13).

Final Separation

The false teachers are called "wandering stars" most likely as a comparison to planets visible in the night sky. Unlike the stars whose courses were fixed and reliable, the planetary bodies seemed to wander off course. Thus they were unreliable guides, just as the false teachers were.[60] Because of their error, God had destined them for "the black darkness" that lasts "forever." The black darkness suggests the same fate as that of the fallen angels who were being "kept in eternal bonds under darkness" (v. 6) until the final judgment. In that way, the text is similar to others we have seen thus far that show demonic beings and unrepentant sinners heading for the same fate (cf. Matt. 25:41). That destiny is of course entirely different from that of Jude's readers who were bound for "eternal life" (v. 21).

Unending Experience

The term "darkness" is best understood in light of Jesus' own teaching, which describes hell in these terms:

> **Matthew 8:12** "But the sons of the kingdom will be cast out into the outer darkness; in that place there will be weeping and gnashing of teeth."
> **Matthew 22:13** Then the king said to the servants, "Bind him hand and foot, and throw him into the outer darkness; in that place there will be weeping and gnashing of teeth."

---

59. BDAG, s.v. δίκη, 1.
60. Schreiner, *1, 2 Peter, Jude*, 467–68.

Matthew 25:30 "Throw out the worthless slave into the outer darkness; in that place there will be weeping and gnashing of teeth."

In every one of these texts from Matthew, Jesus describes this darkness in terms that he uses elsewhere of the fires of hell (cf. Matt. 13:42, 50). Thus, it is likely that Jude employs "darkness" to refer to the same place that Jesus referred to—hell. In Jesus' teaching, the people consigned to this darkness experience weeping and gnashing of teeth. That suggests consciousness of their punishment, which Jude says lasts for the entirety of the age to come—which is unending in its duration. It is a conscious experience that will never end.

Just Retribution

We have already seen that God's punishments in Jude are examples of his righteous judgment (cf. *dikē*, v. 7). As an everlasting punishment, the penalty of darkness partakes of that same retributive idea.

Foundation #9: Revelation 14:9 - 11

The following two passages from John's apocalypse are two of the most important passages in Scripture describing the final state of the wicked. Both passages partake of John's rich theology of eternal life which issues forth from the double resurrection at the end of the age (cf. John 5:28–29). Revelation 14:9–11 is a scene of the final judgment that describes what happens to those who worship "the beast and his image" (v. 9).

Final Separation

Those saints who persevere in faithfulness to Christ are "blessed" even if they "die in the Lord" (14:12–13). As John observes earlier in his vision, those who persevere "eat of the tree of life" (2:7), are "not hurt by the second death" (2:11), eat "hidden manna" (2:17), "rule" with Christ (2:27), are "clothed in white garments" (3:5), and never go out from the presence of God (3:12). The destiny of those who persevere is far different from those who worship the beast and receive his mark on their forehead (14:9). Those who worship the beast fall under the "wrath of God" and are "tormented with fire and brimstone" (14:10). The contrast between the final state of those who die in the Lord and those who do not is decidedly separate.

Unending Experience

John describes the damned as "tormented with fire and brimstone" (v. 10). Again, the imagery of fire shows up here as an expression of God's holy and painful judgment on sin. The verb for "torment" *(basanizō)* in verse 10 means to subject someone to severe distress.[61] The noun for "torment" *(basanismos)* in verse 11 likewise refers to "the severe pain experienced through torture."[62] Both terms indicate the infliction of pain and distress. John says that the pain and distress do not end but go on everlastingly.[63] If the language was not clear up to this point, John clarifies the endless duration of their experience: "they have no rest day and night" (14:11).

Just Retribution

This torment falls on these people as a direct response to their worship of the beast. They fail to do what the saints do: "keep the commandments of God" (v. 12). God inflicts pain and distress on the ungodly, not to prepare them for salvation or to annihilate them altogether, but to punish them for their failure to worship God and the Lamb.

Foundation #10: Revelation 20:10, 14-15

We would be hard-pressed to find a more vivid depiction of the final judgment than the one found in Revelation 20. Here God casts the devil into the lake of fire for everlasting torment (v. 10). God's final judgment of all humanity immediately follows. In fulfillment of Daniel 12:2–3, there is a general resurrection of everyone who has ever lived as the sea, death, and Hades bring forth all those who have died (v. 13). These now appear before God to be judged according to their deeds (v. 12). At last, God will pronounce a verdict on the final destinies of everyone who has ever lived.

---

61. BDAG, s.v. βασανίζω, 2.b.

62. BDAG, s.v. βασανισμός, 2.

63. BDAG says that the phrase εἰς αἰῶνας αἰώνων (14:11) is formulaic and is synonymous with "eternal." See BDAG, s.v. αἰών, 1.b. As Keener observes, "That the smoke of their torture rises 'for ever and ever' … must mean eternal torment rather than annihilation; this same phrase applies to God's and Christ's eternality (Rev. 1:18; 4:10; 10:6; 11:15; 15:7), to the reign of the saints (22:5), and to the eternal suffering of the beast (20:10)." See Craig S. Keener, *Revelation*, NIV Application Commentary (Grand Rapids: Zondervan, 2000), 374.

Final Separation

The quality of each person's life is accounted for in books that are opened (v. 12). One of the books opened is the "Book of Life," which contains the names of all those who are to inherit eternal life in the new heavens and the new earth (vv. 12, 15). Those whose names are written in the Book of Life enter the holy city (21:2), dwell with God (21:3), have their tears wiped away, experience no more crying or pain (21:4), and are called God's children (21:7). Those found in the Book of Life are separated once and for all from those who are not found there. Those not in the Book of Life are raised from the dead in bodies fit to endure their final punishment,[64] and they are thrown into the lake of fire (20:15). It is the "second death" that never ends — the dissolution of all that matters for everlasting ages.

Unending Experience

After the resurrection of the just and the unjust (vv. 4–6, 13), both groups receive bodies fit for their destiny. For those whose names are not written in the Book of Life, they obtain bodies supernaturally fit to endure the same torment as the devil and his minions. We know that the experience of the lake of fire is everlasting because the devil, the beast, and the false prophet experience conscious torment "day and night forever and ever" (v. 10). Moreover, we have already seen in chapter 14 that people who worship the beast experience torment forever and ever: "they have no rest day and night" (14:11). So it is clear that everyone who enters the lake of fire has an everlasting conscious experience of suffering. As Grant Osborne writes, "The second death is not death in the same way as physical earthly death, that is, the cessation of earthly existence. There is no cessation here but rather ongoing conscious punishment."[65]

Just Retribution

The opening of the books and the judgment according to deeds indicate that the final assize will render to each person what is owed to them. Again, there is no hint of renewal or annihilation, only of divine retribution for the deeds that each person accomplished while living.

---

64. So Peterson, "The Foundation of the House: Scripture," 165.

65. Grant R. Osborne, *Revelation*, Baker Exegetical Commentary on the New Testament (Grand Rapids: Baker, 2002), 723–24.

Concluding Implications

The Bible teaches that God has created the world for the purpose of exalting the glory of his own name (Isa. 42:8; 43:7). He means to manifest both his justice and his mercy in his disposition of sinful humanity (Ex. 34:7). Those who follow Christ are "vessels of mercy" who show forth "the riches of His glory" (Rom. 9:23). Those who do not follow Christ and go to judgment are like Pharaoh, whom God raised up "to demonstrate My power in you and that My name might be proclaimed throughout the whole earth" (Rom. 9:17). In short, God is glorified in both mercy and justice, and the existence of hell serves to demonstrate eternally the glory of God's justice in his judgment on sin.[66]

There are numerous objections to the traditional doctrine of hell as it is presented in Scripture—certainly too many to answer in this brief space. The weight of the scriptural arguments above should be enough to settle the issue even if our lingering objections are never fully resolved in this life. On this point, Augustine once reproved those who act as "if the conjectures of men are to weigh more than the word of God." He thunders, "They who desire to be rid of eternal punishment ought to abstain from arguing against God."[67] Indeed, anyone who argues against what Scripture teaches is arguing against God. And that is not a position any disciple wants to be in. Rather, we should try to understand why God has revealed to us this doctrine. How are our lives changed by this knowledge? If hell really is a place of eternal conscious torment for all of those who fail to trust in Christ, there are some urgent implications for all of us to consider. I will conclude with two of them.

First, the biblical doctrine of hell teaches us whom to fear. God is not only the treasure of heaven. He is also the terror of hell. What makes hell terrifying is not the presence of the devil but the presence of God's wrath and indignation forever. If you have been frightened of hell because you are frightened of the devil, you are not fearing the right person. The Lord Jesus himself teaches us this, "Do not fear those who kill the body, but are unable to kill the soul; but rather fear Him who is able to destroy both soul and body in hell" (Matt. 10:28). Who destroys

---

66. Jim Hamilton lists seven ways in which hell glorifies God. See James M. Hamilton Jr., "How Does Hell Glorify God?" *9Marks eJournal* 7, no. 4 (Sept.–Oct. 2010): 20–22.

67. Augustine, "The City of God," XXI.23.

soul and body in hell? Is it the devil? Of course not.[68] The devil himself is being punished there. Who is the one destroying soul and body in hell forever? God "afflicts" the wicked in hell, and the Lord Jesus deals out "retribution" to his enemies (2 Thess. 1:6–8). Going to hell means being left in the presence of God's wrath forever (Rom. 2:5–8). Hell is scary because "it is a terrifying thing to fall into the hands of the living God" (Heb. 10:31). And that is what happens when people go to hell.

Second, the biblical doctrine of hell compels believers to see the urgency of evangelism. Have you considered the great mercy of God toward you in Christ? Have you begun to fathom what he rescued you from through Christ's sacrificial death on the cross? If his mercy was big enough and wide enough to include you, is it not sufficient for your neighbor as well? Shouldn't the terrors of the damned move you to share the mercy of God with those who have not experienced it while there's still time? Perhaps Spurgeon has said it best:

> Oh, my brothers and sisters in Christ, if sinners will be damned, at least let them leap to hell over our bodies; and if they will perish, let them perish with our arms about their knees, imploring them to stay, and not madly to destroy themselves. If hell must be filled, at least let it be filled in the teeth of our exertions, and let not one go there unwarned and unprayed for.[69]

---

68. Contra N. T. Wright, *Jesus and the Victory of God*, Christian Origins and the Question of God 2 (Minneapolis: Fortress, 1996), 454–55.

69. Charles Haddon Spurgeon, "Sermon XX: The Wailing of Risca," in *Spurgeon's Sermons*, vol. 7 (Peabody, MA: Hendrickson, 2014), 333–34.

JOHN G. STACKHOUSE JR.

Denny Burk and I hold many doctrines in common, of course, surrounding this area of eschatology. It would be inefficient for our purposes for me to list them all, but it is important always to recall that our disagreements lie within broad agreements about God, Christ, sin, and salvation, among other key loci in systematic theology.

In particular, we agree that our view of God is at stake in our view of hell. So I grasp the nettle to suggest that Burk's view of God is rather more focused on God's greatness than upon God's goodness and particularly, it seems, at the expense of celebrating God's love for his creatures.

Despite Burk's claim to be rigorously biblical, I submit that his argument is essentially deductive: Since God is infinitely great, any sin against such a God deserves infinite punishment. Furthermore, God insists on such infinite punishment, because "God has created the world for the purpose of exalting the glory of his own name (Isa. 42:8; 43:7)."

There are several things to notice about such an argument. But initially let's clear away a little brush that confuses the nature of theological reasoning. Burk starts by taking swipes at his theological counterparts for being "emotional"—as if emotions are not conveyors of information that theologians, like any careful thinkers, ought to pay attention to. Why *does* this formulation of doctrine repel me? Why *does* this view of God horrify me? Perhaps it is because I have unsanctified feelings that need to be corrected by God's Word. But perhaps instead, those are *sanctified* feelings, or even just good, basic human feelings remaining of the *imago dei,* that are warning me that I am on the wrong theological path. To be "emotional" is simply to be humanly alert to what's going on, and we are wise to take the feelings into account, although not, of course, to be dominated by them.

Now, then, to the argument. First, it is, as I say, deductive. In fact, Burk begins with, of all things, a story not from the Bible. In fact, it is a story he learned from a preacher that, like all good preacher stories, does indeed appeal immediately to our emotions—or, to put it more carefully, our ethical intuitions. (I myself don't think there's anything wrong with such a move; it simply seems incongruous from someone who has just taken pains to warn us about the emotionalism of his opponents.) The purposely disgusting story of progressive victims of dismemberment concludes that "to sin against an infinitely glorious being is an infinitely heinous offense that is worthy of an infinitely heinous punishment."

The immediate problem here, and one that shows up in all the exegetical work that follows, is that Burk shows precisely nowhere in the Bible a single passage in which this argument is actually made. Nowhere in Scripture does any biblical author say, "Because God is infinitely great, sin against God is infinitely bad and therefore entails infinite punishment." I suggest that it is Burk who is guided by his emotions and intuitions expressed deductively and that the actual data of Scripture are entirely against him when freed from the interpretative presupposition he brings to it from reasoning such as this.

The second point to note is that Burk's view of God has God pursuing primarily his own glory: "God has created the world for the purpose of exalting the glory of his own name (Isa. 42:8; 43:7)." Let's notice first that the former of the two proof texts offered here does not in fact make the point in question, and that the latter one actually speaks of God's *love* for Israel, not that Israel is some means God uses merely to glorify himself.

Indeed, this view of God as preoccupied with his own glory, so popular among some evangelicals today, is a dangerously narrow view of God's purposes in the world. It is narrow because it leaves out lots of scriptural teaching: "For God so *loved* the world that he gave his only Son" (John 3:16)—not so that God would get more glory but so "that whoever believes in him shall not perish but have eternal life." Likewise, Jesus suffered and died for us "for the joy set before him" (Heb. 12:2)—the joy of a lover who gets to save the beloved. God is deeply invested in the whole cosmos and in making shalom (peace") everywhere, and so he undertook "to reconcile to himself all things, whether things on earth or things in heaven, by making peace through his blood, shed on the cross" (Col. 1:20).

This view is narrow and also dangerous, because Burk's God is preoccupied with his own magnificence and so can do nothing else than insist that he get his due. If that means the unending torture of the damned, so be it. Such a God would be pleased thereby. But the Bible's God loves human beings, loves the whole world, and finds enjoyment in our salvation even at his own terrible cost. Such a God seems unlikely to enjoy the torture of his creatures, and while his holiness demands that justice be done to the unrepentant and determinedly alienated, there is no pleasure in it, and that justice is administered only as long as necessary: you pay for your crimes, and then you're done.

Burk's view of God's agenda entails a monstrously egotistical God who deals loftily with his hapless creatures as mere instruments of his self-aggrandizement. I do not mean to caricature here: I am truly afraid that this is what is actually on offer from those who I am sure mean to praise God, but in doing so incorrectly—as certain traditions of Nominalism, Calvinism, and Islam have done—end up reducing God to an ignoble cartoon of self-absorption and frightening indifference toward everything else.

The third point to note is that Burk, following Robert Peterson, focuses on ten Scriptural texts. To be sure, each of the contributors to this volume faces the challenge of limited space in which to argue, so choices have to be made about texts. But it must be remembered that very many texts in the Bible speak to the issue of the destiny of the enemies of God and, as Edward Fudge (among others) has detailed, these very many texts speak with virtual unanimity when it comes to describing the outcome of opposing God: judgment, suffering, and extinction.

In passage after passage of Burk's analysis, moreover, he adds meanings that are not in the text—especially the idea that the suffering depicted therein is eternal, which is, after all, begging the question. Isaiah 66, to begin with, speaks of worms and fire that do not die, but they are consuming *corpses*, not zombies or some other form of perpetually living "undead." The deathlessness of the symbols of judgment, worms and fire, speak of the perpetuity of God's holy antipathy toward sin, but the corpses themselves *are dead*. They're finished. And Burk has the integrity in this case to admit that he is, indeed, adding information to the text: "Though not mentioned specifically in this text, this scene seems to assume that God's enemies have been given a body fit for an unending punishment." I suggest that it is not "the text" that is doing the assuming here.

His next passage, Daniel 12, speaks of "shame and everlasting contempt." But this text says literally nothing about whether the damned are conscious forever to be ashamed of their contemptible reputations. Their reputations live on in ignominy, so to speak, whether they are alive or dead. That's all Daniel is saying.

In his third passage, Matthew 18, Burk again confuses the fire (which is a figure of God's eternal repugnance and resistance toward evil) and the experience a (mortal) being might have of that fire of judgment: "eternal fire ... expresses the pain that must be endured by those in hell." In fact, Burk rightly quotes the gospel passage as speaking of "perishing" and "complete destruction," phrases that really don't sound like "staying alive in a conscious state forever."

The question-begging goes on and on. The passages Burk adduces simply do *not* speak about bodies that are made fit for enduring eternal suffering. (To his credit, we must note, Burk avoids the non-Christian idea of an "immortal soul.") But space forbids me dealing with each one in turn, and I have dealt already in my own essay with the key texts in Revelation.

A fourth point to make, then, is that God's wrath is fierce, but it does not last forever, as we are told in Scripture again and again (Ps. 30:5; 103:9). So either terminal punishment is in view—proportionate suffering and then disappearance—or universalism is correct. And since universalism is not correct (as I shall argue further in response to Robin Parry), terminal punishment remains as the view consistent with scriptural teaching.

In Burk's view, alas, God's wrath does last forever, he punishes forever, and he does so because it makes him look good to do so (equal to increasing his glory). I respectfully suggest that the view of God as keeping human beings conscious in torment forever does nothing to achieve God's other purposes of saving the creatures he loves and enhancing shalom. I suggest further that such a view doesn't even achieve its desired result: to enhance God's glory. Quite the contrary: It poses an unbiblical and therefore unnecessary stumbling block to genuine faith. Such a view is, to speak more bluntly, sadistic, and the God of the Bible, the God and Father of our Lord Jesus Christ, is the exact opposite of one who gets joy from the suffering of others: he gets joy from suffering *for* others (Heb. 12:2 again).

Praise this God, then, "For his anger is but for a moment; his favor is for a lifetime. Weeping may linger for the night, but joy comes with the morning" (Ps. 30:5 NRSV).

A UNIVERSALIST RESPONSE

ROBIN A. PARRY

I want to commend Denny Burk for his clear commitment to the authority of Scripture and for helpfully highlighting the biblical presentation of final judgment followed by a division between those who inherit life and those who inherit destruction. This theme is not only consistent across the New Testament, as Burk shows so well, but was also a part of the "rule of faith" in the early church—that core of central Christian beliefs.[70] So it is not a take-it-or-leave-it doctrine, but a *central* one. On this we agree. My focus here, however, will be on areas of disagreement.

Methodological Concerns

Burk tells us that the burden of his essay is "to explain what the *relevant* texts of Scripture *actually* say" (italics mine). Now, while I agree that the ten passages he considers are *some of* the relevant texts in this discussion, I don't think that they are *the* (most? only?) relevant texts. And I certainly don't think that we can settle the question of hell simply by considering these texts without considering them *alongside* others. Presumably texts that appear to be universalist or texts about God's loving desire to save all people through Christ, and so on, would also be relevant.

The critical hermeneutical aspect to the hell debate is how one deals with the fact that some biblical texts seem to speak of annihilation, some of everlasting conscious torment (ECT), and some of universalism. The issues for evangelicals is how to affirm *all* of these texts as sacred Scripture, how to interpret them in relation to each other, and how to hold their teachings together.

---

70. Irenaeus, *Against Heresies* 1.10.1; 3.4.2; Tertullian, *On the Prescription of Heretics* 13; *On the Veiling of Virgins* 1.3–4; *Against Praxeas* 2; Hippolytus, *Against Noetus* 1, 18; Origen, *On First Principles*, preface.

So I worry that Burk maintains that the weight of his biblical arguments "should be enough to settle the issue" in favor of ECT without
so much as a sideways glance at other relevant texts. I do not doubt for
a moment that he would agree that he should offer a plausible ECT
interpretation of these other passages. But would he not be approaching
all such texts with the fixed conviction that they *must* be compatible
with ECT? And how is that not just as influential for his interpretation
of those texts as he fears the prejudiced emotional readings of annihilationists and universalists are for his ten texts?[71]

With regard to the ten texts, we might even agree that, other things
being equal, some of the texts appear *at face value* to teach ECT. But
other things are *not* equal—I have argued in my paper that there are
important biblical factors that weigh against such a view of hell. I cannot ignore these when considering the ten texts and their relevance.

How I would approach the ten texts should be mostly clear from my
chapter, so I'll try not to repeat myself here. My contention is simply
that they are not clear enough to rule out any of the views under discussion in this book.

Burk offers two key arguments to tip the scales in favor of his readings: (a) that the texts provide no suggestion of hope beyond condemnation for the lost; (b) that some of the texts describe the punishment/
destruction as *aiônios*. I will briefly respond to each.

Two Destinies

Let's begin by deviating briefly from the topic. Mark's Gospel says
divorce and remarriage are forbidden (10:1–11). There are *no exceptions*
mentioned. If Mark was all we had, then we would think that biblical Christians must *never* divorce and remarry. However, Matthew's
Gospel mentions an exception: sexual immorality (19:1–9). But it is the
only exception mentioned. If the Gospels were all we had, then Christians would have *only one* ground for divorce and remarriage. However,
Paul adds another: desertion (1 Cor 7:15).

My point? Any Christian wondering about the Bible's teaching on
divorce and remarriage and its application today cannot read Mark as if

---

71. As an aside, unlike Burk, I think that emotion has a critical role to play in theological
and ethical rationality.

we didn't have Matthew and Paul. We must seek to do justice to what *all* of them wrote. It may be, as many scholars think, that Mark himself did not believe that there were any exceptions to the ruling and that Matthew himself thought there was only one.[72] Even if that is the case, we cannot take such stances if we wish to be true to the *whole* of Scripture. We affirm the truth of what Mark wrote, but we do so aware of the qualifications offered by other texts. We affirm Mark, but go beyond Mark.

Let's get back to the case in hand. Burk is correct that most of the two-destinies passages do not suggest any salvation after the division of people into two groups. And if we had no reasons from Scripture to hope for ultimate universal salvation, then these texts would certainly count strongly against it. But we *do* have biblical grounds for universalism. So how can we affirm the truth of *both* of the two-destinies texts *and* the global salvation texts (both of which can be found side-by-side in Paul, John, and Revelation—who presumably thought they belonged together)? The typical universalist proposal, embraced by many in the early church, is that we can do so by understanding the condemnation as qualified by the ultimate salvation texts and thus as a *pen*ultimate fate. The failure of the two-destinies passages to mention post-condemnation salvation, while suggestive, does not in itself rule out such salvation any more than Mark's failure to mention an exception to the ban on divorce and remarriage rules one out.

Consider, too, that the lack of qualification of the two destinies may play an important rhetorical function. Think of a policeman warning a criminal: "If you do that, you'll go to prison!" He doesn't add, "But don't worry, you'll get out eventually." Such mitigation would serve to undermine the impact of the warning, even if it is true. In the same way, there may be good reasons in certain speech contexts why God would not want to undercut the seriousness of two destinies by qualifying them.

Eternal?

What about "eternal punishment" and "eternal destruction"? I have already indicated my approach, and I was pleased that Burk notes that *aiônios* "is an adjective that means 'pertaining to an age,'" and, as

---

72. Or it may be that Matthew and Paul help alert us to the unspoken assumptions behind Mark.

Stackhouse observes, "often means 'of the age to come.'" This is correct, and it is part of the reason that I don't think we can "be confident that *kolasis* is a punishment ... that is unending." In the case of *kolasin aiônion* (Matt. 25:46), we cannot settle the question of the duration of the punishment from this word, even if the age to come (in which the punishment occurs) is everlasting.[73] The need for caution is illustrated by the "eternal fire" (*puros aiôniou*) of Sodom's punishment (Jude 7), which — contra Burk — did *not* burn forever.

We also do well to note the numerous examples in which universalists among the early church fathers would happily speak of eschatological punishment as *aiônios* and consider such biblical terminology as *fully compatible* with their universalism.[74]

This leaves the ECT interpretation of the ten texts a possible way to make sense of them. But I contend that it becomes more difficult to read them that way once they are situated within the canon as a whole. And the passages only function as authoritative Scripture when read within the canonical framework.

Other Concerns

Thinking Biblically

Burk mentions some common objections to eternal conscious torment (ECT) in his introduction, but worries that they are "based on human estimations of the way God ought to behave" rather than on "specific passages of Scripture."

However, thinking theologically is not simply about explaining "specific passages of Scripture," but of indwelling the Bible and allowing the Bible to indwell us, such that our mind and emotions are reshaped in biblical ways. One can think biblically *beyond* what any specific biblical text says. The point is this: the problems that Burk dismisses are problems that arise when Christians are trying to think biblically. There

---

73. It is worth noting alternative universalist approaches here. Origenists do think that the aionial punishment lasts for the duration of the age to come. However, they do not see the age to come as everlasting, but as a prelude to the final restoration *beyond all ages*. Thomas Talbott thinks that aionalial punishment is punishment of any duration that (a) has its origin in the eternal God, and (b) has everlasting corrective effects. Alternatively, it could *even* be understood as an ECT from which God will deliver any who repent and are united to Christ by the Spirit. Thus, even *if* Burk is correct, it does not rule out universalism.

74. See Allin, *Christ Triumphant*, 93–98; Konstan and Ramelli, *Terms for Eternity*, chs. 3–4.

may not be a specific verse that says that eternal torment is incompatible with divine love, but that does not mean that the worry does not arise *precisely from* biblical teaching about God. It is too easy to dismiss this as "human estimations of the way God ought to behave." If the lack of a specific proof text was considered enough to exclude such concerns, then along with them would go other matters for which specific proof texts are lacking—doctrines such as the Trinity. There be dragons!

Rejoicing in Damnation?

I find Burk's vision in which never-ending punishment "will ultimately become a source of joy and praise for the saints as they witness the infinite goodness and justice of God" disturbing. We will look upon the damned, which will include people we love deeply, and see them in desolate turmoil of soul, with *absolutely no hope*, and our hearts will overflow with happiness. No thanks. God does not delight in the death of sinners, even if it is just (Ezek. 33:11), and I do not wish to either. The reactions of the saints to the punishment of sinners will be mixed. We will rejoice that the enemies of God are no longer free to cause harm and that sinners have not "gotten away with it." Nevertheless, how could we not also feel sadness that human beings are suffering?

The Happiness of the Redeemed

This raises another concern: Can the saints ever be *fully* happy in the new creation if those they love are suffering ECT (or are annihilated)? In the resurrection, how could a mother ever find perfect joy if her beloved daughter is burning in hell? The God-given love she has makes her yearn for her daughter's entry into divine life. But this can *never* be. So it is not only the daughter who has no hope—*the mother* has none either. And how can this do anything but diminish her heavenly joy? (Unless God causes her to *hate* her daughter. No!)[75]

---

75. Stackhouse suggests God will wipe our memories of the lost, but this would in reality shred our pre-death memories into an incoherent mess (see Gregory MacDonald, *The Evangelical Universalist*, 2d ed. [Eugene, OR: Cascade, 2012], 16–17).

The Parable

To help us align our theological presuppositions with the Bible in preparation for rightly interpreting the texts, Burk offers a parable about pulling legs off various creatures. The aim is to help us appreciate that the seriousness of a sin is determined in part by the status of the one sinned against. I agree. He then argues that God's infinity makes any sin against God "worthy of an infinitely heinous punishment."

Burk is telling us about the principle underpinning his essay. It is intended to clear away any distorting presuppositions, freeing us up to hear what the texts "actually say." However, this kind of argument did not make an appearance before St. Anselm (1033–1109), and it is certainly not found in Scripture. More than that, it appears to be incompatible with Scripture. Here is why. All sins are sins against God, and on this argument, as God is infinitely glorious, they all incur infinite demerit. You cannot get worse than infinite demerit, so it seems that *all sins* are as bad as each other—infinitely bad. If you steal a sheet of paper from the office, you have committed a sin that is worthy of infinite punishment in just the same way that you have if you torture and kill children.

Now, this certainly offends our deepest moral intuitions, and that has to set off alarm bells, but it also runs into the problem that in the Bible sins are differentiated in degrees of seriousness: not all sins are as bad as each other, and not all deserve the same punishment. There is certainly no suggestion that they all deserve "an infinitely heinous punishment." So my worry is that this argument, rather than guiding us to rightly understand the biblical texts, may have the *opposite* effect.

God is indeed infinitely glorious, but it does not follow from this truth that sins against God incur infinite demerit. The seriousness of sin is determined *not only* by the status of the one sinned against, but also by the nature of the sin itself (the motivation, the intentions, the effects, etc.). Finite creatures are simply not capable of committing sins that warrant never-ending punishment.[76] Such punishment is disproportionate, undermining the principle of retribution on which it depends. Thus, ECT seems *un*just.

---

76. Unless God ensures that they keep on sinning to eternity so that he can keep on punishing them—a suggestion with nothing to commend it.

Further, I worry that on this view of hell God ends up *perpetuating* sin and an evil world without end. It is true that he is forever balancing them out with the appropriate amount of punishment, but it remains the case that instead of removing sin from creation, God actively keeps unreconciled, sinful wills around *forever* in hell. I find that theologically problematic.

Burk says that the question of ECT comes down to the question of who God is and that "our emotional reflex against the traditional doctrine of hell reveals what we really believe about God." I agree. But this is precisely the *problem* for ECT! The very reason Christians struggle with it is that it seems incompatible with divine goodness, love, and—yes—justice.

JERRY L. WALLS

I find myself in a curious situation in responding to Denny Burk because I agree with him against the other contributors that hell is eternal, conscious misery. I agree broadly with his exegetical case for eternal hell, and I think the burden of proof remains on those who subscribe to conditional immortality and universalism. I do not, however, think the biblical case for eternal hell is decisive by itself, and in fact, I think both advocates of conditional immortality and universalism can make impressive exegetical cases for their views. But it is clear where the overwhelming consensus lies in the history of theology, and that is why I think the burden of proof remains on those who reject the traditional doctrine of hell as conscious, eternal misery.

Going forward, I believe the debate must focus more on larger theological, philosophical, moral, and aesthetic issues and assess the various competing positions in light of these criteria. These issues should not be set in contrast to exegetical considerations, of course, nor is giving them their due an alternative to sound exegesis. To the contrary, these issues inevitably arise out of exegetical claims and conclusions, and they must be central to the conversation as we argue our case for whose exegesis is finally most convincing. These matters will not be resolved simply by arguments about etymology and Greek and Hebrew grammar.

I will accordingly focus my comments on these larger issues in my response to Burk. As he notes, the big issue for many people with hell is that they "can hardly comprehend how the traditional view can be reconciled with the ways of a just and loving God." Broadly speaking, I want to know more about how Burk understands the justice and love of God as it relates to hell. Near the end of his essay, he writes, "In short, God is glorified in both his mercy and justice, and the existence of hell serves to demonstrate eternally the glory of God's justice in his judgment of sin."

Early on, Burk attempts to generate a sense of the justice of eternal punishment in hell with a parable that succeeds, I think, in showing that there is a correlation between moral guilt and the worth of the one who is sinned against. However, I also think there is profound disanalogy in the parable that undermines the central point he wants to establish. This resides in the fact that we do not have the power to do anything to God that is remotely analogous to the harm the character in the parable inflicts on helpless creatures ranging from grasshoppers to human infants. Indeed, God is so far above us in power, glory, and moral perfection that we are utterly incapable of harming him. In any case, the point Burk wants to establish is that "to sin against an infinitely glorious being is an infinitely heinous offense that is worthy of an infinitely heinous punishment."

This sort of argument has an illustrious pedigree, and variations of it have been defended by thinkers ranging from Anselm of Canterbury to Jonathan Edwards. However, the attempt to deduce "infinitely heinous offense that is worthy of an infinitely heinous punishment" from the notion of infinite glory is rather dubious. Indeed, the notion of infinity is a difficult one, to put it mildly, and it is far from clear how infinity in one thing entails infinity in another that bears some sort of relation to it. Consider an analogy: Suppose I say that I understand that there is an infinite series of numbers between 1 and 2. Does it follow that my understanding is infinite? Obviously not. I have a certain understanding of infinity, but that hardly makes my understanding infinite. Likewise, it does not follow merely from the fact that sin is against an infinitely glorious being that sin is infinitely heinous.

Indeed, a more plausible claim is the following: A finite being, with only finite time and power, can do only finite harm and, therefore, deserve only finite punishment. So far then, I am dubious that Burk has made the case that eternal hell as he conceives it is just.

Let us pursue further the issue of justice. It is not clear to me how Burk conceives of human freedom and its role in moral responsibility and guilt. Is it the case that sinners who reject God are free in the sense that they really could have accepted the gospel, but chose not to do so?

Does he believe God gives all persons enabling grace that is sufficient to empower them freely to accept the gospel and be saved? Is God just in the sense that he treats like cases alike? Are all fallen sinners given the same opportunity to experience the joy of salvation and eternal life?

This question is complicated by Burk's view that the Bible teaches that eternal misery in hell is "the lot of every person who dies in an unrepentant state. All those who fail to experience saving faith in Jesus while they are alive in this age will be resurrected and condemned when Christ returns." Now, the reason this complicates things is that it certainly appears that many people have far more and better opportunities to hear the gospel and accept it in this life than many others who are less fortunate. The person who is raised in a loving family that regularly attends a healthy Bible-believing church, let's say, has far more opportunity than a person raised in a slum whose mother is a prostitute and whose father is a violent drug dealer. Suppose the latter is exposed only to a garbled view of the gospel, which he rejects, and he is later killed as a teenager by a street gang. If the opportunity to receive Christ ends with death, it appears this person had little, if any, meaningful chance to receive grace and be saved.

Burk writes that "Jesus depicts hell as the just and punitive response to unrepentant sin." Is the justice in this punishment due to the fact that these impenitent sinners refused grace that was available to them? To put the question another way, do these impenitent sinners receive the *same* offer of grace and mercy that those who are saved receive? Or is it the case that those who go to hell receive justice, while those who are saved receive mercy?

I raise these several questions to ask Burk to lay his cards on the table, and in fairness, I will lay mine on the table. Indeed, it is probably pretty apparent what cards I am holding. What I am driving at is this: I believe the doctrine of hell is morally indefensible, given theological determinism. I am wondering whether Burk agrees with this, or whether he believes God is glorified by choosing some for salvation and passing over the rest who remain dead in their sins and are consigned to reprobation. Does he believe God is glorified in giving irresistible grace to some, while damning others who are not given such grace, and who consequently cannot do other than sin and disobey God? Is this what he means when he says "the existence of hell serves to demonstrate eternally the glory of God's justice in his judgment on sin"?

Is hell somehow necessary to demonstrate God's justice? Does God *need* eternal hell fully to glorify himself? Assuming Burk affirms substitutionary atonement, was God's justice not sufficiently demonstrated in the death of Christ?

The questions I have been pressing become even more pointed when we raise them in terms of God's love. Does Burk believe that God truly loves all sinners? Does God sincerely desire the salvation of all? Is his offer of grace genuinely motivated by love for fallen sinners, or does he only offer grace so it will be clear that he is just in damning those who reject it. (Again, it is far from clear how damnation can even be just in the case of sinners who are simply not able freely to accept the offer of grace, let alone compatible with God's perfect love for all).

The notion that the opportunity to repent is over at death is hard enough to defend as a matter of justice, given the seemingly obvious reality that many people have little if any real opportunity to respond to the gospel in this life. But it is impossible to square with the claim that God truly loves all persons and sincerely prefers the salvation of all. I do not think the Bible teaches that the opportunity to repent ends at death, and the reasons that have traditionally been given to support this claim are dubious. For instance, Aquinas held that it is impossible to repent after death because a disembodied soul cannot change its fundamental orientation. If God, whose mercy endures forever, is not willing that any should perish, but that all will come to repentance, wishes to extend his grace after death, he is certainly capable of enabling sinners to repent, with or without a body.[77]

Admittedly, the doctrine of eternal hell is a difficult one to deal with regardless of one's view of grace and human freedom. But if hell is freely chosen by sinners who are given every opportunity to repent, but who persistently refuse the offer of grace, it is at least clear that they have chosen their own lot. Despite God's sincere love for them, they have chosen to reject that love, and accordingly they experience the misery that inevitably results for persons who decisively reject the true end for which they were created.

But how can it be said with a straight face that God loves persons from whom he withholds the saving grace that would, in the words of the *Westminster Confession*, determine them to that which is good,

---

77. For further discussion of these issues, see my *Heaven, Hell and Purgatory* (Grand Rapids: Brazos, 2015), chapter 8.

"effectually drawing them to Jesus Christ, yet so as they come most freely, being made willing by grace."[78] For theological determinists, human freedom is no barrier to salvation for anyone God is willing to save. Irresistible grace determines people to want to come to Christ in such a way that they come "most freely."

I press these questions because Burk concludes his essay with a flourish that sounds very much as if he believes God truly loves and desires the salvation of all. He asks: "If his mercy was big enough and wide enough to include you, is it not sufficient for your neighbor as well?" This sounds like he means to say there is grace sufficient to save all persons so that those who end up in hell do so because they have persistently rejected grace that was available to save them. This is conveyed all the more in the famous quote from Charles Spurgeon with which he concludes his essay.

So here is my final question for Burk: Does he believe God loves all fallen sinners with a heart of true compassion as suggested in the lines from Spurgeon? Or does he believe only that *we* should exert this sort of effort to win them to Christ, but that *God* may not love them in the same way? If so, this puts us in the ironic situation of loving these sinners more than God does.

But again, ironically, on Spurgeon's own theology, God could give all such sinners his irresistible grace that would determine them gladly, joyfully, and most freely to come to Christ. And if they persist in going to hell, it is because he did not favor them with such grace. I am left wondering how Burk understands grace and human freedom.

---

78. *Westminster Confession*, X.1.

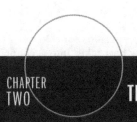

TERMINAL PUNISHMENT

JOHN G. STACKHOUSE JR.

"As I passed the fire I did not know whether it was Hell or the furious love of God."

— G. K. Chesterton

Any proper doctrine of hell must take thoroughly into account the goodness of God, an attribute that can be viewed as having two poles, both of which are essential to its definition. The former pole is that of God's holiness: God's moral rectitude and cleanness, God's detestation of all that is wrong and his relentless action to make everything right. God is, in a word, a perfectionist. The latter pole is that of God's benevolence: God's kindness, generosity, forgiveness, and self-sacrifice. God is, in a word, a lover. The same book of the Bible thus makes these complementary points: "God is light" and "God is love" (1 John 1:5; 4:8, 16).

Any doctrine being offered for our approval thus must give fully adequate attention to both God's fierce holiness and God's fervent affection, God's justice and God's generosity. In the following presentation, I shall outline and defend the view sometimes called "annihilationism" or "conditional immortality," but what I think is better termed "terminal punishment" — the view that hell is the situation in which those who do not avail themselves of the atonement made by Jesus in his suffering and death must make their own atonement by suffering and then death, separated from the sustaining life of God and thus disappearing from the cosmos. And I will contend that this view best takes into account these two poles of God's goodness. (In my rebuttals to my colleagues, I will contend that one or the other pole suffers in their alternatives.)

My more central affirmation, however, is that "terminal punishment" is the view of hell most fully warranted by Scripture. The other views, to be sure, can plausibly adduce certain Scriptures to their respective cases, and I certainly would want to allow for my own considerable limitations as a theologian.[1] I make bold to contend, nonetheless, that terminal punishment enjoys about as strong a warrant in Scripture as I have seen can be offered for any doctrine. And as an evangelical Christian who has devoted years of study to church history and historical theology with great profit, I nonetheless stand where evangelicals ought to stand: on what one thinks the Bible says, whatever the tradition might be.[2] I beg the reader's indulgence, therefore, if I argue rather robustly for this view.[3]

What Is Hell?

It is crucial to begin with a proper understanding of what hell is, in the light of the Bible. Any doctrine of hell that fails to live up to such a proper definition, whether by claiming too little or too much (as I think the alternatives do), should be set aside in favor of one that does correspond to the biblical portrayal of it.

The Christian understanding of hell stands in significant contrast

---

1. I offer a wide array of qualifications of our epistemic confidence in *Need to Know: Vocation as the Heart of Christian Epistemology* (Oxford and New York: Oxford University Press, 2014).

2. I therefore am not calling to the dock the several early church figures and documents that sound like they support my view (e.g., Didache, Epistle of Barnabas, Ignatius of Antioch, and so on). Nor, for that matter, am I adducing various important contemporary scholars who share it as well, from John R. W. Stott to Earle Ellis to Howard Marshall to Richard Swinburne (see Christopher M. Date, Gregory G. Stump, and Joshua W. Anderson, eds., *Rethinking Hell: Readings in Evangelical Conditionalism* [Eugene, OR: Wipf and Stock, 2014]). There is no doubt where the weight of the tradition lies, and it doesn't lie here. But the majority of Christians, including Christian theologians, have defended the authority of the Roman Catholic Church, the baptism of infants, and a number of other doctrines many evangelicals don't feel obliged to defend. What we ought to feel obliged to investigate, and then defend, is what the Bible says. That is what I attempt to do here.

3. In this enthusiasm I judge that I do not exceed in vigor my predecessor in the first edition of *Four Views on Hell*, Clark Pinnock, nor my predecessor in the Sangwoo Youtong Chee Chair of Theology at Regent College, J. I. Packer, who pronounced the view I here defend as "a prime case of [Scriptural] avalanche-dodging" ("The Problem of Eternal Punishment," *Crux* 26, 1990: 24).

to its cultural antecedents in both the Hebraic Sheol and the Greek Hades. Like those two other places or conditions (I will use these terms "places" and "conditions" interchangeably, since experientially they are equivalent), hell follows death, and it is a sad situation — a pit of darkness, at best a mere shadow of life on earth (e.g., Ezek. 32:17–32). But hell has at least three main aspects in Christian thought.

First, hell is depicted as a destination. Hell is the logical and metaphysical, and thus inevitable, outcome of the decision to reject God — and thus to reject the good. Hell is not a destination that God arbitrarily assigns to the recalcitrant sinner. Hell is simply the natural result of a moral agent choosing to separate from God, the source of life, and go some other way — and the other way (and we shall see that there is indeed only one other way) is what the Bible depicts as hell — or "destruction" (Matt. 7:13; Phil. 3:19).

Second, hell is depicted as a fire. Fire in the Bible performs two useful and related functions. The first is that of testing, or judging, the essential nature of a thing by destroying anything that lacks value, as fire burns away husks to reveal seeds, if there are any, and destroys dross to reveal precious metals, if there are any. The second, and closely related, function is that of purifying the situation of that thing itself if there is nothing to it of lasting value.

Third, hell is depicted as a dump. For a long time now, Christians have believed that the very term *Gehenna* that Jesus used to speak of hell, which denoted the valley beside the city of Jerusalem, was the municipal garbage dump. The valley did have a terrible past, and given Jesus' description of Gehenna as a place of removal, burning, and maggots, a garbage dump readily came to mind (Mark 9:43–48). Biblical scholars have since determined that the first reference we have to Gehenna as Jerusalem's actual dump dates from a thousand years after Christ. But the image remains because it fits generic biblical descriptions: hell is the place to which evil is removed and in which it is destroyed (Matt. 22:13; 25:30).

Why Is Hell Good?

Let us take each of the three aspects of hell in turn to show how hell in these basic senses is consonant with the goodness of God. Hell as destination respects the freedom and the validity of our choices as human beings created in the image of God and thus given the awful dignity of choosing, or refusing, to obey God and cooperate with God in the glorious calling of gardening the earth (Gen. 1–2).[4] Hell as destination demonstrates that God keeps his word and that we live in an actual world that functions the way God says it does, and not in some illusion: When God gives us choices and challenges, they are real and they thus have real consequences.

Hell as fire points to God's fixed determination to judge all things, to make plain their true character, and to purge God's cosmos of all that is not completely good. Thus the fires of hell mete out the just punishment for sins. They hurt: Suffering is what sin incurs and is that which atones for sin. And those fires also eliminate: The final result of sin is death (Rom. 6:23), as the fire of judgment purges the universe of the truly mortal remains of those who do not possess eternal life as the gift of God. Eventually, that is, all that cannot last forever turns to ash and disappears, no longer to pollute and offend and harm.

We can pause to note in this respect that the fire of God's goodness therefore "never goes out," in the sense that God's resolute resistance to evil and God's commitment to purifying all things are simply part of the divine character and thus never change. God's wrath against sin is not something that is ever extinguished because it is a settled attitude of God, even as it can be satisfied in the crucial sense that there is nothing evil for it to burn: If everything is finally good, as it will be once all evil has been consumed in the very lake of the fire of God's judgment, then God's wrath stands idle.

Hell as dump demonstrates that God intends to remove evil once and for all from his good creation. Hell as dump signifies, to our great relief, that evil has no lasting, legitimate place in God's good order. Hell, therefore, functions as a symbol of God's commitment to sanitation: to purity, health, and freedom from contamination.

Other views of hell suggest that hell is indeed more or less than the picture we derive from these three motifs: perhaps a torture chamber of everlasting punishment or a sort of medical ward of rehabilitation.

---

4. Readers unfamiliar with this way of understanding the commands of God to the first humans in Genesis are invited to consult Albert M. Wolters, *Creation Regained: Biblical Basics for a Reformational Worldview* (Grand Rapids: Eerdmans, 1985); and see also part 3 of my *Making the Best of It: Following Christ in the Real World* (New York and Oxford: Oxford University Press, 2008).

I suggest instead, however, that these three images together tell us all we need to know from the Bible about hell and are best understood together in terms of terminal punishment.

Why Is This Doctrine Resisted?

The main reason why our contemporaries resist the doctrine of hell is that so many of us don't take it seriously enough. We joke about evil, we even praise it as attractive. (Phrases such as "sinfully delicious" and "better naughty than nice" show up with dull regularity in Yuletide advertisements.) Cartoonists trade in silly images of hell that diminish and distort its reality. We are sentimental about forgiveness, believing, in what we like to think are our finer moments, that we eventually ought to forgive everyone—at least, we think that way just so long as we do not actually fasten our attention on any particular evil person and his or her evil deeds. Then we are not so accommodating. (People who have suffered under a specific repressive regime or who have endured personal violence seem not to be sentimental about the cost of forgiveness nor its universal applicability.) And we are generally unaware of the objective problem of evil or its ramifications in the cosmos. We have almost completely forgotten the previously global intuition that evil actions incur guilt, cause damage, incur debt, and so on. (More on this intuition below.)

To be sure, some of us refuse to countenance discussion of the doctrine of hell because we take it very seriously indeed, and we fear that hell will go on forever, as traditional Christian teaching avers. That idea—that God keeps creatures alive for eternity in order that they may suffer without end and without hope—seems so ghastly that even orthodox believers (one might say especially orthodox believers) prefer that the matter not surface at all. It is literally too horrible to consider. The present essay is offered to such believers as a more palatable alternative, to be sure, but fundamentally as a more biblically and theologically sound alternative.

Some Christians instead suggest that hell is not nearly as bad as we have been led to believe, but is merely a kind of purgatory, an intermediate condition in which those who currently are confused about God, or even opposed to God, will have ample time and optimal conditions in which to reconsider their opinions, reorder their lives, and eventually come to see and to worship the one, true, and good God. We will spend the rest of the book discussing the respective merits of these alternatives.

For now, I suggest that careful exegesis of all of the pertinent Scriptures leads to the understanding of hell as a place of limited punishment: "punishment" because sins can be atoned for only by commensurate suffering and death, and "limited" because the sins of any one human being, and the collective sins of unredeemed humanity, can and will be eventually atoned for and thus will be eliminated at some time in the future. Since those human beings, furthermore, are in hell because they have deliberately refused the lifeline that connects them with the "Source of all Good" (Calvin), there is nothing in themselves to sustain or regain their existence, and so they vanish once they have paid their debt. The rest of this essay will set out the grounds for this view.

Hell as Terminal Punishment

We will begin, then, where every biblically minded Christian wants to begin — namely, with the very words of Scripture. Three words in particular are key in this study: "eternal," "destroy," and "death."

The Meaning(s) of "Eternal"

Christians speak of hell as being eternal, but what does the Bible mean by "eternal"?

Shaped as we are by the Greek heritage of our civilization, we tend to think of "eternal" as "having continual existence" or the like. If something is eternal, therefore, it lasts forever. The Bible, however, uses the term sometimes in that respect and sometimes in other respects. Obviously, when God is said to be eternal, the Bible means "forever." When the same adjective is used of mountains, however, sometimes clearly something else is claimed (Gen. 49:26; cf. Hab. 3:6 in which the mountains are subject to drastic change in the Day of the Lord).

In the Old Testament there are ordinances, rituals, and institutions described as "eternal" (the Hebrew word is ôlâm), but they clearly do not last forever (and in at least some cases the context suggests that those who are present know full well that the item in question will not last forever). Exodus 12:24–25, of example, speaks of Passover: "You shall observe this rite as a perpetual [ôlâm] ordinance for you and your children. When you come to the land that the LORD will give you, as he has promised, you shall keep this observance." To this day, observant Jews celebrate Passover. But non-Jewish Christians have set aside the Israel-specific feast of Passover for the universal Christian celebrations of Holy Week and the Eucharist.

Exodus 29:4–9 similarly outlines the rites regarding the ordination of priests and concludes, "And the priesthood shall be theirs by a perpetual [*ôlâm*] ordinance" (v. 9). Again, many observant Jews look forward to the reestablishment of the priesthood in a new temple in Jerusalem. But Christians have seen Christ to be our one and only great high priest who renders the former system, and thus Aaron's priestly descendants, otiose (Heb. 10:1–18).

First Kings 8:6, 12–13 describes the inauguration of Solomon's temple: "Then the priests brought the ark of the covenant of the LORD to its place, in the inner sanctuary of the house, in the most holy place, underneath the wings of the cherubim.... Then Solomon said, 'The LORD has said that he would dwell in thick darkness. I have built you an exalted house, a place for you to dwell in forever.'" Proud as Solomon must have been of the new temple, he was wise enough to realize that no human building could last forever. We need to allow for hyperbole on such occasions and not press the words to literal meaning they could not have had even in Solomon's mind.

When we come to the New Testament, we see that the most common word translated "eternal" (*aiônion*) can mean "everlasting," but often means "of the age to come." Thus the "eternal life" of which John loves to write is not only life that doesn't end (a quantitative idea) but also is the kind of life lived in the light of the coming kingdom of God, the wholesome, flourishing life that will be enjoyed after Jesus returns and yet can be tasted even now (a qualitative idea).

Those who believe in hell as a place of eternal torment would not, of course, have any trouble with the foregoing. They can freely grant that *aiônion* can have qualitative as well as quantitative denotations. Where we disagree, then, is over the contention I now make that "eternal" does not always mean "existing forever." Indeed, the crucial distinction here is between, on the one hand, an event or an action that occurs for only a segment of time, and on the other, the result of that event or action that is indeed "without end." Thus the event or action itself can properly be called "eternal" because of its everlasting implication. We see exactly this distinction in a number of key passages in the New Testament. Let's look at three.

Hebrews 6:1–2 speaks of "eternal judgment": "Therefore let us go on toward perfection, leaving behind the basic teaching about Christ, and not laying again the foundation: repentance from dead works and faith toward God, instruction about baptisms, laying on of hands, resurrection of the dead, and eternal judgment." The author of this epistle cannot possibly have had in view a judgment that goes on forever—as if God could never descend from the heavenly bench! Instead, all orthodox Christians believe in some sort of Last Judgment that God conducts for a certain amount of time and then concludes with final verdicts— while the implications of the decisions taken during that judgment are, indeed, permanent, everlasting, eternal.

Similarly, Hebrews 9:11–12 speaks of "eternal redemption": "But when Christ came as a high priest of the good things that have come, then through the greater and perfect tent (not made with hands, that is, not of this creation), he entered once for all into the Holy Place, not with the blood of goats and calves, but with his own blood, thus obtaining eternal redemption." Once again, no one seriously imagines the author of this epistle believing that Christ is constantly offering his blood up to the Father as propitiation for our sins. The passage itself, in fact, emphasizes "once for all," a theme even more vigorously pressed in Hebrews 10:1–14.[5]

Paul writes of "eternal destruction" in 2 Thessalonians 1:9, by which he cannot sensibly mean an endless process of being destroyed. He obviously means that the destruction, which concludes at some point following the Last Judgment, has the grim ramification of being utter and irremediable: "destroyed" as in "gone forever."

Finally, Mark 3:28–29 speaks of "an eternal sin": "Truly I tell you, people will be forgiven for their sins and whatever blasphemies they utter; but whoever blasphemes against the Holy Spirit can never have

---

5. I pause here to note that Christians who believe that God is timeless may well believe that in the view of God everything is always happening in a timeless "present." Thus, in this instance, Christ could indeed be eternally offering himself up as sacrifice. But if that is the stance taken, then everything is indeed always happening, everything is therefore eternal, and the mind reels at trying to make sense of almost any significant topic of Christian theology, including the one under discussion. So having acknowledged this view, I have to set it aside as sui generis.

forgiveness, but is guilty of an eternal sin." Once again, we cannot imagine the author having in view someone sinning in this particular way on and on, forever and ever. Obviously the idea is that the sin, however briefly or extensively it was engaged in, has eternal consequences.

Serious students of the doctrine of hell, therefore, must be careful not to settle too quickly for ideas that rest on linguistic conventions that may not be followed in the pages of Scripture, and particularly on "what everybody knows" regarding the definition of "eternal." "Eternal" does indeed have something to do with "lasting forever," but in each case in Scripture we have to be careful to understand what it is that lasts forever: the thing or event being described, or its implications? And in the view of hell I am defending, this distinction is basic: between the eternal implication of the doom one receives from the Last Judgment (there will never be an escape), and the nature of that doom (a certain amount of suffering to be endured, proportionate to one's sin, after which one dies and disappears).

The Meaning of "Destroy" and "Death"

Unlike the case of words translated "eternal," when the Bible speaks of something being "destroyed" or something experiencing "death," it generally means termination. And, as Edward Fudge has assiduously demonstrated, the Bible is replete with passages—literally dozens and dozens—that speak of the destiny of the lost as termination, end, disappearance, eradication, annihilation, and vanishing.[6]

Even when one of the words for destroy or destruction can be rendered as "ruin" (*apollunai, apoleia*) it usually means—and always means, when it is linked with "fire"—the disintegration and disappearance of the thing in question. The same idea occurs in English: a bad stain on a silk garment ruins it. It cannot be cleaned. The stain doesn't cause the garment immediately to wink out of existence, of course, but it does render it utterly unfit for its proper use. So what do we do with it? We throw it away: as far as we're concerned, it doesn't exist anymore. So with ruined wineskins (Matt. 9:17), to use a more biblical image.

---

6. Edward Fudge, *The Fire That Consumes: A Biblical and Historical Study of the Doctrine of Final Punishment* (Houston: Providential Press, 1982). Anyone who wants to think seriously about hell must reckon with Fudge's astonishingly industrious biblical work on this topic.

We likewise say that "a person's reputation was destroyed." We don't have to mean that he subsequently had no reputation at all, but that what remained of his reputation was useless, even harmful, for social standing or employment. And it has become, in fact, irremediable. This point perhaps seems obvious, but in this particular conversation it is important to underline the idea that "destruction" and, *a fortiori*, "death" truly mean extinction: the thing destroyed is gone; the thing that has died is gone. There may indeed be "remains," but no one considers those to be equivalent to the thing that used to be there, nor is there anything to be salvaged. The true essence of the thing has vanished, whatever happens to remain.

Psalm after psalm and proverb after proverb reiterate the same biblical teaching (e.g., Ps. 1:4–6; Prov. 1:18–19). The wicked eventually and inevitably come to the same end: They will vanish from the face of the earth. Psalm 37 is just one of these many examples as it speaks of the wicked withering and dying like plants, disappearing so that they cannot be found, dissipating like smoke, being "cut off" so as to leave no trace (vv. 9, 22), and, finally, being simply "destroyed" (v. 38). The vision of the good world to come is one in which the wicked are simply, wonderfully, and eternally absent—"as though they had never been" (Obad. 16). They are not off somewhere else being punished: They are gone.[7] Jesus himself, as a rabbi steeped in the Old Testament, speaks over and over in the Gospels of the wicked being destroyed, being cut down and thrown into the fire, and utterly collapsing—and those figures come from a single chapter, Matthew 7.

Sodom and Gomorrah are clearly the paradigm cases of destruction. These entire cities are, literally, killed by God, and nothing remains of them except the smoke of their burning. New Testament descriptions of hell or, more broadly, of God's judgment upon the unrepentant typically draw on Sodom and Gomorrah and on the prophetic portrayals of the Day of the Lord that echo that story (especially in Isaiah, as we shall

---

7. Universalists might try to argue that the wicked aren't there because they have been redeemed. But to argue thus would be not only to add substantial content to what the passages say but actually to reverse the evident meaning of such passages. Others might argue that since the Old Testament doesn't talk much about an afterlife, we wouldn't expect it to talk about the everlasting existence of the sinners or the saints. Again, however, to take refuge in the vagueness of the conception of Sheol is to miss the clear implication of these verses as negative judgment resulting in eradication (usually meaning "not even leaving offspring").

see) to a Jewish audience that would be expected to easily recall these graphic examples of utter devastation. Consider, for instance, 2 Peter 2:6: "and if by turning the cities of Sodom and Gomorrah to ashes he condemned them to extinction and made them an example of what is coming to the ungodly." As clear as day, Peter says that the "extinction" of Sodom and Gomorrah is "an example of what is coming to the ungodly." This verse—and many others like it—is clear proof for the terminal punishment view of hell. Other interpreters must read this verse against its clear and natural meaning.

Similarly, the interpretation of other New Testament references to Old Testament passages should give priority to the original meaning of the text. Edward Fudge rightly affirms,

> New Testament terms such as "unquenchable fire," "smoke ascending forever and ever," and "the worm that does not die" are borrowed from the prophetic literature of the Old Testament. Legitimate exegesis requires that the meaning of these expressions in the New Testament at least begin with their meaning in the Old Testament and be enlarged only with justification from the text itself.[8]

Revelation offers us several grim examples of such usage as the great multitude cheers the victory of God over the evil empire of Babylon: "Hallelujah! The smoke goes up from her forever and ever" (19:3). Similarly, Revelation 14:10–11 depicts relentless torment in the presence of God's goodness—"angels and ... the Lamb"—culminating in an incineration of fire and sulphur that is directly evocative of Sodom and Gomorrah, who had "fire and sulphur" rain down on them ... and were no more.

Then, again in Revelation 19, an even more graphic picture is painted, one clearly drawn from ancient battlefields with a lake of sulphurous fire (shades again of Sodom and Gomorrah) being reserved for the worst of God's enemies:

> Then I saw an angel standing in the sun, and with a loud voice he called to all the birds that fly in midheaven, "Come, gather for the great supper of God, to eat the flesh of kings, the flesh of captains, the flesh of the mighty, the flesh of horses and their riders—flesh

---

8. Fudge, *The Fire That Consumes*, 29.

of all, both free and slave, both small and great." Then I saw the beast and the kings of the earth with their armies gathered to make war against the rider on the horse and against his army. And the beast was captured, and with it the false prophet who had performed in its presence the signs by which he deceived those who had received the mark of the beast and those who worshiped its image. These two were thrown alive into the lake of fire that burns with sulfur. And the rest were killed by the sword of the rider on the horse, the sword that came from his mouth; and all the birds were gorged with their flesh. (vv. 17–21)

Only a woodenly literal reading would press the details of these descriptions as to temporal sequence and extent: "How could smoke go up forever and ever? Is fuel being constantly added?" Or it would be a tendentious reading: "See? These passages—admittedly in the vivid, even fantastic, language of apocalyptic—support our view of eternal torment." The ancient audience would readily understand instead that the extravagant phrasing John uses here depicts a total defeat of God's enemies and the destruction of all who opposed God. They are well and truly dead, with only smoke to mark the spot, so to speak (Deut. 29:23; Isa. 34:10; Mal. 4:1). Just as it was in the case of Sodom and Gomorrah, this is a death from which no one, and no city, returns.

One might fairly ask whether Revelation 14:11's depiction of the damned enjoying "no rest day or night" implies that they never arrive at the relief of death and that they are instead forever conscious. But "rest" in the Old Testament (upon which, of course, Revelation draws heavily) doesn't mean merely the cessation of experience, but carries positive connotations of Sabbath—particularly Sabbath as enjoying the presence of God forever in the Promised Land. Thus the condemned are doomed never to enjoy rest, they will never escape their doom—for they suffer and die outside God's rest (Heb. 4:9).

Similarly, in Isaiah 66:24, the corpses of God's enemies are left to be consumed by the "worms" and "fire" of God's wrath. There is no reason to conclude from this passage that the corpses last forever! How could they, if they are being consumed? Eventually, every last bit must vanish into the maw of worm or flame. But the agents of their destruction, the worms and the fire, symbolize God's hatred and judgment of evil to death, an attitude that never disappears, as we have noted, since it is intrinsic to God's character. "Our God *is* a consuming fire" (Heb. 12:29; cf. Deut. 4:24; cf. Isa. 33:14).

As the account continues in the book of Revelation, we read, "Then Death and Hades were thrown into the lake of fire. This is the second death, the lake of fire; and anyone whose name was not found written in the book of life was thrown into the lake of fire" (20:14–15). The similar language would lead the conscientious reader to a similar conclusion: Death and Hades are destroyed (cf. 1 Cor. 15:24–26) and "anyone whose name was not found written in the book of life" is similarly destroyed, dead, gone—not immediately, as we shall see, but eventually. Being thrown into a lake of fire surely incurs pain, and that suffering might last a while, depending on what or who is being judged. The beast and the false prophet are contained therein for a millennium: (Rev. 19:20). But it is impossible to imagine "Death and Hades" suffering. The "second death" means, ultimately, to disappear.

Yet what about Revelation 20:10? "And the devil who had deceived them was thrown into the lake of fire and sulfur, where the beast and the false prophet were, and they will be tormented day and night forever and ever." Surely this passage teaches eternal torment for the wicked?

This passage is not as obvious in its meaning, however, as it might first seem. Later in the same passage, as we have just noted, we find "Death and Hades" thrown into the same lake of fire (v. 14). And the next verse sees "anyone whose name was not found written in the book of life" thrown into the lake of fire. So does that mean that lost humans will be "tormented day and night forever and ever," as traditional teaching says?

Well, if it does mean that, then we have the problem of conceiving of how "Death and Hades," who show up in the story between the other two references, are to be tormented forever and ever as well. That doesn't make any sense, and the passage doesn't claim that they will be tormented. Instead, the passage makes better sense if Death and Hades were understood to end, and indeed that is what the passage says: "Then Death and Hades were thrown into the lake of fire. This is the second death, the lake of fire." Since the very next verse is the one that speaks of lost humans, the most natural reading is to conclude that they, too, experience the second death. To state the obvious, the passage does not say that humans will be tormented forever and ever, and in fact the passage seems, in its basic literary elements, to suggest otherwise.

What, then, to make of the "forever and ever" torment of the devil, the beast, and the false prophet? Some scholars have suggested that these three are, like Death and Hades, abstractions, and their eternal torment is simply a mythical representation of the utter defeat of all evil by the power of God. Other Christians believe, however, that Satan, the beast, and the false prophet are actual persons, in which case it is at least conceivable that they are capable of experiencing eternal torment, should God will it. And perhaps they do.

When we recall, however, that the language of apocalyptic in general, and of this passage in particular, is typically extravagant, poetical, and allusive, we ought not to press the language of everlasting torment into a metaphysical construction of an actual state of affairs in which these strange beings suffer forever. Indeed, Hebrews 2:14 claims that Jesus destroys the devil—in fulfillment, perhaps, of Ezekiel 28:19. In this passage in Revelation 20, that is, it is more likely that we are encountering a highly symbolic representation of a fundamental, historical truth: The enemies of God will be soundly, eternally defeated and receive the full recompense for their crimes. And since they are the worst sinners imaginable, the author sees them receiving the worst punishment imaginable and expresses that in the most powerful language imaginable. (See a suggestive parallel in the difference in punishments in Revelation 19:20–21.) And that may be the point, which we should be careful not to mistakenly press into the wrong category: metaphysics instead of poetry.

To be fair, however, even if we grant that it is possibly the case that Satan and his minions literally suffer forever, we must be sure to note that Revelation teaches only that they do, and we are focusing in these essays on the destiny of human beings. This passage, like the many others we have surveyed even in this brief space, teaches instead the eventual termination of human beings in "the second death."

Occasionally when the matter of "death" arises in Bible study, someone points out that Adam and Eve did not drop dead in the Garden of Eden immediately upon disobeying God by eating of the Tree of the Knowledge of Good and Evil. Nor did they die later that day. Yet God said, "In the day that you eat of it you shall die" (Gen. 2:17). The interpretation of this verse, of course, is a problem for anyone, not just for proponents of the view I am commending. But what precisely no one can conclude is that God was threatening that "in the day you eat of it you shall die—by which I mean, you will actually live forever, if very unpleasantly." Given the pains God later takes to keep Adam and Eve from the Tree of Life (Gen. 3:22), we can be sure that by "die" God does not mean "not die."

We therefore must be careful not to interpret phrases that sound pretty plainly like termination (passages that speak of "destruction" and "death") to somehow mean not destroyed and not dead, but instead "kept painfully alive forever." Edward Fudge, who perhaps has given more attention than anyone to the linguistic challenges in this debate, concludes with a certain understandable asperity,

> If we ignore the Bible's own use of its language, we can make these terms mean whatever we please. But if we let the Bible interpret itself, we have far less choice. For all of Scripture's language on this subject leads us time and time again to the same conclusion: the wicked will finally perish completely and forever in hell.[9]

Let's be clear: I am not saying that God could not keep creatures alive forever in pain. But I am saying that there is no good reason to think that God will do so, and especially not from Scripture. Quite the contrary.

Some defend the traditional view by pointing to capital punishment as the worst of all punishments and to euthanasia as a horrible crime. Thus they argue that it is merciful of God to keep sinners alive forever, even if their existence is that of perpetual and hopeless misery. But this argument is importantly confused. In the first place, Christian opponents of capital punishment and euthanasia typically oppose them on the grounds that mere human beings ought not to be playing God. But God can, and does, rightly end people's lives. In the second place, and more to the present point, consider that the circumstances of hell are not that of a modern prisoner enjoying the very limited pleasures of life while incarcerated. I do not mean to whitewash the horrors of

---

9. Edward W. Fudge, "The Final End of the Wicked," in *Rethinking Hell: Readings in Evangelical Conditionalism*, eds. Christopher M. Date, Gregory G. Stump, and Joshua W. Anderson (Eugene, OR: Wipf and Stock, 2014), 41.

imprisonment, but at least some food might taste good, at least some friendships might be formed, at least imagination and memory might offer consolations—and there is always the hope of escape or other release. The same view might be taken of people suffering from certain forms of chronic illness or other disability: Life is sufficiently blessed by God such that many people in such situations still prefer a badly compromised life to no life at all.

The situation in hell, however, is one of unrelenting misery, of sheer punishment. And those of us who have cared for badly wounded or diseased people whose every moment is agonizing and for whom there is no prospect of relief have been glad for their suffering to end when God mercifully terminates their lives. No, terminal punishment is far more consonant with the goodness of God.

Part of the problem in this discussion, of course, is that down through church history Christians have taken for granted something that ought instead to have been questioned: the immortality of the soul. Yet our souls are not intrinsically immortal: only God has the property of life in himself. Nor is there a single verse of Scripture that says that God somehow, at some time, renders everyone's soul immortal. Eternal life is a gift of God to believers (John 3:16; 1 Cor. 15:50–54). Our sinning ancestors were kept from eating of the Tree of Life (Gen. 3:22–23), and we Christians look forward to the eternal city lined with abundant trees of life (Rev. 22:2). Immortality is clearly something we must get, not something we already have. So why would we keep believing that hell is a place of eternal torment of an immortal soul? We should not.

Finite Punishment and the Cross

It is frequently alleged that the view I am commending asserts that the lost are resurrected before the judgment seat of Christ only to be summarily judged and then immediately annihilated. And perhaps there are some who do teach that. But it seems evident to me that unless the lost have atoned for their sins during the so-called intermediate state (between their deaths and that last judgment), those sins, and the implications of those sins, remain—and they cannot simply be allowed by God's goodness to remain in God's good cosmos indefinitely.

God ensures that justice is done, that pollution is cleansed, that debts are paid, that all becomes well. At least one fundamental element of the biblical understanding of sin is reflected in various cultures around the world, from the dharma/karma structure of Indian religion to the sets of tabus in tribal religions on every continent. This element is the idea that human wrongdoing somehow damages the cosmos (e.g., Deut. 19:13; 21:9. In the Old Testament, the concept of guilt is some sort of thing that needs dealing with—not merely an abstract designation or emotional state—from the Torah through the Prophets: e.g., Lev. 4; Zech. 3:9).[10] Each sinful action makes a damaging mark on the goodness of the world, and the moral order of the world thus somehow requires this damage to be repaired. This idea helps to explain why God cannot "just forgive" our sins without anyone suffering. Not only must our relationship with God be repaired through reconciliation, and not only must our spiritual state be repaired through regeneration, but reality itself must be repaired. And not even God can dodge that problem—as Jesus' anguished conversation with his Father in Gethsemane acutely demonstrates. Atonement has to be made.

In the Bible, suffering and death are understood to be the "wages of sin" (Rom. 6:23), and the elaborate sacrificial system of the Torah was ordained by God to symbolize this fundamental reality. We note, again, that suffering and death are not arbitrarily associated with sin by God as if God could choose some other implications. Suffering and death are just what happens as a result of sin.

As the New Testament makes clear, however, the blood of animals can never atone for the sins committed by the human masters who offer them up. Only the suffering and death of humans can suffice to atone for the transgressions of those humans. The logic of justice is basic and inescapable: Someone has to pay, and pay fully, the debt—or fill the hole, or clean the dirt, or fix the break. Atonement is required to make straight the crooked and to level the uneven.

The glory of the gospel is that God graciously chooses to become human in order to do for us what we cannot do for ourselves: fully atone for sin and yet emerge, resurrected, to new life. All we can do for ourselves, that is, and what we must do for ourselves, is to atone for our sins by likewise suffering and dying—unless, indeed, we gladly accept the saving work of Jesus as the Lamb of God offered in our stead. In short, someone has to pay for our sins: either Jesus does, or we do.

---

10. Gary A. Anderson, *Sin: A History* (New Haven, CT: Yale University Press, 2009).

The doctrine of terminal punishment, therefore, says that those whose names are not written in the Book of Life arrive at the same destiny as all those (the devil, the beast, the false prophet, Death itself, and Hades) who oppose or otherwise deface God's good order: the lake of fire (Rev. 20:15). Therein, according to their nature as moral beings who have sinned, they make atonement via suffering and death. And God's cosmos cannot remain entirely and forever good if remnants of Satan or Death or wicked humans persist.

There simply is no other passage that comes close to suggesting that human beings suffer forever. Daniel 12:2–3 speaks of the lost incurring everlasting shame and contempt. But those terms refer to people's reputations, not to their own existence. And Matthew 25:46 is utterly ambiguous in terms of this debate. "Eternal life" certainly means life experienced for an infinite duration, even as it includes the qualitative goodness we mentioned earlier. But "eternal punishment" can easily be seen, as we have shown above, to be suffering and death that has, in the nature of the case (namely, death), eternal implication without eternal conscious experience. Recall, again, our understanding of capital punishment. It is punishment that terminates life and the implication is understood to be everlasting: You don't come back from it. What none of us mean by capital punishment is some enduring state of suffering.

Hell, therefore, is the final place of suffering and death. The suffering is commensurate with the sin: the Judge of all the earth always does right. Some therefore suffer worse than others, since some sinned worse than others. And the eventual death of all who are not united to God is as inevitable as the death of any astronaut who leaves the spaceship and then cuts all his life-supporting tethers of heat, air, and water: He briefly enjoys a kind of self-chosen autonomy, but ultimately, and relatively soon, he finds himself "free" only to suffer and die. That result is not arbitrary, either, but the natural consequence of his behavior.

Moreover, just as Jesus' suffering on the cross had a certain duration that culminated in his declaring, as he died, "It is finished" (John 19:30; *tetelestai*, which also means "paid in full"), so anyone who makes atonement suffers and dies condignly with the sin to be covered. Just as Jesus did not suffer eternally, even for the sins of the whole world, so each person who makes atonement on his or her own will not suffer eternally, either. Finite beings can perform only a finite amount of sin, and therefore a finite amount of suffering is sufficient to atone for it.

My friendly theological opponent may reply that Jesus is divine, and so he could suffer infinitely in our stead. So perhaps the lost suffer an infinitely long time. Even supposing that we know what we are talking about when we posit an infinite duration and thus an amount of suffering being experienced by Jesus in a state of (finite) incarnation during a finite amount of time on the cross (and I am not at all sure that these are coherent ideas), what we do not have in Scripture is any of this talk of infinity.

We do not encounter much of this language in the history of Christian thought, either, for the first thousand years or so. Anselm, Aquinas, and others do their best to sort things out during the high Middle Ages, and they have recourse to such concepts. They suggest, in brief, that because God's majesty and honor are of infinite quality, any sin against them deserves an infinite punishment. But with all due respect to such great figures in the tradition of the church, we yet must not take their conceptualizations for granted. Rather, we must submit any such idea to proper tests of both rationality and Scripture.

One can easily argue quite differently than did the medieval scholastics: that finite creatures can wreak only a finite amount of damage in and on the universe, and so a finite amount of suffering must suffice to atone for it. Are we therefore talking about finite or infinite quantities of sinfulness requiring finite or infinite quantities of suffering to atone for them? The mind begins to spin.

Again, however, even if we charitably grant each other the legitimacy of each other's deductive arguments, we must let Scripture decide the matter, and Scripture speaks decidedly on one side: "the wages of sin is death" (Rom. 6:23) and death means, if nothing else, termination. The one thing death does not mean is "not dying." The overwhelming and consistent scriptural testimony about atonement consisting of suffering and then death gives us the right lens through which to view the cross: the God-man finishing his work of atonement in his suffering and death—and then rising on Easter to bring believers new life (Rom. 5:6, 8; Heb. 2:9; 1 John 3:16).

The Goodness of God

The Bible thus clearly and uniformly supports the doctrine of terminal punishment as entirely commensurate with the goodness of God. God is indeed not willing that any should perish, and at the end of days it will be clear that God has done all God can do to draw people to himself—but in a way that honors our dignity as moral agents, just as God has honored the dignity of angels as moral agents. And just as some angels, such as Satan, are allowed by God to choose rebellion and its consequences, so some humans are allowed to do the same.

(We ought to note, in this respect, that the doctrine of terminal punishment is consistent with any orthodox view of predestination, whether monergistic or synergistic. The end result of human sin is the same, whatever one makes of the mysteries of the interaction of God's will and human wills: either Jesus suffers and dies for our sins, or we do.)

The punishment fits the crime: God does not keep rebellious angels and humans alive forever, but only so long as is absolutely necessary for them to pay their debts and purge their guilt. The view in both Testaments is that when the truly good God finally judges sin, that judgment is truly final. The cosmos is thoroughly purified of all evil—including evildoers. Indeed, in God's mercy, even the memory of evildoers might vanish, thus letting all proceed forward in the age to come without grief for those once loved and lost (Isa. 65:17; Rev. 21:4). Jesus thus renews the cosmos (Rev. 21:5). And thus God can truly be "all in all" (1 Cor. 15:28).

Hell therefore is bad, horribly bad. I stoutly reject the charge that the view of hell I am commending here somehow lets anyone off easily. No one gets "let off" at all. Everyone gets their just deserts, if they are not covered by the mercy of Christ. Hell is terrible. And it is final. John R. W. Stott offers this massively convincing summary:

> The Lausanne Covenant's expression "eternal separation from God" ... is a conscious echo both of Jesus's words "depart from me" (Matt. 7:23; 25:41) and of Paul's "shut out from the presence of the Lord" (2 Thess. 1:9). We surely have to say that this banishment from God will be real, terrible (so that "it would be better for him if he had not been born," Mark 14:21), and eternal. The New Testament contains no hint of the possibility of a later reprieve or

amnesty. The biblical phraseology includes, in contrast to "eternal life" and "eternal salvation," "eternal judgment" (Heb. 6:2 and possibly Mark 3:29), "everlasting contempt" (Dan. 12:2), "eternal punishment" (Matt. 25:46), "everlasting destruction" (2 Thess. 1:9), and "eternal fire" (Matt. 18:8; 25:41). And the imagery supporting this phraseology includes the pictures of the door being shut (Matt. 25:10–12) and the great chasm being fixed (Luke 16:26).[11]

But hell also is no worse than it has to be. Thus the doctrine of terminal punishment exonerates our good God from the appalling image of a perpetual tormenter. There is no joy here in the suffering of the wicked, but only sad justice.

I submit, then, that the Bible's express teaching, the Bible's logic, and the Bible's images nicely coincide in the doctrine of terminal punishment. So also coincide the wrath of God and the love of God, for God loves the good and does whatever God can to produce as much good as possible.

Chesterton, that is, saw both: hell is the furious love of God.

---

11. John R. W. Stott, "Judgment and Hell," in *Rethinking Hell: Readings in Evangelical Conditionalism*, eds. Christopher M. Date, Gregory G. Stump, and Joshua W. Anderson (Eugene, OR: Wipf and Stock, 2014), 50.

AN ETERNAL CONSCIOUS TORMENT RESPONSE

DENNY BURK

I commend John Stackhouse for making his argument on the basis of Scripture. Scripture alone is the only proper authority to bind the Christian conscience. Nevertheless, for a number of reasons, I remain unconvinced of the author's argument for "terminal punishment."

1. God's wrath and love are not at odds with one another.

Stackhouse argues that the goodness of God has two poles: holiness and benevolence. His holiness is his moral rectitude and abhorrence of sin. His benevolence is his kindness and mercy to sinners. Any biblical doctrine of hell has to account for both of these attributes of God. The implication of these statements would rule out both universalism (because it is out of step with God's holiness) and eternal conscious torment (because it is out of step with God's benevolence). This sets the stage for "terminal punishment" to be the Aristotelian mean between two unbiblical extremes.

Yet I would question this framing of the issue. Yes, the Bible plainly reveals that God is both wrathful and loving (e.g., John 3:36; 1 John 4:8). But nowhere are these attributes presented in conflict with one another or as two poles to be balanced against one another. God's wrath is a reflection of his holiness and consists in his anger against anything that contradicts his character and goodness. In short, wrath is the appropriate response to sin. Sin separates us from God, enslaves us, and destroys us. It prevents us from having a relationship with God. Thus, it would not be loving for God to be indifferent about that which so utterly desolates us and dishonors Him. If God would be loving, he would rightly be angry at and judge anything that affronts his glory and his creatures that way. In this way, God's love and wrath are complementary facets of the godhead, not contradictory attributes that need to be balanced against one another.

We might mention one other way in which God's love and wrath appear as complements. We cannot know the depth of God's love for us in Christ if we fail to grasp the greatness of God's wrath against sin. The Bible teaches us to understand God's love in light of his judgment on sin: "But God demonstrates his own love for us in this: While we were still sinners, Christ died for us" (Rom. 5:8). God shows his love to sinners by pouring out his wrath on Christ instead of us. What would have taken us an eternity in hell to suffer, Jesus Christ endured for us in his painful experience on the cross. Thus, the measure of his sufferings—which included his bearing the eternal wrath of God against sin—is the measure of his love for us. To diminish God's wrath would be to diminish the measure of Jesus' sacrifice on our behalf and thus our experience of his love. Charles Spurgeon has described it well:

> The whole of the tremendous debt was put upon his shoulders; the whole weight of the sins of all his people was placed upon him. Once he seemed to stagger under it: "Father, if it be possible." But again he stood upright: "Nevertheless, not my will, but thine be done." The whole of the punishment of his people was distilled into one cup; no mortal lip might give it so much as a solitary sip. When he put it to his own lips, it was so bitter, he well nigh spurned it—"Let this cup pass from me." But his love for his people was so strong, that he took the cup in both his hands, and
>
> > "At one tremendous draught of love
> > He drank damnation dry,"
>
> for all his people. He drank it all, he endured all, he suffered all; so that now for ever there are no flames of hell for them, no racks of torment; they have no eternal woes; Christ hath suffered all they ought to have suffered, and they must, they shall go free.[12]

It would be a mistake, therefore, to treat God's wrath as the opponent of his love. Both attributes exist without contradiction within the character of God.

---

12. Charles Haddon Spurgeon, "Sermon XX: Justification by Grace," in *Spurgeon's Sermons*, vol. 3 (Peabody, MA: Hendrickson, 2014), 298.

2. The depiction of hell as a "fire" and as a "dump" falls short.

Stackhouse acknowledges that scholars have shown the "garbage dump" interpretation of *Gehenna* to be an anachronism. Nevertheless, he goes on to argue as if the garbage dump metaphor is relevant because it "fits generic biblical descriptions: hell is the place to which evil is removed and in which it is destroyed." This anachronism is not supported by Scripture and weakens his case that "hell" is a place where things are destroyed. There is no evidence that a garbage dump is in view here. Thus, to use that image as a basis for understanding how things are "destroyed" in hell is a mistake. For that reason, it is an error to suggest that things are "destroyed" in hell in the same way that items are destroyed and disintegrate in a garbage dump. The degree to which he is still relying on that discredited image of hell is the degree to which he has undermined his own argument.

3. Hellfire as annihilation introduces eschatological absurdity.

Stackhouse correctly acknowledges the biblical description of hell as a place of fire. Nevertheless, he incorrectly identifies what the fires of hell represent. He says that hellfire has two functions: testing and purifying. By that, he means that fire *tests* the "essential nature of a thing, by destroying anything that lacks value." Likewise, fire *purifies* objects that have no lasting value. He does not argue that the fire purifies people who go to hell. He argues that the fire erases them from existence and thereby "purges" God's universe "of all that is not completely good."

This view is problematic because the cosmos still would not be as it should be after the final judgment. God's creation would still be defiled by the existence of sinners. His fires would yet burn for ages until he completely erases sinners from the cosmos. But this does not comport with the biblical depiction of the final judgment, after which evil has been decisively dealt with and the cosmos has been restored to its rightful order (Rev. 21:5). Yet, in Stackhouse's argument the very existence of the damned in hell—even though temporary—leaves the matter of evil still unresolved after the final judgment. In that sense, it extends the "already/not yet" eschatology of the New Testament for ages beyond the final judgment. This is an absurdity not warranted by the imagery of hellfire.

Stackhouse further argues that "God's cosmos cannot remain

entirely and forever good if remnants of Satan or Death or wicked humans persist." Yet we have to ask where the biblical warrant is for such a statement. The Scripture repeatedly says that God's justice is magnified by his judgment on the wicked, not by the elimination of the wicked.

One stark example of this is Revelation 19:1–6, the account of the "great harlot." Even as the smoke rises up from the damned, a great multitude in heaven offers up a fourfold "Hallelujah" for God's glorious justice revealed in his judgments on the damned. It does not say that generic smoke rises up forever—as if the fire is everlasting but the damned are not. It says that "*her* smoke rises up forever and ever" (v. 3 NASB), which implies that the existence of the damned is coextensive with that of the everlasting fire. Again, the "hallelujahs" are for God's judgment of the wicked, not for the elimination of the wicked. And God's justice is not called into question because of her existence while burning. His justice is vindicated by her burning. Everything is good in God's cosmos when God's judgment falls on the damned.

The Bible depicts hellfire primarily as an image of God's holy wrath against sin. It suggests nothing about the finite existence of that which it burns. It is all about the unending fury that God has against sin and against those who in the end refuse to repent. In light of the special properties that God gives to resurrected bodies, it overrides the imagery to say that fire implies an ontological statement about the temporary existence of the damned. Nor does the imagery suggest that the existence of the damned is a smudge on God's restored universe after the final judgment. After the final judgment, God leaves no loose ends to tie up after ages of incinerating judgments in hell. On the contrary, the fires are a statement about God's just and unyielding anger toward sin.

4. The "palatability" of terminal punishment does not make it true.

Stackhouse says that orthodox believers often find the idea of eternal conscious torment to be "ghastly" and "too horrible to consider." He therefore offers the terminal punishment view as a more "palatable alternative" to the abhorrent idea that God would keep "creatures alive for eternity in order that they may suffer without end." To be sure, Stackhouse says that Scripture must ultimately bind the conscience. But this emotional framing of the issue constitutes an unbiblical prejudice against the interpretation that has been the dominant view among orthodox Christians over the entire 2,000-year history of the Christian church.

If Stackhouse wishes for consciences to be bound to a different interpretation, this kind of prejudicial statement does not help. Ultimately, the matter must be settled on biblical grounds. In the end, the Bible is our final authority, not our own conjectures about how God ought to behave in the world. After all, what may seem "palatable" to sinners might not be at all palatable to a holy God.

5. The exposition of key biblical texts remains unconvincing.

In this brief response I cannot refute in detail every biblical interpretation offered in Stackhouse's chapter. To do so would be a virtual rewrite of my own chapter. Nevertheless, I would raise again objection to his exegesis of key biblical material. Stackhouse rightly observes that "eternal" has a semantic range that sometimes describes something that "lasts forever" and that at other times describes something that does not last forever. The semantic range of "eternal," however, is not really the issue. The question is what the term means in the context of the texts that are in dispute.

That '*ôlām* may indicate something temporary in some texts is no argument against its meaning *everlasting* in a text like Daniel 12:2. In that verse, both righteous and wicked are "awake" to consciousness of their destiny. The term '*ôlām* describes their destinies and suggests that their destinies are equally extended into the future — a future that is obviously conscious and everlasting for the righteous. There is nothing in the text to indicate that it would be unconscious and temporary for the unrighteous.

Stackhouse argues that biblical language for "destruction" and "death" generally means "termination." This is a well-worn argument for annihilationists, and Stackhouse follows closely the arguments that Edward Fudge has made elsewhere and that Robert Peterson has decisively refuted.[13] Stackhouse's exposition in this book is unconvincing in large part because he adduces a string of biblical references that teach about temporal judgments (e.g., Ps. 1:4–6; 37; Prov. 1:18–19; Obad.

---

13. Edward William Fudge and Robert A. Peterson, *Two Views of Hell: A Biblical & Theological Dialogue*, Spectrum Multiview Books (Downers Grove, IL: IVP Academic, 2000).

16). But these references to temporal "destruction" and "death" hardly constitute evidence against everlasting death and destruction taught in texts like 2 Thessalonians 1:9. (See my exposition of this text in my chapter.)

6. The "immortality of the soul" is no argument against the resurrection of the damned.

Stackhouse argues that the eternal conscious torment view relies on a view of the "immortality of the soul" that is foreign to Scripture. He says that there is not "a single verse of Scripture that says that God somehow, at some time, renders everyone's soul immortal.... So why would we keep believing that hell is a place of eternal torment of an immortal soul? We should not." But this isn't exactly what traditionalists believe about immortality.

The Bible teaches the immortality of whole human beings, not merely the immortality of their souls. This is not to deny that the soul is often distinguished from the body in Scripture (e.g., 1 Thess. 5:23). Nor is it to deny that the Scripture speaks of the soul's existence apart from the body (e.g., 2 Cor. 5:8). It is to say that both the righteous and the unrighteous will be resurrected in physical bodies at the end of the age (Dan. 12:2–3; John 5:28–29). This means that both the saved and the damned have physical bodies in the age to come. They are not body-less spirits either in glory or in damnation. They are human beings given bodies that are fit for their everlasting destiny.

Even if the Bible lacked teaching on the so-called immortality of the soul as Stackhouse alleges, it is beside the point. The question is what happens to resurrected human beings in the age to come, not merely what happens to their souls. And the Bible teaches that some are resurrected to everlasting judgment.

7. The finite duration of sin does not imply a finite duration of punishment.

Stackhouse argues that "Finite beings can perform only a finite amount of sin, and therefore a finite amount of suffering is sufficient to atone for it." Again, this is a statement without biblical warrant. It fails to recognize that the seriousness of sin—and thus of the punishment due to sin—is not measured by the duration of the sin by the dignity of the one sinned against. The reason that sin deserves an everlasting punishment is because of the holiness of God. God is the first and best of beings. His dignity and worth cannot be measured. Thus, to sin against an infinitely glorious being is an infinitely heinous offense that is worthy of an infinitely heinous punishment. The penalty of hell — eternal conscious suffering under the wrath of God — is not an overreaction on God's part. It is an eternal, glorious testimony to his holiness and justice. And in the age to come, every saint will celebrate that truth (Rev. 18:20).

ROBIN A. PARRY

I would like to thank John Stackhouse for a clear presentation of the annihilationist view, which helpfully blends exegetical and theological reflection into a coherent whole. I have a lot of time for annihilationists — or what I should now perhaps call "terminators"; I used to be one. I think that on several issues terminators have the edge over tormentors. In particular, I think that their arguments against the *never-ending* nature of hell's torments are often compelling. Nevertheless, it seems to me that the view remains problematic.

Jesus and the Failure of God?

I agree with Stackhouse that termination is less theologically troublesome than torment. ECT seems to be incompatible with divine justice and love, while termination certainly has a good claim on being just (at least, if retribution exhausts our notion of justice) and might even be compatible with divine love. However, it seems to me that both tormentors and terminators find themselves on the horns of a dilemma.

The question is this: Can God bring it about that all people freely embrace salvation in Christ? If one is a Calvinist then the answer is *yes;* if one is an Arminian then the answer given is usually *no*[14] — God wants all people to freely embrace the gospel, but God cannot compel a free choice. Consequently, for Arminians, God cannot ensure that all people are saved. The problem is that we seem to be confronted with two alternatives, neither of which is very attractive.

1. *If God can* deliver all people without violating their freedom but chooses instead to send some of them to hell (for torment or termination), then while such an act may be just (in

---

14. Though, as I argue in my essay, I think it could be yes.

retributive terms), it seems to be incompatible with the claim that God loves such sinners and desires what is best for them. (After all, by saving them through Christ he is in no way compromising his justice.)

2. *If God cannot* deliver all people without violating their freedom, then while God desires a restoration of all things, in fact he is very likely to be forever thwarted in his desires. How can we then speak of God's eschatological victory?

So if universalism is not true, it seems to me that the pressure is on to surrender either the claim that God is love or the claim that God completely wins.

Stackhouse takes the second option. He speaks of human freedom and its inherent consequences and how God does "*all God can do* to draw people to himself" and "whatever he can to produce *as much good as possible*" (italics mine), but in the end God must reconcile himself to the fact that many reject him and find themselves forever lost. God takes no joy in this—"only sad justice." (As an aside, Stackhouse says that "God has done *all that he can do* to draw people to himself," but if he also claims—as he seems to—that there are no opportunities for salvation beyond death, then this seems implausible. Can we really claim that for all those who have died there was *nothing more* that God could have done to solicit their acceptance of the gospel before they died?[15])

It seems to me that if eschatological destruction is something that God reluctantly allows creatures to inflict upon themselves, then it represents God's permanent failure to bring about his purposes in the case of all such creatures. He tried to stop them before it was too late, but they slipped through his fingers like sand. If, on the other hand, it is something that God actively inflicts on sinful creatures, then it represents God's permanent abandonment of his purposes in the case of such creatures. God tried to woo them over, but they thwarted his attempts,

---

15. In addition, I am unclear, given Stackhouse's account of atonement, why he is not a universalist. He says that sin must be atoned for by death—either our own or that of Christ. But he then says that *Jesus has paid the debt in full for all people*, making a universal atonement. In that case, on Stackhouse's logic, no sinners need atone for sin with their *own* death. So why do any go to hell? As it stands, Stackhouse's account is problematic—incomplete at best. Jesus' death seems only to *potentially* atone for sin. Behold the Lamb of God, who potentially takes away the sins of the world!

so he gave up trying and condemned them to hell or blasted them out of existence. Either way, God reluctantly settles for second best.

I appreciate that some are prepared to bite the bullet on this one, but it seems something akin to Orwellinan doublespeak to call the end of this narrative "God's triumph over sin" or "divine victory." The problem is that this notion of divine victory is theoretically compatible with a state in which every rational agent in creation freely chooses to reject God and embrace destruction. We would look at the eschatological state in which the whole cosmos was burning in hell or has been terminated, in which none of those for whom Christ died has been saved, in which none of God's intentions for creation are realized, and we would say, "*This* is God's triumph over sin!" But to me it looks more like the triumph of sin and Satan over God's purposes. It seems to make "God wins" worryingly close in meaning to "God loses."

Annihilationists raise the objection against eternal torment that, on the traditional view, evil is never removed from creation, but is simply contained in an everlasting stasis chamber. Indeed! Better to be done with sin and banish it from creation. Annihilationism removes that problem with the guillotine. There are no sinners in the new creation — God is all in all.

The problem is that God's answer to evil here is not a *gospel* solution (i.e., to eradicate sin from the sinners), but a terminator solution (i.e., to eradicate the sinners themselves). This is a drastic way of winning creation — like winning all the votes in an election by killing those who would have voted differently. Hypothetically, God could annihilate the vast majority of human beings and then claim to have won a glorious triumph in a universe filled with creatures that love him. But is this not a pyrrhic victory? The cost of winning was so *very* high. And given that this was a cost that God really did not want to pay, then it is as much a failure as a victory. It looks to me as if on this view sin and death have their wicked way in the end — forcing God to abandon and obliterate many of those he loves. Here is Nik Ansell:

> It is worth reminding ourselves ... that the annihilation and destruction of God's good creation is precisely the aim and goal of evil, not evidence of its defeat. The destruction, including the self-destruction, of those made in God's image represents a victory

for the forces of darkness. In the transformation of everlasting punishment into final judgment [i.e., annihilation], evil still has the last word.[16]

One attraction of universalism is that it allows one to affirm *both* divine love *and* divine victory.

Over-Reading Biblical Imagery?

Sometimes I feel that terminators, like tormentors, can push biblical imagery (e.g., of consuming fire) and language (e.g., "destroy") farther than necessary. I agree that Scripture uses *very strong* language and imagery to describe the fate of sinners—language that can, when contextually appropriate, indicate final ruin and annihilation. As such, terminators like Stackhouse are right to appeal to it.

However, the debate is not thereby settled. We must not leap too quickly from such powerful imagery to the proclamation that hell is *terminal* punishment. Why? Because we must remember that the biblical God who destroys is *also* the God "who gives life to the dead" (Rom. 4:17). This relativizes destruction talk, for *one cannot be destroyed beyond divine recovery*. Destruction need not be terminal when the Lord God is involved. As I briefly argued in my essay, Scripture makes no apology for its rhetoric of wrath, which allows the deployment of end-of-the-road termination language, only to subsequently speak of restoration.

Let's take as an example the instance that Stackhouse rightly makes paradigmatic: Sodom and Gomorrah. They are the models par excellence of "eternal punishment" (Jude 7)—and, says Stackhouse, "nothing remains of them except the smoke of their burning." Thus, he sees in Sodom and Gomorrah "clear proof of the terminal punishment view." I, however, think they serve to caution us against giving up on hope. Jesus talked about how Sodom and Gomorrah would be treated on the coming day of judgment (Matt 10:15; 11:24). Yet, presumably Jesus cannot have thought of the inhabitants of the towns as having no existence whatsoever; otherwise they could not be judged in the future.

Perhaps a terminator may say that they are resurrected into existence again before being annihilated a second time. Perhaps. But what are

---

16. Nik Ansell, "Hell: The Nemesis of Hope?" Online: http://theotherjournal.com/2009/04/20/hell-the-nemesis-of-hope/.

we to make of Ezekiel's prophecy? Ezekiel pictures Judah as being the sister of Sodom, whose own wickedness exceeds that of Sodom. God says that he "removed" Sodom when he saw their sin (16:48–50). Judah too will bear her public disgrace (16:52, 57–59). But God is a God of restoration, and in an unexpected gesture of grace he promises to restore the fortunes of Sodom and her daughters as well as those of Samaria and Judah (16:53) so that they all return to their former state (16:55); indeed, Judah will be ashamed of her sin and God will make atonement for her and an eternal covenant. Then he will give Sodom to Judah as a daughter (16:60–63). So here we find a prophet taking Sodom—the paradigm case of sinful behavior and fiery punishment—and promising her *a post-annihilation restoration*.

At the very least, this ought to caution us against taking the *seemingly* final language and imagery of judgment in the Bible as ruling out the possibility of final restoration. If Sodom really is the core biblical paradigm of final punishment—and it is—then why can it not also be a biblical basis for hope beyond final destruction?

Death

Using death language to suggest annihilation is more problematic, and here I side with Burk. It seems to me that some of Stackhouse's arguments are based on the assumption that death and nonexistence are interchangeable notions. To take but two instances: (a) "the one thing death does not mean is 'not dying'"; (b) we must be cautious not to interpret termination language to mean "not dead, but instead 'kept painfully alive forever.'"

However, this argument works by equating "death" with nonexistence and "life" with existence. But this is to beg the question. If language of "death" is not simply interchangeable with "nonexistence" (and that of "life" with "existence"), then the argument does not work. And it seems to me that the biblical usage of this terminology does not track notions of existence or nonexistence. After all, the dead were not considered utterly nonexistent. In the Old Testament they had some quasi-existence in the shadowy underworld of sheol/hades. In the New Testament this notion of hades was filled out some more and was certainly not nonbeing.

Sure, the dead may well vanish from the earth (as Stackhouse helpfully shows), but that is not the same as *utterly* vanishing. Furthermore, the Bible is more than happy to use the notions of life and death in a theological sense, indicating one's relation (or lack of relation) to God, the source of life. Thus, those out of relation with God are considered to be dead in sin (e.g., Eph. 2:1). This does not mean that they do not exist. On the flipside, those who are in Christ participate in his life and are alive to God (e.g., Eph. 2:5). This, again, has nothing to do with existence and nonexistence, and everything to do with knowing God. Thus, say, talk of the lake of fire as the "second death" cannot be assumed to mean "the second annihilation," unless one already knows that death-talk equals annihilation-talk. But if it indicates alienation from divine life in the age to come, then the language seems to me to make complete sense.

If I am correct, then death, even the second death, cannot be taken to extinguish hope for resurrection. The gates of the New Jerusalem are never shut, not even to those kings of the earth and rebellious nations that oppose the Messiah and find themselves in the lake of fire (Rev. 21:22–27). The blood of the lamb ever avails, offering hope in the place beyond all hope.

JERRY L. WALLS

I want to begin my response to John Stackhouse by urging that he has considerably overstated the biblical support for his view. He writes that "terminal punishment enjoys about as strong a warrant in Scripture as I have seen can be offered for any doctrine." Then later in his essay, in arguing against the view of eternal hell, he claims that "Scripture speaks decidedly" against that view.

The conditional immortality view, or terminal punishment, as he labels it, has been recognized as a viable evangelical option for some time now, and it can claim a number of distinguished theologians and biblical scholars in its ranks. The view, moreover, enjoys the energetic — and I would add, intelligent — support of an official organization that exists for the very purpose of challenging the traditional view of hell and defending conditional immortality as the truly biblical option.[17] So it is perhaps not surprising to hear this view confidently asserted as *the* biblical view.

But the very existence of this volume gives the lie to any such pronouncements. Surely Stackhouse was engaging in a bit of hyperbole when he said terminal punishment has about as much scriptural warrant as any doctrine. Surely he would agree that the incarnation, the bodily resurrection of Jesus, and salvation by grace through faith enjoy a higher degree of biblical support.

Of course, I am happy to concede that there are numerous biblical texts that, *prima facie*, seem clearly to teach terminal punishment. The problem, of course, is that there are similarly numerous texts that seem clearly to teach that hell is eternal conscious misery, and still others that appear clearly to teach universal salvation. At the heart of the ongoing debate is the question of which contestants in this dispute can best

---

17. I refer to *Rethinking Hell*.

explain and interpret the other two sets of texts in light of the texts they find to be most clear. And the ongoing debate makes it reasonably clear that any claims to victory by the advocates of conditional immortality are rather premature.

Moreover, despite the gains of the conditional immortality view in recent decades, as well as those of the universalists, the fact remains that the traditional view still enjoys a broad consensus and the burden of proof is still on those views that wish to displace it. As I suggested in my reply to Burk, this debate will require making the case on broader theological, philosophical, moral and aesthetic grounds, and I will comment on some of these that I think are relevant.

But I want to say more about why the traditional view should be presumed correct unless shown to be false beyond reasonable doubt. Indeed, I think we should be wary of pitting tradition against Scripture, as Stackhouse seems to do when he urges that evangelicals should stand "on what one thinks the Bible says, whatever the tradition might be." Now, some tradition, of course, is extrabiblical, and I would certainly agree with Stackhouse concerning *that* sort of tradition.

However, when a traditional doctrine is one that is rooted in biblical exegesis and enjoys centuries of consensus going back to the earliest Fathers and across all branches of the church, one should give it every benefit of the doubt. One should do so precisely out of respect for the authority of Scripture as God's definitive written revelation. Here is why. If Scripture is revelation, then God successfully revealed his truth through it. And if so, then it makes sense to think that the church, making its best effort to correctly interpret Scripture, would succeed in doing so. If they fail to correctly interpret it, that raises questions about the clarity of Scripture and its status as divine revelation.

Now, I do not want to overstate my case here. I am not saying the traditional doctrine of hell is on the same level as, say, the doctrines of the Nicene Creed. The doctrine of eternal hell does not enjoy that level of consensus, nor is it central to the biblical revelation the way those creedal doctrines are. So it is open to challenge in a way classic creedal doctrines are not. Still, the doctrine of eternal hell has the sort of weight in tradition that it deserves the benefit of the doubt. Generations of Christians across the ecumenical spectrum have found the traditional doctrine of eternal hell to be a credible component of the biblical drama, even as they might wish the doctrine were not true. Indeed, I have recently defended the doctrine as part of a larger account of the Christian view of the last things that provides powerful resources to address fundamental questions ranging from the problem of evil to the meaning of life.[18]

What this means is that advocates of conditional immortality (and universalism) must demonstrate that their view is theologically, morally, and aesthetically superior to the traditional view of hell and gives us a more satisfying account of the biblical drama than the traditional view that most Christians down the ages have endorsed. Moreover, they need to give us a convincing "error theory" to explain how and why the tradition went wrong in affirming the dominant view of hell. If they can succeed in doing this as integral to their exegetical case, they will have reason to claim their view is indeed the one most warranted by Scripture.

However, I think this is a tall order for the terminal punishment view, and it does not fare as well as its advocates claim it does against rival views. Here are a few particulars. First, I think a significant part of the appeal of the terminal punishment view comes from the sense that it represents a more fitting punishment than eternal misery. Finite creatures, after all, can only do a finite amount of evil and cause a limited amount of harm in the space of their short lives, so infinite punishment seems way out of proportion to the crime. Moreover, traditional pictures of hell have often depicted it as the supreme torture chamber, which only exacerbates the sense that it is an excessive form of punishment that is morally indefensible. As Stackhouse puts it, the idea that God keeps creatures alive for eternity that they might suffer endless misery, with no hope of respite, is so "ghastly" that many believers try to suppress the idea. "It is literally too horrible to consider." The view he offers is not only more biblically sound, he claims, but also "a more palatable alternative."

These alleged advantages largely dissipate, however, on the view of eternal hell I defend and its account of optimal grace. In my view, hell is not an eternal punishment that is imposed for sins committed in this life. Rather, hell is eternal because some sinners persist in rejecting

---

18. Jerry L. Walls, *Heaven, Hell, and Purgatory: Rethinking the Things That Matter Most* (Grand Rapids: Brazos, 2015).

the love and grace of God for all eternity. Because God is love in his essential nature, his love to sinners never ceases, but those who resist his love refuse the only thing that can possibly make them happy, and consequently they remain in misery. Indeed, I am sympathetic to a theological tradition, particularly in Eastern Orthodoxy, that, in the words of David Hart, "makes no distinction, essentially, between the fire of hell and light of God's glory and that interprets damnation as the soul's resistance to the beauty of God's glory, its refusal to open itself before the divine love, which causes divine love to seem an exterior chastisement."[19]

This picture of eternal hell is, I think, rather different from the notion that God keeps hapless creatures alive to punish them forever, with no hope of respite. Indeed, on my view, God's love is forever extended to those in hell, and it is possible that some of them may receive it and decide to return home to the Father, as the prodigal son did when he finally came to see that things were much better back home.

Next, I think the traditional view of hell better accounts for the significance of human freedom and its role in the drama of salvation and redemption. I quite agree with Stackhouse when he writes: "Hell is not a destination that God arbitrarily assigns to the recalcitrant sinner. Hell is simply the natural result of a moral agent choosing to separate from God, the source of life, and go some other way." Of course, we disagree about what this natural result is, and this difference arguably hinges on different views of how freedom is related to our very nature as human beings.

Perhaps the very essence of a human being is to be eternally related, either positively or negatively, to the God of love in whose image we are created. R. Zachary Manis has recently advanced a Kierkegaardian argument along these lines and has suggested that the possibility of eternal damnation is an entailment of the sort of freedom that allows the highest goods.

> [W]e are creatures made for the highest good of eternal communion with God and the saints in heaven. The features of human nature that make this end possible for human beings — including

---

19. David Bentley Hart, *The Beauty of the Infinite: The Aesthetics of Christian Truth* (Grand Rapids: Eerdmans, 2003), 399.

immortality and maximal creaturely moral freedom—are the very features that endow humans with the power of eternal self-damnation. The capacity for salvation (eternal communion) and the capacity for damnation (eternal disunion) are two sides of the same coin; they are metaphysically inseparable.[20]

I can hardly do justice to Manis's argument in this brief response, but I do want to emphasize that the argument hinges on both moral and metaphysical judgments. In particular, the argument depends on claims about the nature and significance of human freedom and how that freedom is essentially related to our very identity as human beings.[21]

Next, I want to challenge Stackhouse's claim that his view has something like an aesthetic advantage over the traditional view because, according to it, all evil will be completely destroyed and eliminated. He writes: "The vision of the good world to come is one in which the wicked are simply, wonderfully, and eternally absent—'as though they had never been' (Obad. 16)."

Now here is the problem. These wicked persons were still human beings who were created to love God and other persons, and they were someone's children and parents and brothers and sisters and so on, many of whom will be blessed to enjoy happiness of "the good world to come." So, given this reality, the painful memories of their evil choices and final destruction will remain a part of ongoing reality. Unless God simply erases all memories of these persons—a suggestion that raises more problems than it solves—the good world to come will still contain some painful unredeemed evil. As Stackhouse himself remarks, while commending his account of hell as "no worse than it has to be," it nevertheless remains a matter of "sad justice." If sad justice remains as a terminal aspect of reality, this view does not give us a conclusion to the story that is entirely free of the shadows of evil.

This is all the more so if Stackhouse concedes that it is possible that "Satan and his minions literally suffer forever." Final reality would then

---

20. R. Zachary Manis, "'Eternity will nail him to himself': the logic of damnation in Kierkegaard's *The Sickness unto Death*," *Religious Studies* (2015), 22. I have argued similarly in *Hell: The Logic of Damnation* (Notre Dame: University of Notre Dame Press, 1992), 136–38.

21. Manis particularly devotes the second half of his essay to answering the question, "Why Not Annihilation?"

include not only the unredeemed evil of memories of wicked persons finally destroyed, but conscious eternal misery as well.

In view of these considerations, I think the terminal punishment view loses whatever advantages it may initially appear to have over the traditional view of hell I defend.

A UNIVERSALIST VIEW

ROBIN A. PARRY

Introduction

Christian universalism is the view that in the end God will reconcile all people to himself through Christ.[1] Let me spell this out a little. Universalists take sin very seriously. Sin rots creation from the inside out, and humans need to be rescued from it and its consequences. Only God can deliver us from this predicament, and that is precisely what God has done through the atoning work of Christ. What makes universalism universal is simply its insistence that "God will reconcile *all* people." Does this mean that universalists don't believe in eschatological judgment? No. There *is* eschatological punishment, but "in the end" there will be deliverance.

Christian universalism is a minority voice within the church, but it is not some new-fangled liberal theology. It is, rather, an ancient Christian theological position that in the early church stood alongside annihilation and eternal torment as a viable Christian opinion. The view is perhaps most closely associated with the great biblical scholar and pastoral theologian Origen (c.184–c.254), but precursors to his thought can be found in Bardaisan of Edessa (154–222), Clement of Alexandria (c.150–c.215), and texts such as *The Apocalypse of Peter*. And it seems that Origen was followed in his universalism by other names of note, arguably including Theognostus (c.210–c.270), Pierius †309), Gregory the Wonderworker (c.213–c.270), Pamphilus (†309),

---

1. I would like to thank Thomas Talbott, David Congdon, Andrew Torrance, and Alex Smith for constructive feedback on an earlier draft.

Methodius of Olympus (†c.311), Eusebius (c.260–c.340), Athanasius (296–373), Didymus the Blind (†c.398), Basil of Caesarea (c.329–79), Gregory of Nyssa (c.335–c.395), Gregory of Nazianzen (c.329–c.390), Evagrius Pontocus (345–99), Diodore of Tarsus (†c.390), Theodore of Mopsuestia (c.350–428), the younger Jerome (c.347–420), Rufinus (c.340–410), Dionysius the Areopagite (sixth century), Maximus the Confessor (c.580–662), Isaac of Nineveh (†700), and John Scotus Eriugena (c.815–c.877).[2] St. Augustine (354–430)—who himself seems to have endorsed universalism in his early Christian life, though he later strongly rejected it—implies that universalism was very common in the churches of his time.[3] My point in listing these folk is simply to highlight that universalism is an ancient Christian view that arises from impulses deep within Christian theology itself.

Madness in the Method

In the past the debate on hell has often gotten bogged down in proof texting. One frequently finds those who think that they can settle the matter one way or the other simply by pointing to a few verses. I recall once having a very long discussion with someone who insisted, on the basis of the parable of the rich man and Lazarus (Luke 16:19–31), that universalism was wrong. He was utterly immovable, no matter how many biblical arguments I went through in favor of universalism (none of which he had an answer to). In his mind, whatever those other biblical passages are about, they simply *cannot* teach universalism. His reflections on the issue started and ended with Luke 16. Now such texts are, of course, important, and they should not be avoided,[4] but the problem is that *all sides* can point to verses that *seem* to support their view. For instance, consider:

2. For a detailed defense of the claim that these people were universalists, see Ilaria Ramelli, *The Christian Doctrine of Apokatastasis: A Critical Assessment from the New Testament to Eriugena.* *VC* 120. (Leiden: Brill, 2013). On the question of whether universalism was declared heretical, see Gregory MacDonald (ed.), *"All Shall Be Well": Explorations in Universal Salvation and Christian Theology, from Origen to Moltmann* (Eugene, OR: Cascade, 2011), 2–13.

3. Augustine, *Enchiridion*, sec. 112.

4. On Luke 16:19–31, see David Powys, *"Hell": A Hard Look at a Hard Question: The Fate of the Unrighteous in the New Testament* (Carlisle: Paternoster, 1998), 218–28; Richard Bauckham, "The Rich Man and Lazarus: The Parable and the Parallels," *New Testament Studies* 37 (1991): 225–46; Kim Papaioannou, *The Geography of Hell in the Teaching of Jesus* (Eugene, OR: Pickwick, 2013), 111–35; Gregory MacDonald, *The Evangelical Universalist*, 2d ed. (Eugene, OR: Cascade, 2012), 145–47 (hereafter *TEU*). (As an aside, Gregory MacDonald is the pen name under which I wrote *TEU*.)

1. Eternal torment (Matt. 25:45; 2 Thess. 1:6–9; Rev. 14:11; 20:10–15)
2. Annihilation (Matt. 7:13; 10:28; John 3:16; Rom. 6:23; Heb. 10:39)
3. Universalism (Rom. 5:18; 11:32; 1 Cor. 15:22; Phil. 2:11; Col. 1:20)

Showing that a specific passage seems at face value to support your particular view of hell is not going to settle the issue. *Everyone* in this discussion who thinks that the Bible is not contradictory will need to interpret some passages in ways that run counter to their *prima facie* meaning.

Is there a guide to help us interpret in theologically sensitive ways? Yes. The church has always recognized that the gospel narrative of the triune God manifest in Christ's incarnation, ministry, death, resurrection, ascension, and return must be at the core of the interpretation of Scripture. This Trinitarian, gospel-shaped narrative was known as "the rule of faith," and it was the orthodox standard for genuine *Christian* interpretation of the Bible. So we need a theological hermeneutic, rooted in the gospel itself, that is sensitive to the contours of this story.

I do not have the space here to explore all the detailed exegetical matters that need attention, so I will focus my gaze on the big picture—the biblical grand narrative, at the heart of which lies Christ. The reader may feel frustrated that I am devoting so much space to passages that don't explicitly mention hell. Please bear with me. My contention is that if we are to think clearly about hell, we need to consider it, and individual passages about it, in the context of this theological framework.

Putting Hell in Its Place
In the Context of the Christ-Centered Biblical Metanarrative

A doctrine of hell needs to make good sense in its place in the biblical metanarrative, the grand story that runs from Genesis to Revelation. I shall argue that when located in the plotline of Scripture, a universalist doctrine of hell makes good sense.

Let's start at the most general level—with God. Paul writes that creation is "from" God, "through" God, and "for" God (Rom. 11:36). God is the context of the world—the origin and the destiny of creation.

That, I suggest, is the very broad theological framework within which we must operate.

Let's zoom in a little closer. As an introduction to my telling of the story, consider the Christ hymn of Colossians 1.

> For in him [the Son] all things were created: things in heaven and on earth, visible and invisible, whether thrones or powers or rulers or authorities; all things have been created through him and for him.... God was pleased ... through him to reconcile to himself all things, whether things on earth or things in heaven, by making peace through his blood, shed on the cross. (16, 19–20)

We see here a story that runs from the creation of all things through Christ to the reconciliation of *the same* all things through Christ (notice the parallel between the "all things" in creation and redemption).[5] To avoid the universalism of this text is a challenge for non-universalists. Some argue that reconciliation here means, "to put in order." So, we are told, believers are "reconciled" by being saved, while unbelievers are "reconciled" by being damned. The problem here is that this proposal runs roughshod over the concept of reconciliation in general, and of the concept of reconciliation in Paul in particular (Rom. 5:10; 1 Cor. 7:11; 2 Cor. 5:18–20; Eph. 2:16; Col. 1:22). Being defeated and condemned is *not* being reconciled! Rather, this reconciliation is spelled out in terms of "*making peace* through his blood, shed on the cross" (Col. 1:26). As Miroslav Volf comments: "At the heart of the cross is Christ's stance of not letting the other remain an enemy and of creating space in himself for the offender to come in."[6] Try as I might, I struggle to see how "making peace" through the cross can concern damnation, *even if* the damned acknowledge the justice of their punishment.[7]

So I propose we explore this Christ-centered creation-to-new-creation plot as a context for considering hell. This hermeneutical judgment—that Christ is the norm for interpreting Scripture—underpins my entire approach.

---

5. While sin is not mentioned, the fact that reconciliation is required clearly presupposes it.

6. Miroslav Volf, *Exclusion and Embrace: A Theological Exploration of Identity, Otherness, and Reconciliation* (Nashville: Abingdon, 1996), 126.

7. On Colossians 1, see *TEU*, 41–53.

Creation: All Things Are from Him and for Him

Christians are universalists about creation — God created *all* things, through his Word. And the doctrine of creation is not simply about origins (everything comes *from* God), but about purpose and destiny. Created things have a *telos*, a destiny, and that *telos* is God. The end of creation is there in its beginning: creation is *from* God, *for* God, and oriented *toward* God, reaching toward its potential and completion *in* God. So the question of universalism can be framed in terms of whether or not God will manage to bring all creation to the goal for which he intended it.

Take humans — the subject of this debate. Christians agree that *all* humans are created in the image of God (Gen. 1:24–26). But while God did create humans as "good," he did not create humans as finished and completed creatures — he created them with a destiny to grow toward. This *telos* of human creatures is, in community, to be filled with God and to image God in the world.

The gospel revelation of Jesus Christ deepens and sharpens our understanding of the human *telos*. The risen and ascended humanity of Christ is the climax of our human nature. One day we shall be like him (Rom. 8:11; 1 Cor. 15:12–57; 1 John 3:2). In one sense, for us, being human is a yet-to-be completed journey. Jesus is the only person ever of whom it can be said that he is *fully* human. Humanity has reached its goal *in him*. And in the gospel it becomes clearer to us that the creation of humanity was always a two-phase project: the first Adam was earthly; the second Adam was heavenly (1 Cor. 15:42–49). Humanity was made with a destiny, and that destiny was to be conformed to the image of the true human, the origin of the new, phase-two humanity — Jesus.

Fall

Genesis suggests that the move from phase-one to phase-two humanity was interrupted by sin. Sin corrodes humanity at every level and makes it impossible for us to reach our destination. Instead we spiral away from God, the source of life, into corruption, decay, and death.

Christians are universalists about sin — *all* have sinned and have fallen short of the glory of God (Rom. 3:23). Without divine redemptive grace, human beings (and creation as a whole) are doomed to futility.

Do we deserve divine punishment? Yes. Do we deserve divine rescue? No. Will God deliver us? Well, remember, even broken humans are still in God's image (Gen. 9:6), still valuable, still beloved:

> [A]ll creatures participate in God's goodness, especially rational creatures who were made in God's image.... The rational creature is, essentially, a being bearing the divine image and ordered toward union with God.... God can no more cease to value rational creatures—even if they fall into sin—than He can cease to value Himself, because rational creatures are a reflection of His own essence. Therefore, He is always faithful to them, even when they are unfaithful to Him, and must seek to destroy their sin.[8]

To hate creatures made in his image, even fallen ones, would be a form of indirect self-hatred, and this God cannot do. "God is angered by human sin not *although* he loves human beings but *because* he loves them. He says No to sin because he says Yes to the sinner."[9]

So the question here is this: Will God allow sin to thwart his purposes to beautify the cosmos? The answer comes in the gospel story— *no freaking way!* Sin may be as deep and dark and deadly as it can, but Christ annihilates it! The first Adam may have wrought havoc, but the Second Adam more than undoes that destruction (Rom. 5:14–21). So here is another (loaded) question: Does Christ undo *all* the damage caused by sin, or does he only undo *some* of it? Where sin abounds, does grace abound *all the more* (Rom. 5:20), or does it just abound *quite a lot*?

Redemption: All Things Are Through Him

(i) Incarnation[10]

The divine Word, the second person of the Holy Trinity, became flesh (John 1:14). As the Second Adam, Jesus represented the whole race—he is the sinless and obedient one in whom God's covenant relationship with humanity finds fulfillment. Most Christians have been

---

8. John Kronen and Eric Reitan, *God's Final Victory: A Comparative Philosophical Case for Universalism* (New York: Bloomsbury, 2011), 38. Some readers will be uncomfortable associating the divine image with rationality. If that is you, simply substitute "human" for "rational" in the passage.

9. Jürgen Moltmann, *The Coming of God: Christian Eschatology* (London: SCM, 1996), 243.

10. Of course, to tell the story fully would require speaking of God's way with Israel, but space prohibits. On Israel and universalism, see *TEU*, 54–73, 90–96, 229–33.

universalists about Christ's humanity—he represents *all* humans in his humanity. Here, for instance, is Hilary of Poitiers (†367): "Christ has become the body of the whole of humanity, that, through the body that he was kind enough to assume, the whole of humanity might be hidden in him...."[11]

Christ's being fully human is fundamental to our salvation. As Gregory of Nazianzus observed: "that which He has not assumed, He has not healed."[12] He became human so that he could heal our humanity in himself, through his death and resurrection. This is suggestive. Listen to Athanasius: "Flesh was taken up by the Logos to liberate all humans and resurrect all of them from the dead and ransom all of them from sin."[13]

(ii) Death

Most Christians, past and present, are universalists about Christ's crucifixion—Jesus died for *all* people in order to save *all* people.[14] This belief is well grounded in Scripture and tradition. Consider the following:

> [Christ] is the atoning sacrifice for our sins, and not only for ours but also for the sins of *the whole world*. (1 John 2:2)

> For Christ's love compels us, because we are convinced that one died for *all*, and therefore all died. (2 Cor. 5:14)

> This is good, and pleases God our Savior, who *wants all people to be saved* and to come to a knowledge of the truth. For there is one God and one mediator between God and mankind, the man Christ Jesus, who gave himself as a ransom for *all people*.... (1 Tim. 2:3–6)

> But we do see Jesus, who ... suffered death, so that by the grace of God he might taste death for *everyone*. (Heb. 2:9)

---

11. In *Psalmos*, 51.16–17.

12. Gregory of Nazianzus, *Epistle 101*.

13. Athanasius, *Letter to Adelphius*.

14. Obviously many (though not all) Calvinists are an exception to this rule, with their doctrine of limited atonement. On this view, Jesus died to redeem only a *subset* of humans, the elect. For a defense of a universal atonement in these texts, see I. Howard Marshall, "For All, For All My Saviour Died," in *Semper Reformandum: Studies in Honor of Clark H. Pinnock*, eds. S. E. Porter and A. R. Cross (Carlisle: Paternoster, 2003), 322–46.

Jesus is "the Lamb of God, who takes away the sin of *the world*" (John 1:29). For remember, "God did not send his Son into the world to condemn the world, but *to save the world* through him" (John 3:17). And he will succeed: "I, when I am lifted up from the earth [on the cross], will draw all people to myself" (John 12:32).[15] Here is Athanasius again: Christ "delivered his own body to death *on behalf of all* ... in order to bring again to incorruptibility the human beings now doomed to corruption."[16]

This teaching emphasizes the mainstream Christian view that God *desires* to redeem all people (1 Tim. 2:4; 2 Peter 3:9) and has *acted* in Christ in order to do so. So the provocative questions here are these: Will God's desire to save all people be satisfied or eternally frustrated? Will the cross save all those for whom Christ died, or will his death have been in vain for some people?[17]

(iii) Resurrection/Ascension

The resurrection of Jesus is new creation, the age to come breaking into the present evil age. And Jesus' resurrection is not simply *Jesus'* resurrection — it is *ours;* it is the destiny of all humanity played out in the person of our representative.

All Christian eschatology must be Christ-centered, and it must be grounded *here*, in this event. Here we see the future of the world, the future of humanity, manifest in his risen flesh. The story of humanity does not terminate on a cross, but passes through an empty tomb and ascends to God. So my question here is this: Is the resurrection of Jesus on behalf of all humanity a foretaste of the future of *all* humanity or only the future of *part of* humanity? If the latter, does Christ's resurrection on behalf of the damned come to nothing? Are they beyond its reach?

Church: A Foretaste of the Age to Come

We live in a time between the resurrection of Jesus and the general resurrection of the dead, between the inauguration of the kingdom of God and our full participation in it. The new age is here *now* — for

---

15. On effectual calling and this verse see *TEU*, 239–41.

16. Athanasius, *De Incarnatione*, 9.

17. There is no agreed Christian understanding of *how* the atonement works. I contend that *however* we understand the mechanism, it coheres best with universalism.

Christ has been exalted and the Spirit has been poured out—but we still await its complete arrival.

This tension between now and not-yet permeates New Testament teaching on universal salvation. On the one hand, in the person of the risen Christ everyone is *already* redeemed. God has *already* reconciled the world to himself in Christ (Rom. 5:18; 2 Cor. 5:19; Col. 1:19–20).

On the other hand, only those who have been united to Christ by the Holy Spirit now participate in that salvation (and even then, only in an anticipatory way, until the general resurrection). So the actual existential participation of all people in salvation is *not* a present reality, it lies in the future: "For as in Adam all die, so in Christ all *will* be made alive" (1 Cor. 15:22).[18]

> [J]ust as one trespass [Adam's] resulted in condemnation for all people, so also one act of righteousness [Christ's] resulted in justi-fication and life for all people. For just as through the disobedience of the one man the many were made sinners, so also through the obedience of the one man the many *will be* made righteous. (Rom. 5:18–19)[19]

So is everyone currently justified? Yes and no. In that Christ has been raised for our justification (Rom. 4:25), we are all already justified in his resurrection. However, it is only as we respond in obedient trust to the gospel and are united to Christ by the Spirit that we participate subjectively in this justification.

This now/not-yet tension is seen throughout Paul's letters. For instance, in 2 Corinthians 5:14–21, Paul addresses the issue of the universal significance of Christ's work. We read that "one died for all, and therefore all died" (v. 14) and that "God was reconciling *the world* to himself in Christ, not counting people's sins against them" (v. 19). From this perspective there are no insiders and outsiders—everyone is an insider. And yet Paul still issues the imperative, "We implore you on Christ's behalf: *Be reconciled* to God" (v. 20). A Spirit-enabled human response to the gospel is still required if people are to share

---

18. For a defense of a universalist reading of this passage, against its critics, see *TEU*, 84–90.

19. For a defense of a universalist reading of this passage, against its critics, see *TEU*, 78–84. On the argument that "all" does not mean all, an argument regularly deployed against universalist readings of certain passages, see *TEU*, 82–83; Thomas Talbott, *The Inescapable Love of God*, 2nd ed. (Eugene, OR: Cascade, 2014), 52–57.

in the salvation already achieved in Christ. And right now many live outside the gospel community. So Paul makes a very clear distinction in all his writings between those who are "in Christ" and those who are not, the church and the world, believers and unbelievers, the elect and those who are not elect. The former are "being saved" while the latter are "perishing" (2 Cor. 2:15; 4:3).

It is critical to note, however, that for Paul the dead in sin can become those alive in Christ, children destined for wrath can become children of mercy (Eph. 2:1–11).[20] This is relevant because we cannot assume that just because Paul sees a *current* divide between those being saved and those perishing, that this divide will remain in place *eternally*. As a case in point, consider Romans 9–11. There, Paul marks a stark division within Israel between those who are "elect" and "the others" (Rom. 11:7), between vessels of mercy and heart-hardened vessels of wrath prepared for destruction (Rom. 9:6–23). It all seems very final. And yet in chapter 11 we discover that the hardening of Israel has only been *in part* (i.e., some Jews, not all Jews) and *temporary* (a hardening *until* ...) (Rom. 11:25). Those vessels of wrath prepared for destruction and cut off from the olive tree *can be grafted back in again* (Rom. 11:17–24), becoming vessels of mercy, participating in election. Indeed, in the eschaton they *will* be grafted back in: when "*all* Israel will be saved" when "the deliverer will come from Zion" (Rom. 11:26).[21] So here Paul sees a current division between the in-group and the out-group within Israel itself, but it's a division that will be overcome in the new age.

It seems to me that underpinning much NT ecclesiology is the vision of Israel's prophets that in the last days Israel would be restored, the Spirit poured out, and the nations would come in pilgrimage and worship the God of Abraham alongside Israel (e.g., Isa. 2:1–4; 11:10–12; 18:7; 60:1–16; 61:5–6; 66:12, 18, 23). To NT authors, this vision is coming to pass *in the ekklesia*—the Spirit is poured out, and Jews and people from among the nations are united as equals, worshipping the God of Israel together. However, we make a mistake if we lose sight of the now/not-yet tension. The church in the present is only a prophetic

---

20. I do not have time to explore the important notion of election. For my understanding of it, see *TEU*, 222–42.

21. Romans 9–11 is an incredibly dense and complex text, and any interpretation is open to challenge. For a fuller treatment of my view see my *TEU*, 90–96, 229–33.

foretaste of the fuller reality to come—an anticipation of the grander fulfillment in the new creation, when "all Israel" is saved (Rom. 11:26) and all the nations and the kings of the earth bring their tribute into the New Jerusalem (Rev. 21:24–27).

Here it may be helpful to consider the current division Paul saw within Israel between the majority, who had not responded to his gospel, and the minority, the Messiah-believing Jews. He was deeply distraught about this situation (Rom. 9:1–5; 10:1), but was not without hope. In Paul's mind, the Messiah-believing Jews are not elect *instead of* the rest but elect *on behalf of* the rest. They are like the firstfruits of a sacrificial offering to God, a sign that the rest of the harvest (i.e., *all* Israel) will return in due course (Rom. 11:16).

Consummation: All Things Are to Him

In the light of the story so far, we can see where things are heading. This is a story for which universal salvation seems a fitting ending. Thus, Paul speaks of "the mystery of [God's] will according to his good pleasure, which he purposed in Christ, to be put into effect when the times reach their fulfillment— *to bring unity to all things in heaven and on earth under Christ*" (Eph. 1:9–10).[22] All creation is made "for" and oriented "to" God—and it is summed up and brought to its fitting conclusion and destiny in Jesus. Then at Jesus' name *every* knee will bow—in heaven, and on earth, and under the earth (i.e., the dead)—and *every* tongue confess him as Lord (Phil. 2:9–11).[23] All will be subject to Christ, and then Christ will subject himself to the Father on behalf of creation, so that God will be "all in all" (1 Cor. 15:28).[24] *That* is the kind of end I would expect for the biblical story.

Now, we are so used to the traditional story of hell as the final fate of some/many/most people that we usually fail to notice how out of sync it is as a conclusion to *this* story. Surely we need a *very* good explanation for this tale ending in tragedy for some/many/most people. What possible reasons could there be for such an unexpected climax? Even if we think we can find an answer to that question (and finding a good

---

22. For a universalist reading of Ephesians, see *TEU*, 184–91.

23. For a defense of a universalist interpretation of this text (against the often-made claim that some are *forced* to bow the knee *against their will*) see *TEU*, 97–100.

24. For a defense of a universalist reading of 1 Corinthians 15, see *TEU*, 84–90.

answer to it is a major challenge), it is hard to avoid the conclusion that the biblical story told in a non-universalist way ends in a tragic partial failure for God.

In the Context of the Doctrine of God

Every doctrine of hell implies a doctrine of God, and every doctrine of God will shape one's theology of hell. Let's consider some fundamental Christian claims about God.

"God is light; in him there is no darkness at all" (1 John 1:5). Christian theology sees God as *essentially* good. God doesn't just happen, by a stroke of good fortune, to be good. Nor is it that he has chosen in an arbitrary way to be good, as if he could have chosen otherwise. His perfection is such that *he could not fail* to be good. More than that, Christian theology has always unwaveringly insisted that the God of the gospel is love (1 John 4:8, 16). Again, he does not just *happen* to be loving; he is essentially—*in his very being*—love. For God to fail to be good or to be love would be for God to fail *to be God*, which is literally incoherent.

Now the Christian instincts here are simple and clear: if God is love then God loves all his creatures.[25] And to love someone is to want the best for them. For a human creature, the best—from a Christian perspective—would be union with God through Christ. So it seems clear that if God is love then God will at least *desire* to bring all people into union with him (which in a sinful world will require salvation from sin). Furthermore, if God is love then God will continue to love those in hell, desiring their best.

Christians also insist that God is essentially just, so our doctrine of hell must comport with God's justice. Things get a little complicated here, because what we mean by justice is somewhat contested. However, I would contend that universalism is compatible with all serious proposals on the nature of divine justice.[26] Be that as it may, I have only one point to make here: We must be very careful not to set divine love and

---

25. While the Trinity can be love even if there is no creation to love, if there is a creation to love, then the Trinity must love it. On the implications of "God is love," see Talbott, *The Inescapable Love of God*, 102–19.

26. On hell and justice, see Talbott, *Inescapable*, 133–52; John Kronan and Eric Reitan, *God's Final Victory: A Comparative Philosophical Case for Universalism* (New York: Bloomsbury Academic, 2011), 91–126. Both books argue that hell can *only* be said to satisfy the demands of divine justice if universalism is true.

justice in *opposition* to each other, as if some of God's acts are loving (like saving people) while others are just (like punishing people in hell).[27] We are in danger of dividing God, as if he were internally conflicted and had to switch between being loving and being just. It is important to appreciate that *everything* God does is true to who God *is*, as a just, holy, and loving God. His love is holy love, and holy love is not soppy, fuzzy love, but a persevering love that cannot be compromised. God's love can even manifest at times as a severe mercy. "His is a love of cauterizing holiness and of a righteousness whose only response to evil is the purity of a perfect hatred. Wrath and justice are but ways in which such love must show itself to be love in the face of its denial."[28]

What we need is a theology of hell in which it can be seen as a manifestation of divine goodness: of loving justice, and of just love.

Hell: "Abandon Hope All Ye Who Enter Here"?[29]

Having set the stage, I want now to offer a skeleton sketch of a view of hell I think compatible with the God of the gospel.

Judgment

In Scripture, divine judgment serves various ends. It has, as the tradition rightly points out, a retributive aspect. Someone is punished because they *deserve* to be. It is not hard to find this instinct in Scripture. But we err if we think that retribution exhausts what biblical justice and punishment are about. Biblical justice is about putting wrong things right. As such, while retribution may possibly be a necessary condition of justice, it cannot be a sufficient condition, because retribution cannot undo the harms done and put right the wrongs.[30] The primary end of God's justice, with respect to creation, is not punishment, but salvation.[31] And punishment itself is not merely suffering inflicted as a

---

27. This is a danger into which the mainstream tradition often falls, against its better instincts.

28. John A. T. Robinson, *In the End, God . . . : A Study of the Christian Doctrine of the Last Things*. 1950; special edition (Eugene, OR: Cascade, 2011), 99.

29. Dante, *Inferno*, Canto III.9.

30. On the limited role of retribution in justice, see Talbott, *Inescapable*, 133–52.

31. On biblical justice, wrath, and punishment being *far* more than retribution, see Stephen Travis, *Christ and the Judgment of God: The Limits of Divine Retribution in New Testament Thought*, 2d ed. (Milton Keynes: Paternoster, 2009); Patrick Dale, *Redeeming Judgment* (Eugene, OR: Cascade, 2012); Christopher Marshall, *Beyond Retribution: A New Testament Vision for Justice, Crime, and Punishment* (Grand Rapids: Eerdmans, 2001).

deserved consequence for wrong deeds. Punishment also functions as a deterrent (e.g., Deut. 13:11), as a warning to repent (e.g., Rev. 14:7 in context), and as a means of delivering victims from their abusers (e.g., 2 Thess. 1:6–7a). Furthermore, it is also a corrective for those being punished—a means by which they can come to appreciate the true significance of what they have done, and its consequences (e.g., 1 Cor. 5:1–5; 11:29–32; Titus 2:11–12; Heb. 12:5–11; Rev. 3:19).

And these different purposes of punishment need not be mutually exclusive. God's punishment of Israel, say, can be *simultaneously retributive and restorative.* In specific contexts one aspect or the other may come into focus, but we should not let that mislead us into supposing that its partner is missing.

I would argue that a specific pattern of divine punishment occurs again and again in the Bible, acquiring the status of a normative paradigm. This is the pattern of *judgment followed by restoration.* This pattern is played out time and again for both Israel and the nations. I will illustrate this with examples from Jeremiah, though examples could be drawn from across Scripture. In chapter 30, Jeremiah speaks of God's people facing horrible judgment (vv. 5–7c) *followed by* wonderful salvation (vv. 7d–11); an incurable wound that is beyond healing (vv. 12–15) *followed by* God's healing (vv. 16–17); a storm of divine wrath (vv. 23–24) *followed by* covenant renewal (31:1). This pattern—judgment and salvation, exile and restoration, death and resurrection[32]—is God's way with Israel.

What of the nations? Here Jeremiah's oracles against the nations are worth a look. They are full of doom, but we find that the oracles against Egypt, Moab, Ammon, and Elam end, inexplicably, with a promise of restoration (46:26; 48:47; 49:6; 49:39). And note that the language of judgment in the oracles looks final—"Moab will be *destroyed* as a nation.... Yet I will restore the fortunes of Moab in days to come" (48:42, 47); "I will *shatter* Elam ... until I have made an *end* of them.... Yet I will restore the fortunes of Elam in days to come" (49:37, 39). The prophetic rhetoric of wrath may lead us to think that these nations have

---

32. The language of death and resurrection to speak of Israel's exile and restoration is not Jeremiah's. I am evoking the imagery of Ezekiel 37 (the Valley of Dry Bones), but also hinting at a forward-looking theological association with the Messiah's own resurrection (as Israel's representative). See *TEU,* chs. 3–4 for an exploration of the connections between Israel's exile-restoration and Christ's death-resurrection.

reached the end of the road. Not so. We are reminded of God's promise to restore *even Sodom*, the very model of sinners destroyed in divine fire (Ezek. 16:53), and Isaiah's prophecy about Egypt: "The LORD will strike Egypt with a plague; he will strike them *and heal them*. They will turn to the LORD and he will respond to their pleas and will heal them" (Isa. 19:22).[33]

The underlying theo-logic is that of Lamentations:[34]

Because of the LORD's great love we are not consumed,
for his compassions never fail …
For no one is cast off
by the LORD forever.
Though he brings grief, he will show compassion,
so great is his unfailing love.
For he does not willingly bring affliction
or grief to anyone. (Lam. 3:22, 31–33)

Now I propose that we think of hell in precisely the same way. It is not a wild leap to suppose that the punishment of the age to come follows the same pattern set throughout Scripture. In fact, John's Gospel suggests that the condemnation that people experience in this age is an anticipation of eschatological condemnation (John 3:18). If that is the case, then we have reasonable grounds for thinking that condemnation in the coming age is *more than* retributive; that it is also *restorative*. In other words, we have grounds to look beyond the final judgment to salvation. (Such a proposal is not new. Various second- and third-century Christian texts speak of a postmortem salvation for the damned, sometimes as a result of the prayers of the saints.[35])

This instinct is reinforced when we remember that hell has to make sense in its place in the plotline of the Bible and in the context of the God of the gospel. We have to show how it is a manifestation of the

---

33. My reply to the objection that this teaching concerns groups, not individuals, can be found in *TEU*, 218–20.

34. For reflections on Lamentations, divine wrath, and hell, see Robin A. Parry, *Lamentations*. Two Horizons Old Testament Commentary (Grand Rapids: Eerdmans, 2010), 193–201.

35. The *Apocalypse of Peter*, the *Apocalypse of Elijah*, the *Epistula Apostolorum*, Book 2 of the *Sibylline Oracles*, the *Odes of Solomon*, the *Gospel of Nicodemus*, the *Apocalypse of Paul*, the *Acts of Paul and Thecla*, the *Passio Perpetuae et Felicitatis*. On these texts, see Ramelli, *Christian Doctrine of Apokatastasis*, 67ff.

loving justice of the God who cares for unworthy sinners. If your theology of hell is not compatible with God's love for the damned, then your theology of hell is wrong.

Can One Come to Christ after Death?

Critical to most versions of universalism is the claim that it is possible to be saved *after* one has died.[36] Many Christians take it as a given that death is a point beyond which the opportunity to embrace the gospel does not extend. If that is the case, then universalism, in its historic versions at least, has a problem.

What does the Bible say? Well, it does not *directly* address the issue. There are no biblical texts that say death is a point of no return, but neither are there texts that unambiguously say that one can repent after death.[37] Of course, some appeal to passages like Hebrews 9:27, but all that this text claims is that all humans die once and then face judgment, and *all* sides of this debate will agree with *that* claim. To go further and insist that this judgment leads to irreversible punishment is to go beyond anything said in the text.

So the Bible does not *directly* settle this question. However, this does not mean that biblical teachings have no bearing on our theological reflection on the issue—far from it![38]

On the one hand, one has to ask after the theological rationale behind the mainstream claim that death is the point at which one's fate is forever fixed. *Why* would that be the case? Is it impossible for people to change their ways and to repent after death? Does death somehow fix us in some eternally sinful state? This seems highly unlikely. So might it be that God simply chooses not to seek the lost after the barrier of death is crossed? But again, why? Has God stopped loving them? Does he no longer want them to turn from sin back to him? Will he now ignore any genuine repentance or faith? Again, all this seems out of kilter with the God of the gospel, the God who keeps on seeking a lost sheep *"until* he finds it"* (Luke 15:4).

On the other hand, in favor of post-mortem salvation, universalists

---

36. Some Barthian universalists would deny that God gives extra time after death to repent.

37. Though see later on Revelation, and 1 Peter 3:18–20; 4:6.

38. See Stephen Jonathan, *Grace beyond the Grave: Is Salvation Possible in the Afterlife?* (Eugene, OR: Wipf & Stock, 2014).

would contend that it has the benefit of being highly consistent with the doctrine of divine holy love and the doctrine of God's eschatological victory over sin. "The love which won the scepter on Calvary will wield it as a power, waxing ever, waning never, through all ages; ... [T]he Father will never cease from yearning over the prodigals, and Christ will never cease from seeking the lost, while one knee remains stubborn before the name of Jesus, and one heart is unmastered by His love."[39] Furthermore, if we believe that Scripture teaches *both* that all people will be saved *and* that some people will go to hell—and it does seem to teach both—then it is arguable that we can legitimately infer that those in hell will be saved out of hell. If postmortem salvation can be legitimately inferred from teachings that have good claims to being biblical, then the doctrine itself can claim to be biblical, at least in a secondary sense.

Tricky Texts

But does not Scripture explicitly teach a view of hell that excludes postmortem salvation and universalism? There are some biblical passages that may appear to do so, so I will need to say a little about a few of those texts. I begin with what is likely the earliest Gospel text on hell.

Mark 9:42 - 50

Jesus warns about the dire consequences of causing one of "these little ones ... to stumble" (v. 42). He says to his disciples that "if your hand causes you to stumble, cut it off. It is better for you to enter life maimed than with two hands to go into hell, where the fire never goes out ... where 'the worms that eat them do not die, and the fire is not quenched.' [For] everyone will be salted with fire" (9:43–44, 48–49).

First, the word translated in the NIV as "hell" is *Gehenna*. Gehenna was the name of a valley next to Jerusalem—a valley strongly associated in Israel's past with idolatry (2 Kings 23:10; 2 Chron. 28:3; 33:6) and divine judgment. Jeremiah had prophesied a great slaughter of apostate Israel in that valley. It will be filled with corpses and then set alight, becoming a "valley of ashes" (Jer. 7:29–34; 19:1–15; 31:40). Jesus is picking up on that association.

---

39. James Baldwin Brown, *The Doctrine of Annihilation in the Light of the Gospel of Love* (London: Henry King, 1875), 118–19.

Many have argued that by the time of Jesus Gehenna was a well-known term for a place of everlasting punishment and therefore Jesus' audience will have understood his teaching in this same way. However, the evidence for this claim is less than compelling. *All* the early Jewish texts outside the NT that mention Gehenna[40] were written *after the destruction of Jerusalem in AD 70*, the earliest of them appearing about half a century after Jesus' ministry.[41] (And even these later Jewish musings on Gehenna were still fluid and varied. To some it suggested eternal torment after death; to others, annihilation; to yet others, salvation from Gehenna was possible.[42]) We need to be very cautious when considering how much these later texts may serve as a background for interpreting Jesus' words. Indeed, I tentatively suggest that our current evidence indicates that Gehenna was *not* a common term with a widely shared meaning in Jesus' day.[43] Jesus could possibly have been the *first* person to use the word in an apocalyptic judgment context. All of which is simply to say that we must allow Jesus to do his own thing with the image and that we would do well to take Jeremiah more seriously as a backdrop for interpreting his words.

Second, the imagery of fire and worms is drawn from a vision in Isaiah 66:24. Isaiah 66 is an eschatological picture of the restoration of Jerusalem, but outside the city walls (in the Valley of Hinnom?) lie the dead bodies of the wicked enemies of God (both apostate Israel and Gentile armies), slain in battle. Of the corpses, the prophet says, "the worms that eat them will not die, the fire that burns them will

---

40. *4 Ezra* 2:29; 7:36; *2 Baruch* 59:10; 85:13; *Ascension of Isaiah* 1:3; 4:14–18; *3 Enoch* 44:3; 48D:8; *Apocalypse of Abraham* 15:6; Gk *Apocalypse of Ezra* 1:9; *Sibylline Oracles* 1:104; 2:292; 4:186. For a discussion of these texts, see Edward Fudge, *The Fire that Consumes: A Biblical and Historical Study of the Doctrine of Final Punishment*, 3rd ed. (Eugene, OR: Cascade, 2011); Powys, *"Hell": A Hard Look at a Hard Question*; Papaioannou, *The Geography of Hell*.

41. Indeed, the cataclysmic impact of the fall of Jerusalem may have been one of the contributing factors in the evolution of the notion. This, too, cautions against retrojecting post-destruction developments back into Jesus' day.

42. On the surprising Rabbinic notion of the salvation of some from Gehenna, possibly after a year, see *Rosh Ha-shannah* 16b, 17a. (This Talmudic account was written down long after the time of Jesus, but preserves early Jewish traditions. It is possible, though not certain, that the salvation from Gehenna idea was around in Jesus' time.) My point is not that the early Rabbis were universalists—they were certainly not—but simply that even when the notion of Gehenna was more fully developed, the idea of being sent to Gehenna *and then delivered from it* was neither incoherent nor inconceivable.

43. There is no mention of Gehenna as a place of postmortem judgment in the post-Jeremiah books of the Hebrew Bible, the Apocryphal books, the LXX, or the Dead Sea Scrolls. This is an argument from silence, but it is a loud silence.

not be quenched, and they will be loathsome to all mankind." So Jesus is drawing on texts in Jeremiah and Isaiah about divine judgment on Israel and Israel's enemies, blending them, and saying that such judgment is coming again and should be avoided at all costs. Some NT scholars argue that this judgment, like that spoken of by Jeremiah, is a historical, this-worldly judgment on Jerusalem—its coming destruction at the hands of Rome (AD 70)—and does not concern a postmortem punishment at all.[44] That is certainly possible. The graphic language used to describe it may simply be a prophetic way of speaking about the catastrophic nature of the judgment. *If* this is correct, then this passage cannot be used to attack universalism. But we'll assume—for the sake of argument—that Jesus *is* speaking of postmortem judgment.

Third, we must be very careful how we interpret the imagery. That the fire will not be quenched and the worms will not die need mean no more than that the fire and the worms will be *unceasingly and unstoppably active* until they have finished their work.[45] One does not need to postulate eternal torment in hell by everlasting fire and worms to make sense of this image.

Fourth, notice that the final sentence quoted above (Mark 9:49) is introduced by the word "for" (Gk, *gar*). (The NIV omits it, so I have reinserted it.) The choice of either removing the offending hand/foot/eye or facing the fires of judgment in Gehenna is explained by the phrase, "*for* everyone will be salted with fire." The point appears to be that one must face one mode of salting with fire or the other—either cutting off the hand/foot/eye or being thrown into Gehenna. The former is the fire that they should choose (cf. 9:50)! But notice that Jesus describes the process either way as being "*salted* with fire." Salt was used for purification, so Jesus may be hinting that even Gehenna's fires serve a purificatory purpose. This is a suggestive aside, possibly offering hope beyond hell.

It seems to me that Jesus' words about Gehenna here need not be taken as requiring an everlasting hell. The horrible imagery would not be negated, even if people were saved from Gehenna once the fire and the worms had done their work. That is a big "if," and Jesus is not discussing that question. However, if we have good grounds for

---

44. Best known among them is N. T. Wright.
45. This case is made very convincingly by various annihilationist interpreters.

considering such a possibility from other biblical teachings—and I am convinced that we do—then this text would not rule it out (nor, I would argue, would any of the other Gehenna texts).

Matthew 25:31 - 46

In the parable of the sheep and the goats Jesus sets out the destiny of the two groups as follows: "Then they [the goats] will go away to *eternal* punishment, but the righteous [the sheep] to *eternal* life" (25:46). Earlier the King had said to the goats, "Depart from me, you who are cursed, into the *eternal* fire prepared for the devil and his angels" (25:41).

Understandably, this text is taken by many traditionalists as settling the issue once and for all. It is often pointed out that in verse 46 "eternal life" and "eternal punishment" are set up by Jesus in parallel. From this observation, the case is made that if we wish to argue that the punishment is not everlasting then we must also say the same thing about the life. In other words, the price to be paid for getting rid of everlasting hell is the loss of everlasting life!

The key area of debate here surrounds the Greek word translated as "eternal," *aiônios*—the adjectival form of *aiônion* (a period of time, an age). In many New Testament texts it refers not simply to any age, but to the age to come. We could very plausibly render Jesus' words as referring to a parallel between the punishment of the age to come and the life of the age to come.[46] That is to say, the life and punishment that (a) belong in the age to come, and (b) are appropriate to the age to come.[47] How long will this life and this punishment last? Jesus does not say. That question is simply not the issue here. Perhaps forever. Perhaps not. To settle *that*

---

46. There is some debate on the word *kolasis* (punishment) here. Schneider links the original meaning with *kalazô*, "to cut" (*TDNT* III, 814). Thus, it could be used of pruning trees (Theophrastus, *De casius plantarum* 3.18.2). In secular Greek it seems to be a term referring to punishment done for the *correction and betterment* of the one being punished (Aristotle, *Rhetoric* 1369b13; Plato *Gorgias* 476A–477A; *Protagoras* 323e). However, this distinction was not always retained in later texts. The word could simply be used in a generic way to speak of punishment, irrespective of whether or not it was corrective. In the LXX, *kolasis* seems to be more generic (2 Macc. 4:38; 3 Macc. 1:3; 7:10; 4 Macc. 8:9; Wis. 11:3; 16:2, 24; 19:4; Jer. 18:20; Ezek. 14:3–4, 7; 18:30; 43:11; 44:12). *Kolasis* in Matthew 25:46 could *possibly* mean "correction," but while such a conclusion would strengthen my case, I am inclined to think that Jesus is using the word generically (cf. 1 John 4:18, its only other use in the NT).

47. This is the view of Konstan and Ramelli in their study of *aiônios* in ancient Greek, Jewish, and Christian literature. See Ilaria Ramelli and David Konstan, *Terms for Eternity: Aiônios and Aïdios in Classical and Christian Texts* (Piscataway, NJ: Gorgias, 2013).

question we must look elsewhere. This conclusion may be reinforced by a consideration of the description of the fate of the goats: *to pur to aiônion* ("the eternal fire," 25:41). The same phrase (*puros aiôniou*/eternal fire) is used in Jude 7 to describe the fate of Sodom and Gomorrah. Now in terms of its duration, Sodom's fire *only lasted for a day*. Thus, while not lacking a temporal aspect, *aiônios* is being used in a *qualitative* (rather than a quantitative) way here, as in many other NT texts.[48]

Don't panic. The life of the age to come is indeed everlasting. We know this, however, *not* because Jesus called it *aiônios* in Matthew 25, but because eternal life is a participation in Christ's own incorruptible resurrection life (1 Cor. 15) and his relationship with the Father (John 17:3). But punishment is of a different order. Eschatological punishment lacks any Christ-centered theological basis for being everlasting. So eschatological life and punishment are parallel in belonging to the age to come, but are *not* parallel in needing to endure for the entirety of the age to come. To argue that both must be everlasting is to go beyond the parable.

2 Thessalonians 1:5 - 10

The Pauline text that provides the biggest problems for universalism is 2 Thessalonians 1:5 – 10. Paul is speaking to a church that has suffered persecution (1:5). He reassures them that

> God is just: He will pay back trouble to those who trouble you and give relief to you who are troubled.... This will happen when the Lord Jesus is revealed from heaven in blazing fire with his powerful angels. He will punish those who do not know God and do not obey the gospel of our Lord Jesus. They will be punished with everlasting destruction and shut out from the presence of the Lord and from the glory of his might [or, perhaps better, "punished with everlasting destruction, *which comes from* the presence of the Lord and the glory of his might"[49]].

---

48. See Papaioannou, *Geography of Hell*, ch. 3.

49. The text says, "punished with 'eternal' [of the age to come] destruction from the presence of the Lord." The issue is: what does "from the presence of the Lord" qualify? Is it *the persecutors* (destroyed from the presence) or *the destruction* (which comes from the presence)? I think the latter.

On the face of it, this looks like a text that teaches everlasting destruction. Does it?

The first thing to point out is that we cannot simply assume that *olethron aiônion* must mean *everlasting* or *eternal* punishment/ruin.[50] We have already claimed that the adjective *aiônios* can refer to the age to come. I think a rendering of this expression as "the punishment of the age to come" is perfectly possible in this context. Of course, such punishment *may* still be eternal, but equally, it may not. We cannot settle *that* issue by means of *this* word.

Now in this context in 1 Thessalonians, Paul has no interest at all in discussing the question of whether or not those who experience the punishment/ruin of the age to come can subsequently find salvation. He is not interested either in the question of whether this punishment/ruin can serve an ultimate redemptive function. His focus is purely and simply on divine retributive punishment on the enemies of God's people,[51] a punishment that will bring relief from persecution to the church. That is all perfectly appropriate to the situation.

The hermeneutical and theological question is this: can we extrapolate an anti-universalist theology of divine justice and eschatological punishment from this text? Remember, Paul's purpose in writing this passage was not to provide a general theology of judgment and punishment or a doctrine of hell, but to speak a specific word from God to a specific situation. Now we can, and should, dig down to discern the theological underpinnings of Paul's context-specific word, and we can, and should, seek to integrate them with other things that Paul says on such matters. Furthermore, the resulting "Pauline theology" will play an important role in ongoing Christian theological reflections on eschatological judgment. However, we must *not* assume that simply because Paul does not address the issue of post-punishment salvation for the enemies of the church in this rhetorical context—and it would hardly have been appropriate to do so—that such a possibility is incompatible with his wider theology or with what he says in this text. We need to situate this text within a much wider context when we consider its appropriate place in our own consideration of hell.

---

50. *Olethron* can mean punishment or ruin. It is unclear which rendering is best here.

51. Note that "pay back" implies some proportioning of punishment to the suffering inflicted on the church. This counts against *everlasting* punishment.

Revelation 14:9 - 11 and 20:10 - 15

The two texts in the Bible that provide the strongest evidence for eternal torment come from the book of Revelation. In the first, all those who bear the mark of the beast will "drink the wine of God's fury" and will be "tormented with burning sulfur in the presence of the holy angels and of the Lamb. And the smoke of their torment will rise for ever and ever.[52] There will be no rest day or night for those who worship the beast and its image, or for anyone who receives the mark of his name" (14:10–11). The second concerns the image of "the lake of burning sulfur" in which the devil, the beast, and the false prophet are thrown—"they will be tormented day and night for ever and ever" (20:10). After the final judgment "death and Hades" joined them, and "anyone whose name was not found written in the book of life was thrown into the lake of fire" (20:14–15).

I have dealt with these texts at length elsewhere,[53] so a few simple comments must suffice here. First, it is critical that we situate both texts in their literary context. What we find in both cases is that the fierce judgment passages are followed by salvation postscripts, which relate back to them. So our interpretations of these passages must take into account the frame within which they are situated. In both cases the postscripts are universalist, envisaging salvation for the damned. Thus, the judgment of 14:9–11 (and of the whole of 14:6–20) is followed by a salvation postscript in which the delivered saints sing the praises of God: "Just and true are your ways, King of the nations. Who will not fear you, Lord, and bring glory to your name? For you alone are holy. *All nations will come and worship before you*, for your righteous acts have been revealed" (15:3–4, emphasis added). To grasp the universal implications of this we need to appreciate that in Revelation "the nations" are the bad guys (11:18; 13:7b; 14:8; 16:19; 17:15; 18:3, 23). They fail to heed a final call to repentance and join in the final battle against the saints and the Lamb (20:8), thus becoming the objects of God's eschatological wrath (11:8; 12:5; 19:15). In Revelation, the saints are *never* identified with the nations. Rather, they are those who have been redeemed "*from* every nation" (7:9). So there can be no doubt who the nations in 15:4 are—they

---

52. "... unto ages of ages."
53. *TEU*, 106–32.

are those who were "tormented with burning sulfur" (14:10). And yet *after that*, the saints declare that all these damned nations will come and worship God. And we should note that the word used here for worship (*proskunçsousin*) refers to voluntary, not forced, worship—a point reinforced by the allusion to Psalm 86:9–10, which underlies our passage.

In a similar way, the lake of fire passage (20:10–15) is followed by an amazing vision (21:22–27) in which we read the following of the new Jerusalem: "The nations will walk by its light, and the kings of the earth will bring their splendor into it. On no day will its gates ever be shut, for there will be no night there" (21:24–25). These nations are coming into the city from outside. What, in the geography of this vision, lies outside the city? Only the damned in the lake of fire (22:14–15). That makes sense. As shown above, by this point the audience of Revelation knows full well who "the nations" are—the enemies of Christ—and where they are—in the lake of burning sulfur. The same can be said of "the kings of the earth." They too are Christ's enemies, defeated in the last battle (6:15; 17:2, 18; 18:3, 9; 19:19, 21). They too were cast into the lake of fire. Now we see them coming into the New Jerusalem, through its ever-open gates, having washed their robes in the blood of the Lamb, with their names in the Book of Life (21:27; 22:14). Now they have access to the tree of life, the leaves of which are "for the healing of the nations" (22:2).

I suggest that this guides us to interpret the two judgment texts (14:9–11 and 20:10–15) in such a way as to permit post-damnation salvation. The language the punishment texts employ is very strong, but it needs careful interpretation in terms of the context of the whole book and in terms of the Old Testament scriptures on which it draws. In an earlier book, *The Evangelical Universalist*, I tried to show how this fierce rhetoric, when so interpreted, is consistent with post-damnation salvation for all.

What About Free Will?

Many will claim that, while I may be correct in much of what I have said, I have forgotten something critical—human freedom. Although God desires to redeem all people, he does not wish to do so in such a way that violates their free will. And free will by its very nature cannot be controlled by God. Consequently God cannot guarantee that all people will freely choose to accept salvation. Those in hell are there, not because God wants them to be there, but because of choices freely made.

I need to be clear that universalists are not suggesting that God saves anyone *against* their will. What he does is to work in differing ways so as to solicit a free response. God can, universalists believe, bring it about that all people freely accept the gospel.

But many claim that this is not possible. Consider, say, St. Peter's decision to follow Jesus. Surely, if Peter's choice to submit to Christ was genuinely free, then *it must have been possible for him to refrain from doing it*. If refusing to bow his knee was not psychologically possible, then — it is alleged — his choice was not free. So, the argument is that if people are *free*, God cannot *ensure* that they will accept the gospel. Consequently, unless God violates our freedom, he cannot *guarantee* that all will be saved. We'll call this the libertarian objection. I will argue that it is mistaken.

Let's reflect a little on the nature of freedom. Thomas Talbott argues that a genuinely free action requires a basic level of rationality.[54] We'll consider an extreme situation to bring this out. If someone performs an action when they have (a) no motive for doing so and (b) a very strong motive for not doing so, we tend to consider their actions utterly irrational, and not genuinely free. Imagine a boy who thrusts his hand into a fire, even though he has no reason for wanting to put his hand into the fire and very good reason for wanting to not to. We would not celebrate his freedom; we'd call a psychiatrist. The only course of action that we would consider free is that in which the boy refused to put his hand in the fire — *even if this choice was so psychologically compelling that no alternative action was a live possibility*.

Of course, most of the time we are not in situations like this. Most of the time the reasons and motives for and against different courses of action are not so clear-cut. Then we are faced with conflicting desires and no one course of action is psychologically compelling. In such situations freedom looks different — the person could either opt one way or the other. The libertarian objector takes such situations to be the paradigm of free will, while Talbott considers them to describe freedom *under certain conditions*.

---

54. See Talbott, *Inescapable*, 167–206. For an excellent defense of Talbott's view, see Kronen and Reitan, *Victory*, 127–51.

Now freedom can be impeded by various factors: external constraints (e.g., a man holding a gun to your head), ignorance or deception about the reality of the choice (e.g., if one thinks that pressing the switch will turn on the light, when it actually detonates a bomb), or bondage to desires (e.g., an addiction to drugs). However, a rational choice made in the absence of such external constraints, ignorance, deception, or bondage to desires will be free, *even if psychologically determined.*

Talbott asks us to consider what it might mean to make a free decision to reject God. If we *really understood* the truth of the situation, we would grasp that God is our *telos*, what we most need and desire at the deepest level of our being. Of course, few people do appreciate the truth of their situation vis-à-vis God, so rejecting God is not hard. But does it make any sense to imagine someone who *fully appreciates* the objective truth of the situation choosing to reject Christ and to embrace hell? This is even more insane than the boy putting his hand in the fire! It's incomprehensible. Such a "choice" could only be the result of external compulsion, ignorance, deception, or slavery to desires—all factors that *inhibit* freedom.

So God simply needs to work in many and various ways (even in hell) to gradually increase awareness of the truth of the situation. The greater our Spirit-enabled appreciation of that truth, the greater will be our desire to choose God and the lesser will be our desire to reject God. Of course, short of an overwhelming revelation, we could still theoretically reject God. Only at the point at which we are *fully* informed could we no longer reject God, and I doubt that many people would need to get to that stage before choosing God. But even if we are fully informed, *we are still free.*

To hold out for a freedom that could still reject God even when one fully grasped the truth is to hold out for something not worth having—utterly irrational, random behavior. Such "freedom" is no "precious gift," but an affliction from which we need saving.[55]

To insist that God is obligated to keep us in ignorance, lest we be overwhelmed by the truth and feel compelled to love him, strikes me as

---

55. However, if we really do want to retain such pointless "freedom" then, given enough time, God could *still* bring it about that all people are saved. For the reason, see Kronen and Reitan, *Victory*, 152–77.

simply weird.[56] If that were so, Christ has some apologizing to do to St. Paul (Acts 9). Removing external constraints, dispelling ignorance and deception, and breaking bondage to irrational desires are not a crime against freedom — unless by "freedom" we mean what Paul called "slavery to sin."[57]

In the End, God . . .

In this essay I have argued that the future of creation depends upon the finished work of God in Christ. There can be no other end than that revealed in the resurrection — death will die, and God will be all in all (1 Cor. 15:28). "The traditional position is ... that God will be all in all *despite* the damnation or destruction of many of his creatures.... The universalist asserts: 'The God I believe in, the God I see in Christ, *could not* be all in all *in these conditions*: such victory *could not* be the victory of the God of love."[58]

We will give the last word to P. T. Forsyth, who helpfully pulls together some of the theological themes we have been considering:

> The purpose of a world created by a holy God must be holiness, the reflection and communion of His own holiness. Can God secure it? ... That is the ultimate question in life.... And to that question Christ and His cross are the answer, or they have no meaning at all. They reveal in the foregone victory the omnipotence of holiness to subdue all natural powers and forces, all natural omnipotence, to the moral sanctity of the Kingdom of God. And if they do not reveal that, we are left without any ground of certainty about a holy ending for the world at all.... It is a tremendous claim. And the improbability of it is either a pious absurdity; or it is the quiet irony of a God who has it already done in the hollow of His hand.[59]

---

56. This is not to say that God does not have good reason to start us off in a situation in which our grasp of the truth is very limited, and our freedom looks more libertarian. On which see Talbott, *Inescapable*, 167–206.

57. But what if I'm wrong? What if the *only* way in which God could stop some people damning themselves forever was to limit their freedom? Then, I suggest, the right thing would be for God to do precisely that. In many situations stepping in to forcibly stop people doing dreadful things, even if freely chosen, is good and right. The *terrible* cost in this case would justify such a course of action.

58. Robinson, *In the End, God...*, 97.

59. P. T. Forsyth, *The Person and Place of Jesus Christ* (London: Hodder & Stoughton, 1910), 228–29.

DENNY BURK

Robin Parry defines "Christian universalism" as the belief that "in the end God will reconcile all people to himself through Christ." This version of universalism is "Christian," Parry argues, because Christ is the only way for people to be saved. It says that eventually all people will come to Christ and be saved—even those who have died without repenting of their sin and trusting in him. But this universalism fails to persuade for a number of reasons:

1. The author falls short of a sound hermeneutic.

Parry argues that the debate about hell often gets "bogged down in proof texting." He argues that this method of cherry-picking verses cannot settle the matter because "*all sides* can point to verses that *seem* to support their view." Because attention to specific texts only leads to contradictory conclusions, Parry argues that the "rule of faith"—the Trinitarian gospel narrative—has to be the standard by which we interpret individual texts that appear to be in tension with one another. So Parry devotes a sizable portion of his essay outlining what he believes are the contours of this overarching Trinitarian gospel narrative.

The problem with this approach, however, is that his "Christ-centered biblical metanarrative" amounts to little more than a string of proof texts supporting his version of universalism. He quotes from these proof texts while italicizing words like "all" and the "whole world" as if the observation of these terms somehow establishes a biblical metanarrative (e.g., Col. 1:16, 19–20; Rom. 5:14–21; 1 John 2:2; 2 Cor. 5:14). However, he never really establishes his point. The biblical metanarrative cannot be constructed apart from biblical texts about resurrection and judgment. These are the themes in dispute, yet they are conveniently left out of Parry's version of the "biblical metanarrative."

The bottom line is that Parry's errant hermeneutic yields an errant understanding of Scripture. Through a truncated account of Scripture, it establishes a theological presupposition of universalism. It assumes what it purportedly sets out to prove. And that unwarranted assumption controls the reading of texts that contradict his thesis.

For example, Colossians 1:16, 19–20 figure prominently in Parry's account of the biblical metanarrative: "For in him [the Son] all things were created ... God was pleased ... through him to reconcile to himself all things." Parry rightly points out that "reconcile" refers to salvation in other New Testament texts, but then concludes that "all" people are therefore reconciled. This universalist rendering of "all" fails to account for the immediate context. After speaking of the reconciliation of "all" things in verse 20, Paul goes on to talk about reconciliation in the life of the Colossians in particular. He warns them that their reconciliation is *conditional* upon persevering faith: [You are reconciled] "if indeed you continue in the faith firmly established and steadfast, and not moved away from the hope of the gospel" (v. 23 NASB).

In short, Paul is clear that unbelief does not lead to reconciliation but keeps people "alienated and hostile in mind" toward God (v. 21 NASB). Parry's universalist explanation of "all" in verse 20 cannot account for the conditionalism of verse 23, which excludes unbelievers from the company of the reconciled. Thus his use of verse 20 as a proof text cannot even account for the immediate context—a context that does not support the universalism that he sees at the heart of the biblical metanarrative.

We all agree that a hermeneutical spiral is involved with any reading of the biblical text. The parts interpret the whole, and the whole interprets the parts. That process is inevitable. But at the end of the day, Parry's spiral is top-heavy. His presupposition becomes impervious to counterevidence from Scripture. A faithful hermeneutic would allow contrary evidence to reshape and refine his presupposition of universalism. In the case of Colossians 1:20, the counterevidence completely overthrows that presupposition.

2. The author makes an unwarranted assumption about the existence of sin.

Parry argues that God purposes to restore "all" things in such a way that does not allow for the continued existence of sinners. If God were to allow sinners to exist eternally in hell, it would derail God's purposes. He writes, "Will God allow sin to thwart his purposes to beautify the cosmos?... *No freaking way!*" Leaving sinners in hell would frustrate God's work to reverse the tragic effects of sin in this world. So Parry asks a leading question, "Does Christ undo *all* the damage caused by sin, or does he only undo *some* of it?" Parry argues that God eliminates all the stains on his universe by graciously saving everyone through Christ.

In this line of argument, Parry makes assumptions about the existence of evil that do not have biblical warrant. Nowhere does Scripture teach us that God must *eliminate* sinners in order for justice to be restored in God's cosmos. On the contrary, the Bible teaches that God must *judge* sinners in order for all things to be renewed. For example, in Revelation God's judgment on the wicked is not viewed as a stain on God's justice but as the demonstration of God's justice.

> **Revelation 18:20** "Rejoice over her, O heaven, and you saints and apostles and prophets, because has pronounced judgment for you against her" (NASB).

> **Rev. 19:1–2** "Hallelujah! Salvation and glory and power belong to our God; BECAUSE HIS JUDGMENTS ARE TRUE AND RIGHTEOUS; for He has judged the great harlot who was corrupting the earth with her immorality" (NASB).

Again, the existence of sinners in hell does not "thwart" God's purposes to "beautify" the cosmos. On the contrary, God's judgment on the wicked is a part of God's putting things right by making all things new (Rev. 21:5, 8). We might add to this the observation that human beings are not the only sinners in God's cosmos. There are other beings—the Devil and his angels—that are also destined for the lake of fire (Rev. 20:10). Unless Parry wishes to argue for the salvation of Satan, he would have to acknowledge that Satan's sinful existence under God's judgment does not thwart God's purposes.

3. The author leaves little room for the wrath of God.

Parry rightly argues that "every doctrine of hell implies a doctrine of God, and every doctrine of God will shape one's theology of hell." He also correctly warns against setting "divine love and justice in *opposition* to each other." But in his own account of things, Parry does just that. Parry wrongly construes how goodness, love, and justice come together in the godhead and how they are revealed in the age to come. For Parry, God's love is the dominant aspect of God's character—so much so, that God's love appears to leave little room for his wrath. In fact, he argues that God loves all people at all times. Parry treats God's love as the defining feature of God's relatedness to people: "If God is love then God loves all his creatures. And to love someone is to want the best for them."

For Parry, therefore, God's love will not allow him to punish unrepentant sinners in an everlasting hell. He argues that God continues to love those who are in hell and that God still desires for them to be saved. So even in hell, God's wrath takes a back seat to his love. Parry even goes so far as to suggest that God's wrath and justice are but "ways" in which God's love manifests itself.

Again, this account of God's love leaves little room for God's wrath. For Parry, God's wrath and justice get completely absorbed by God's love. Parry reduces God's wrath to a "severe mercy"—one way in which God's "love must show itself to be love in the face of its denial" (quoting John A. T. Robinson). This is not the biblical portrayal of God's wrath. God's wrath in Scripture is the necessary response of a holy God to sin. God's wrath is his personal opposition to and anger against not only sin, but also sinners. Sinners who do not trust in Christ have the wrath of God "abiding" on them right now (John 3:36). As long as they refuse to repent, they are "storing up" wrath for themselves—a wrath to be revealed in the age to come (Rom. 2:5). God's wrath is not tantamount to love. It is what sinners need to be saved from (Rom. 5:9).

To treat wrath as if it is little more than a Father's temporary disappointment is to miss what the Bible says about it. God's wrath issues forth in incinerating judgments that are punitive in nature, not restorative. God's wrath is his means of executing vengeance—not restoration—on his enemies (Rom. 12:19). God does not love those who are put into hell. On the contrary, his wrath means that he is angry at them forever (Rom. 2:8). But this biblical view of God's wrath disappears in Parry's account of God.

4. The author makes a speculative case for postmortem salvation.

Parry does not deny that there is a place called "hell" in Scripture. He simply argues that the punishments of hell are not punitive, but restorative. He writes, "If we believe that Scripture teaches *both* that all people will be saved *and* that some people will go to hell—and it does seem to teach both—then it is arguable that we can legitimately infer that those in hell will be saved out of hell." So Parry acknowledges that the Bible does not actually say anything explicit about postmortem salvation. It is at best an inference drawn from broader theological themes found in Scripture. Thus in Parry's words, postmortem salvation can only claim to be a biblical doctrine "in a secondary sense."

But it is precisely here that Parry's universalism shipwrecks itself on biblical reality. He has to brush aside biblical texts that treat God's judgment as a final, eternity-defining act of God in the eschaton. Most notable among those texts is Hebrews 9:27: "People are destined to die once, and after that to face judgment." This text teaches that God's judgment on the wicked is final and irreversible. Yet Parry denies that it refers to "irreversible punishment." But his reading would undo the logic of this particular text, which insists that the finality of death and judgment parallels the once-for-all-ness of Christ's sacrificial death and second coming (Heb. 9:28). Thus, to deny the fixedness of judgment in Hebrews 9:27 would imply a denial of the finished work of Christ in Hebrews 9:28. If the former is reversible, then so is the latter. But this is a tortured reading of the text with an implication that no party to this debate would accept.

There are other biblical texts that speak to the irreversibility of God's final judgment. Jesus' parable of the rich man and Lazarus describes an irreversible separation of the righteous from the wicked in the age to come. Lazarus is divided from the rich man by a "great chasm" that prevents people from crossing from torment to blessedness (Luke 16:26). The inability to travel out of torment into blessedness highlights the urgency of repentance before death (Luke 16:30). As I. Howard Marshall comments on this text, "The judgment is thus irrevocable."[60]

There are countless other texts to which we could appeal to establish the point. The bottom line is that there is no explicit evidence anywhere in Scripture for the idea of postmortem salvation. Parry's suggestion that postmortem salvation is implied by Scripture runs aground on the many texts that teach the fixedness of God's judgment. Thus the idea

---

60. I. Howard Marshall, *The Gospel of Luke: A Commentary on the Greek Text*, The New International Greek Testament Commentary (Grand Rapids: Eerdmans, 1978), 638.

of a postmortem salvation is a tendentious speculation with no real grounding in the text of Scripture. If there is no postmortem salvation in Scripture, Parry's case for universalism completely falls apart.

Space forbids a full response to Parry's exposition of seminal texts such as Mark 9:42–50; Matthew 25:31–46; 2 Thessalonians 1:5–10; and Revelation 14:9–11; 20:10–15. I simply refer readers to my chapter in this volume for an alternate interpretation of these texts.

A TERMINAL PUNISHMENT RESPONSE

JOHN G. STACKHOUSE JR.

Universalism has always impressed me as the triumph of hope over exegesis, the pressing of theological conclusions from lovely presuppositions (most of which, to be sure, any Christian should hold) to conclusions that simply cannot stand in the light of Scripture's frequent and stark opposition.

One has to grant to universalism that there is an attractive logic, as well as a pleasing symmetry, to the idea that as God created our cosmos "very good" in its entirety, God will redeem all of it as well. And one also must grant that Paul sometimes enjoys speaking in such categories of "all" and "all," as Robin Parry properly points out (e.g., Rom. 5; 1 Cor. 15; Col. 1).

As we examine the many texts of Scripture that do indeed pertain to this question, however, our hopeful universalism must dim considerably. (To do so is not, of course, to get "bogged down in proof texting," as Parry has it, but to do one's exegetical homework.) The Old Testament uniformly presents a bleak picture of the destruction and disappearance of all of God's enemies. A single verse, Hosea 13:3, speaks for many in its fourfold imagery: "Therefore they shall be like the morning mist or like the dew that goes away early, like chaff that swirls from the threshing floor or like smoke from a window" (NRSV). There is nothing like a universalist hope evident in the Old Testament.

Moreover, Jesus and Paul knew and loved the Old Testament as the Word of God, and nothing they said or wrote ought to be interpreted against it. Furthermore, the eschatological "all" must be interpreted in the light of the prophecies of Jesus and Paul themselves about the judgment, suffering, and destruction of the guilty—as in "all ... who remain on the other side of the Last Judgment." Parry properly notes in this respect,

So is everyone currently justified? Yes and no. In that Christ has been raised for our justification (Rom. 4:25), we are all already justified in his resurrection. However, it is only as we respond in obedient trust to the gospel and are united to Christ by the Spirit that we participate subjectively in this justification.

So each biblical use of "all" has to be interpreted carefully, lest we interpret the reconciliation of all things to include, say, cancers or viruses, as well as the reprobate.

Perhaps, some universalists affirm, hell in the New Testament is like the judgment of God on Israel in the Old Testament: terrible, yes, but with hope of eventual redemption. The grim biblical truth, however, is that only a *remnant* of Israel survived the awful respective exiles of northern and southern kingdoms. So universalism is exactly what is *not* foreshadowed in the career of Israel. Alas for this charitable idea of universalism, moreover, there is simply no scriptural teaching that hell is redemptive and temporary, after which all will be invited into the presence of God forever in happy harmony. Instead, there is a uniform message that hell is both awful and terminal. It is called, therefore, "the second death."

As Jerry Walls rightly avers in his article, the logic of the actual doctrine of purgatory is that Christ has atoned for us; we have received the grounds of that salvation; and in purgatory we are being readied to enjoy the fruits of it. Correctly understood, purgatory is only for Christians, only for those who are already on their way to heaven because they *have* accepted the provisions offered to them by God's grace in the atoning work of Christ. And if purgatory is hinted at as a fire (perhaps 1 Cor. 3:10–15?), it includes a fire of judgment and purgation to prepare the Christian for the remaining sanctification necessary to enter the presence of the holy God.

Parry follows Rob Bell and others in pointing to the intriguing passage in Ezekiel in which even Sodom seems to be redeemed (Ezek. 16). Yet this is a slender and solitary branch on which to hang so heavy a doctrine. Every other biblical reference to Sodom is uniformly negative, and negative in the extreme. Both before and after this revelation through Ezekiel, Sodom is the very picture of evil judged firmly and finally by God. Therefore Jesus warns that the towns that refuse the evangelism of his disciples, as he chides Capernaum for refusing his own, will fare worse than Sodom in the final judgment—which is hyperbole, of course, because any Jew would understand that *nothing can be worse* than the fate of Sodom (Matt. 10:15; 11:24).

Thus most commentators, reading Scripture in concert with Scripture, see in the Ezekiel passage faint hope for Judah (for the "restoration" is only to a "former state" of indictable sinfulness for the northern kingdom of Samaria/Israel and the southern kingdom of Sodom) or none at all (paralleling Jesus's warnings centuries later—as Israel/Samaria, the northern kingdom, is indeed lost to history, vanished even as Sodom has vanished). If the Holy Spirit, that is, intended to teach universalism by the case of Sodom, I suggest that he has done an awfully poor job of it.

(Some universalists similarly seize on the parable of the Unmerciful Servant [Matt. 18:34, cf. Matt. 5:26], as if therein one can find hope of "getting out" once one "has paid the last penny"—even as it seems clear to most commentators that the point of the parable is the *hopelessness* of the villain of the piece ever paying back the monstrous debt he owes. Biblical hyperbole must be recognized as such, or we will end up with Scripture flatly contradicting Scripture.)

For universalism, therefore, only deductive arguments can be seriously mounted, not strong exegetical ones. Universalism has no other recourse than to do what Parry does: Load up on abstract ideas and broad theological schemes and select Scriptural fragments such as "God is love" and "God is not willing that any should perish." Likewise, universalists typically trade in rhetorical questions rather than assertions, and Parry's essay is conspicuously full of them—appealing as they do to the supposed intuitions of the reader rather than to the actual evidence from Scripture or the logic of fully worked-out arguments.

Parry early on, for example, asks, "Does Christ undo *all* the damage caused by sin, or does he only undo *some* of it? Where sin abounds, does grace abound *all the more* (Rom. 5:20), or does it just abound *quite a lot*?" All Christians affirm that Christ will eventually undo all the damage caused by sin. Orthodox Christians have affirmed that hell is part of that project. As for grace abounding, of course it abounds—but that does not mean that grace smothers everything, such as human (or angelic) freedom and responsibility.

Likewise, Parry asks: "Will God's desire to save all people be satisfied or eternally frustrated? Will the cross save all those for whom Christ died, or will his death have been in vain for some people?" Again, the answer is not necessarily a universalist one. Some Christians have said, as Parry later acknowledges, that God sovereignly destines some human beings for hell as he elects only some to salvation. Others, who see the destiny of human beings as resulting from our choices for or against God's gracious offering of salvation, see God's love being refused by some people, and therefore some people enter hell. God gives us freedom to love, and thus he makes himself vulnerable to our refusal to love. Either way, orthodox Christians have looked to their Bibles and come up with answers markedly different from universalist ones — and rhetorical questions thus do not suffice in place of actual arguments.

We also must beware of muddying our terms, such as "justice" and "love" rather than Parry's preferred "loving justice" or "just love." I have agreed with Parry in my own piece that God is always all of what God is, so God is never unjust or unloving. But God's wrath is not, at its worst, a "severe mercy," as Parry hopefully says, but sometimes is only justice, with no mercy at all. Love does all it can, to be sure, but sometimes it must leave justice to do what must finally be done. God hardens Pharaoh's heart and condemns the entire civilization of Canaan. Jesus gives up on the Pharisees and simply stops speaking to them. Satan's head is to be crushed.

Does not the goodness of God, however, eventually triumph over even the most stubborn resistance? Wouldn't Satan himself eventually be won over to God's beauty and love? It might seem so, especially to some tenderhearted believers — or to some theologians who want to press their presuppositions to what they trust to be valid conclusions. But we must beware of the lure of either intuition or speculation: "Given that we hope or believe A, B, and C to be the case, then D seems to follow. Therefore, we believe D follows." Now, if we have no other grounds upon which to reason, then we reason as best we can. But if Scriptural revelation is given to us just at the juncture of A, B, and C with D, then Christians must give the nod to Scripture. And Scripture, particularly in Revelation 20 but in so many other places as well, seems forthrightly bleak on the destiny of Satan and all other creatures who have resisted God until even the last judgment. That destiny is the lake of fire, the second death.

Indeed, it seems counterintuitive (since intuition is not to be scorned, but simply guided by the authority of Scripture) to imagine people being won over to God, even over vast amounts of time, *in the lake of fire.* Having a number of times experienced the opposite—a lake of shocking coldness, when I've fallen off water skis or out of a canoe in northern Canada—I cannot imagine anyone deciding *in that context* to abandon one's resentment of God and instead develop soft, kind thoughts about him. It is one thing to experience the pains of *purgatory* as Christians already reconciled to God and determined to become sanctified, whatever the cost. It is quite another to experience the sufferings of hell and to decide to love the God who is, after all, meting out my just deserts in the teeth of my previous refusal of his offer of grace.

It is this psychological deficiency in universalism that I honestly don't understand. Parry asks us to "imagine a boy who thrusts his hand into a fire, even though he has no reason for wanting to put his hand into the fire and very good reason for not wanting to." Yet no boy puts his hand in the fire unless he has *what he thinks* is a *very strong reason to do so.* Sin addles us to the point that we sincerely believe we are seeking our true interests in ignoring, or even rebelling against, God and God's truth (as we Christians know from our day-to-day struggles). The whole record of the Bible—from the ungrateful generation of rescued Israelites who refused to enter the Promised Land, to the recalcitrance of Judas despite his years in the very company of Jesus, to the doomed but dogged resistance of the fallen angels—warns us that *sinners aren't logical.*

Of course, it is stupid and self-destructive to resist the will of God, but *we all do it every day.* So until our reasoning is fundamentally altered—by the prevenient grace of God—we do not come to the right conclusions about God, Christ, salvation, and the rest of it ... just as Satan has not come to those right conclusions over all these millennia.

Ironically enough, therefore, it is only monergists, or what I call "strong predestinarians," who can be consistently universalist: Only those who believe that God alone can and does reach down and alter our hearts such that we leave off lusting after sin and instead hunger and thirst after righteousness. (Karl Barth's universal election in Christ is, indeed, a very strong form of predestination.) Yet *orthodox* predestinarians—from Augustine through Luther and Calvin—seem uniformly to agree that God predestines some to hell in his *decretum horribile* (as Calvin put it). And why do they agree? Because the Bible seems to them, as it seems to most Christians, to speak unequivocally and terrifyingly of the reality of a hell from which no one escapes, a hell of punishment with no hint of restoring anything *except the final pure goodness of the cosmos*—which, as I have been arguing, is consistent only with terminal punishment (the eventual eradication of evil), and not with eternal torment (an ongoing horror show in God's otherwise good creation).

Alas, then, universalism is consistent with certain wonderful tellings of the biblical story of creation, fall, and redemption. Our tellings, however, must be true to the whole counsel of God, shadows and scares included. The death of the ungodly is a theme from God's initial warning to our first parents in Eden to almost the last chapters of Revelation. "Hoping don't make it so," and instead we must "humbly accept the word planted in you, which can save you" (Jas. 1:21), daunting as some of it truly is.

JERRY L. WALLS

I will begin by saying that although I think Robin Parry is wrong, I hope he is right. I say this as someone who has been defending the doctrine of hell as eternal conscious misery throughout his academic career, and who has perhaps written as many books and essays defending the doctrine as any contemporary Christian thinker.[61]

I disagree with Parry at the exegetical level and also on a big philosophical issue. Despite that, we share a lot of profound theological agreement. I very much agree with his view of divine love and his defense of postmortem repentance. And I am certainly a universalist on the matter of the crucifixion, as he puts it. I heartily believe that God loves all persons, that he sent Christ to die for all, and that God sincerely offers salvation to all and desires all to accept that offer.

In view of all this, there is no reason in principle why all cannot be saved. God emphatically does not need to damn some persons forever to display his wrath in order fully to glorify himself, as some Calvinists believe.[62] Eternal hell is neither a theological, philosophical, moral, nor metaphysical necessity. It is entirely contingent and need not be true. In my view, all persons are given every opportunity to repent and accept God's saving grace, so none need go to hell forever.

The bottom-line reason that I believe hell is conscious eternal misery is that I believe Scripture teaches this. Some people will in fact remain separated from God forever, by their own choice. I do not think this is decisively clear from Scripture, as I have indicated in my response to Stackhouse. But I reiterate the point I made in response to him that there is good reason to give the benefit of the doubt to the traditional

---

61. In addition to my books *Hell: The Logic of Damnation* (Notre Dame: University of Notre Dame Press, 1992) and *Heaven, Hell and Purgatory: Rethinking the Things that Matter Most* (Grand Rapids: Brazos, 2015), I have written some twenty essays defending the doctrine.

62. See John Piper, *Does God Desire All to Be Saved?* (Wheaton: Crossway, 2013).

view, and that the burden of proof remains on those views that seek to displace it. In my view, neither of the alternative views has been sufficiently proven by their advocates.

Of course, I concede the point that both universalists and terminal punishment advocates can cite several texts that *prima facie* seem clearly to support their view, as I noted in my response to Stackhouse. I very much agree with Parry, however, that the hell debate has "often gotten bogged down in proof texting" and that it will take more than this to carry the day.

I recently read Parry's book *The Evangelical Universalist* and very much appreciated his larger theological argument that attempted to make the case for universalism by situating the doctrine of hell "in the biblical metanarrative, the grand story that runs from Genesis to Revelation" (p. 78). This is not to say that he ignored or tried to sidestep the proof texts that traditionalists have cited for their case, but his focus on the big picture allowed him to make the case that these texts can plausibly read differently from how they have usually been read.

I will also concede that his view represents the end of the biblical story that is most to be desired. The universalist view delivers on the promise of a truly perfect end of the story that the terminal punishment view claims to provide, but does not, as I argued in my response to Stackhouse. Parry contends that the traditional doctrine of hell is "out of sync" as a conclusion to the glorious New Testament vision of everything being subject to Christ in the end, with Christ subject to the Father, so that God is "all in all" (1 Cor. 15:28). Insofar as aesthetic considerations are brought to bear in the debate, I cannot deny the appeal of the universalist picture.

Yet, despite the appeal, I do not think this picture is the true end of things. Ironically, one of my deepest disagreements with Parry involves a point of deep agreement. I completely agree with him when he writes the following: "If your theology of hell is not compatible with God's love for the damned, then your theology of hell is wrong."

Indeed, in my view, eternal hell is possible precisely because God is love. The starting point of the biblical drama is that God is love from all eternity, that there was love between the three persons of the Trinity when there was no world and no angels or human beings to receive that love (John 17:24). Moreover, the very kind of love that existed in the

Trinity from all eternity is the kind of love that Christ poured out in his incarnation, death, and resurrection (John 15:9).

Furthermore, it is the same kind of love that Christ showed us that he commands us to give to one another (John 15:12).

But there is the rub for the universalist position. While love is God's very nature, we must choose to love, and that requires that we obey the teaching and example of Jesus. And while love can be elicited, it cannot be coerced, programmed, or determined. The sad truth that the biblical drama makes clear—and human history tragically confirms—is that we may choose not to love either God or each other. Indeed, our freedom in this regard is suggested by these words of Jesus: "Anyone who loves me will obey my teaching. My Father will love them, and we will come to them and make our home with them. Anyone who does not love me will not obey my teaching" (John 14:23–24).

However, Parry, following Thomas Talbott, is convinced that human freedom is not an obstacle to God's saving everyone. He insists, however, that he does not believe God saves anyone against their will. Rather, God can work in various ways to solicit a positive free response from all persons. As Parry says, "God can, universalists believe, bring it about that all people freely accept the gospel."

Now, here it is worth underscoring a striking similarity between theological determinists and universalists. Theological determinists also insist that God does not save people against their will. Moreover, God can choose to save anyone he wants to save, and he does so by determining the will of the elect, not by forcing them against their will. So theological determinists can heartily agree with Parry that God can "bring it about that ... people freely accept the gospel." The difference is that for the determinists, God brings this about only for the elect, whereas Parry believes God can and will do this for all persons. So the question that must be pressed here is what is involved for Parry in God's bringing this about, since he apparently denies theological determinism?

The fundamental reason Talbott thinks the doctrine of eternal hell is incoherent is that there is no intelligible motive for a rational person to choose hell. Such a choice makes no more sense than the choice to put one's hand in the fire. There is no rational reason to do so, and every reason not to do so. Similarly, Parry urges that anyone who is properly informed about the fundamental reality that God is our true end, that he is what we most deeply need for our happiness and fulfillment, simply cannot choose to resist him in the long run. He puts the issue like this: "But does it make any sense to imagine someone who *fully appreciates* the objective truth of the situation choosing to reject Christ and to embrace hell? This is even more insane than the boy putting his hand in the fire!"

Parry's question here is a good one, and indeed, I fully concur that one who "fully appreciates the objective truth of the situation" could not fail to choose Christ. However, the suggestion that this is comparable to the reality that no sane person would put his hand in the fire is deeply misleading. The automatic impulse to withdraw one's hand from the fire is not in any way a morally or spiritually significant reaction. It is a purely animal response, one that the lower animals would make as instinctively as we do. But "full appreciation of the objective truth" about God is another matter altogether. It is very much a rational, moral, and spiritual sort of awareness, and the big question that must be answered is how we achieve or gain this full awareness or appreciation.

Indeed, I have argued against Talbott that precisely here is located an essential aspect of our moral freedom. In other words, we only come to "fully appreciate" this truth as we progressively respond with trust and love to God's self-revelation and internalize what he has revealed to us. This involves far more than processing information or intellectual content. It occurs, rather, as we come to love God with our heart, soul, mind, and strength and allow him to form a character in us that reflects his own holy character. It is when we are transformed in this fashion that the objective truth about God comes fully into focus for us. It is only then that we see with vivid clarity that God is the source of all happiness and joy, and sin is the cause of misery. And in this condition, we freely and gladly embrace Christ and delight to do his will, and indeed, when we have fully internalized this truth and allowed it to shape our character, sin will no longer be an option for us. This is the happy condition of those who have been confirmed in goodness in heaven.

But again, we must freely cooperate with God's grace and own the truth as he reveals it to us. It is important to stress that when God initially begins to reveal himself and his truth to us, we are far from having a holy character, and in this condition, we lack the clarity of vision that we will have when we come fully to appreciate the truth about God—and ourselves. In this condition, we can still reject Christ and the salvation he offers. And if we persist in doing so, instead of perfecting our freedom by coming fully to appreciate the truth about God, we use our freedom to deny the truth and keep it from ever penetrating our hearts.[63]

Of course, the choice to go our own way even to the point of choosing eternal hell is profoundly self-deceptive. The dynamics of this choice are described in the mindset of the church at Laodicea: "You say, 'I am rich; I have acquired wealth and do not need a thing.' But you do not realize that you are wretched, pitiful, poor, blind and naked" (Rev. 3:17). Christ knocks at the door offering all riches, including the inestimable opportunity to sit at the table and dine with him. But as in the passage from John we noted above (14:23–24), we can turn him away in our delusional sense of self-satisfaction and thereby refuse the truth that will set us free.

That is why, as C. S. Lewis famously suggested, the doors of hell are locked on the inside and may remain so forever.[64]

---

63. Here I only sketch an argument I have developed more fully elsewhere. See *Hell: The Logic of Damnation*, 113–38; "A hell of a choice: reply to Talbott," *Religious Studies* 40 (2004), 203–16; see in the same issue, Thomas Talbott, "Misery and freedom: reply to Walls," 217–24; and my "A hell of a dilemma: rejoinder to Talbott," 225–27. See also *Heaven, Hell and Purgatory*, 67–90.

64. C. S. Lewis, *The Problem of Pain* (Harper: SanFrancisco, 2001), 130.

JERRY L. WALLS

Around a hundred years ago, the noted Scottish theologian P. T. Forsyth (1848–1921) suggested that Protestants overreacted when they rejected the doctrine of purgatory. "We threw away too much when we threw purgatory clean out of doors. We threw out the baby with the dirty water of its bath."[1]

There are reasons to believe that later generations of Protestants have at least begun to reconsider what they threw out when they rejected the doctrine of purgatory. For instance, the very fact that the 1992 *Four Views of Hell* volume includes a chapter on "The Purgatorial View" by Roman Catholic theologian Zachary Hayes suggests that at least a measure of openness to the doctrine existed among evangelicals in the late twentieth century.[2] To be sure, two of the other three authors rejected the doctrine, namely, John Walvoord and William Crockett, but the third, Clark Pinnock, expressed sympathy for the doctrine.

Perhaps it is a small indication of how things have changed even further in the intervening years that the current chapter on purgatory is written by a Protestant philosopher. I do not want to overstate things, or to suggest there is a large groundswell of support for purgatory among contemporary evangelicals and other Protestants, but it is fair to say a growing number of Protestant thinkers have recently expressed at least a tentative willingness to reconsider the doctrine.[3]

---

1. P. T. Forsyth, *This Life and the Next* (Boston: The Pilgrim Press, 1948), 37.

2. *Four Views of Hell*, ed. William Crockett (Grand Rapids: Zondervan, 1992).

3. For examples, see Jerry L. Walls, *Purgatory: The Logic of Total Transformation* (New York: Oxford University Press, 2012). See especially chapters 2, 3, and 6.

Of course, Protestant resistance to purgatory is in many ways entirely understandable in light of historical factors that led them to reject the doctrine in the first place. The doctrine of purgatory was at the heart of the controversies that led to the Reformation at that time. Indeed, several of Luther's Ninety-Five Theses dealt with abuses involving purgatory. But here it is important to distinguish between the doctrine of purgatory itself and the abuses that had grown up around it. It was only the abuses that Luther initially protested, and at the time of the Ninety-Five Theses, he still accepted the doctrine, although he later rejected it altogether, as did Calvin. In any case, with this pedigree, it is understandable that many Protestants still reject the doctrine out of hand and find it difficult to think about it objectively.

Still, even apart from Protestant reservations, there is a more fundamental question about the appropriateness of an essay on purgatory in a book entitled *Four Views of Hell*. In particular, is there such a thing as a purgatorial view *of hell*, and if so, what is it? To raise this question is to raise one of the complicated ambiguities in the history of the doctrine, namely, whether purgatory should be understood primarily in relation to heaven, or to hell. Certainly, purgatory has often been understood in terms that are closer to hell than to heaven. That is to say, it has been understood as a place of intense suffering, sometimes meted out by gleeful devils, and is only distinguishable from hell by the fact that it eventually comes to an end and leads finally to heaven. However, it has also been understood primarily in relation to heaven, perhaps classically in Dante. Purgatory so understood is more of ante-room to heaven than a finite variation on hell.

Either way, however, purgatory has been understood traditionally as a temporary abode or stage on the way to heaven. It is only for persons who die in a state of grace and who will eventually make it to heaven.

Answering an Inevitable Question and Expanding Hope

Here it is important to emphasize that the doctrine of purgatory provides an answer to a question that every viable Christian theology must answer, namely, how is it that persons who die in a state of grace, but are less than fully perfect, are made fit for heaven? Scripture makes clear that "nothing unclean" will enter heaven (Rev. 21:27 ESV). Moreover, it charges us to pursue "the holiness without which no one will see the Lord" (Heb. 12:14 ESV). Notice, that this passage is addressed to Christians, and it assumes there is a kind of holiness they have not yet achieved, but must achieve in order to see the Lord.

The doctrine of purgatory provides an account of how this holiness is achieved, and in throwing purgatory "clean out of door," Protestants discarded this solution to a question that must be answered. Of course, Protestants have their own alternative accounts of "purgatory." The most characteristic view is that "purgatory" happens in an instant at the moment of death. In the words of the noted Princeton theologian Charles Hodge, "the Protestant doctrine is that the souls of believers are at death made perfect in holiness."[4]

Before proceeding further, it will be helpful to spell out the essence of the more traditional notion of purgatory a bit more fully, as it will help to focus our discussion below. This account comes from Dorothy L. Sayers, who was a friend of C. S. Lewis and is famous for a translation of Dante, among other things. In her introduction to *Purgatory*, the second part of Dante's *The Divine Comedy*, she stated the essence of the doctrine in six short paragraphs, four of which are of particular interest for our concerns. It is worth emphasizing for our concerns that Sayers was not a Roman Catholic, but rather, like her friend C. S. Lewis, an Anglican. Here are the four points that will be of particular interest for our discussion.

(1) Purgatory is not a place of probation, from which the soul may go either to Heaven or to Hell. All souls admitted to Purgatory are bound for Heaven sooner or later, and are forever beyond the reach of sin.

(2) Purgatory is *not* a 'second chance' for those who die obstinately unrepentant. The soul's own choice between God and self, made in the moment of death, is final. (This moment of final choice is known as the 'Particular Judgment'.)

(3) Repentance in the moment of death (*in articulo mortis*) is *always* accepted. If the movement of the soul is, however feebly, away from self and towards God, its act of contrition is complete, whether or not it is accompanied by formal confession absolution; and the soul enters Purgatory.

---

4. Charles Hodge, *Systematic Theology* (Grand Rapids: Eerdmans, 1966), 3:725.

(4) The Divine acceptance of a repentance *in articulo mortis* does *not* mean that the sinner 'gets away with it' scot-free. What it does mean is that the soul is now obliged, with prolonged labour and pains, and without the assistance of the body, to accomplish in Purgatory the entire process of satisfaction and purification, the greater part of which should have been carried out on earth.[5]

Notice that while purgatory is not a "second chance," it does provide an account of a more expansive view of those who may hope to be finally saved at the end of the day, and this is an important point of connection with the doctrine of hell.

Here it is worth noting a bit of the historical development of purgatory. Historian Isabel Moreira has recently contended that purgatory was given the stamp of approval as an orthodox doctrine by the venerable Bede in the early eighth century. She cites a passage from his *Homilies* from the 720s or early 730s that presents purgatory as a fact, and moreover characterizes it in a way that it includes the essential elements that would be recognized by later medieval theologians. Indeed, Moreira argues that Bede was the first to position purgatory as an orthodox doctrine in response to heresy.

The particular heresy Bede wanted to rebut was Origen's doctrine of universal salvation. The genius of Bede's doctrine of purgatory was that it appropriated the spirit of Origen's theory that made it so appealing. His theology offered the hope of salvation to serious sinners so long as they confessed their sins, took the sacrament, and were willing to do penance (more on this below), even if they delayed repentance to their deathbed. Moreira summarizes it as follows: "Purgatory was, in essence, a highly limited and circumscribed response to the appeal of universal salvation: it was an orthodox variation on universalism."[6]

The relationship here between hell and purgatory is worth emphasizing. In particular, the development of the doctrine of purgatory cuts into the territory of hell. Zachary Hayes put it like this:

---

5. Dorothy L. Sayers, "Introduction" to Dante, *The Divine Comedy II: Purgatory*, trans. Dorothy L. Sayers (London: Penguin, 1955), 59–60.

6. Isabel Moreira, *Heaven's Purge: Purgatory in Late Antiquity* (New York: Oxford University Press, 2010), 165; cf. 154.

As long as there was only heaven or hell, it was not surprising that hell would be heavily populated. But when the possibility of purification after death entered the scene, with it came the tendency to depopulate hell by placing many people in a sort of outer court of heaven until they were more fully prepared for entrance into the presence of God.[7]

Recall the most famous and most despairing line in Dante's inferno, namely the words inscribed over the gate of hell: "Abandon every hope, who enter here."[8] By striking contrast, according to historian Jacques LeGoff, the essential role of purgatory can be summed up in three words: "Purgatory is hope."[9] In short, the doctrine of purgatory modifies the doctrine of hell by providing a theological rationale to hope that more persons can achieve final salvation than Augustine and many of his successors believed. Purgatory is profoundly a doctrine of hope.

But what exactly is this hope? To understand this, we need to look more closely at the purpose of purgatory and how it accounts for how imperfect persons may be made fit for heaven.

Two Reasons for Purgatory: Satisfaction and Sanctification

Notice in Sayers's paragraph number four above that the sinner who repents in the moment of death is obliged "to accomplish in Purgatory the entire process of satisfaction and purification." Those two words "satisfaction" and "purification" summarize the two central reasons for purgatory as it has traditionally been understood. The word "purgatory" itself comes from the word "purge" and pertains to the idea of purging, purifying, or cleansing imperfections or impurities. It can also suggest the idea of purging disease or harmful substances from one's body, so purgatory can also be thought of in terms of healing what is unhealthy or ill.

So whether the image is that of purifying or healing, purgatory in this sense is about a forward-looking process of perfecting that which is imperfect. Understood in these terms, the essential purpose of purgatory

---

7. Zachary Hayes, "The Purgatorial View" in *Four Views of Hell,* 97.

8. Dante, *The Divine Comedy,* trans. Allen Mandelbaum (New York: Alfred A. Knopf, 1995), 68.

9. Jacques LeGoff, *The Birth of Purgatory,* trans. Arthur Goldhammer (Chicago: University of Chicago Press, 1984), 306. LeGoff specifically says this about purgatory in the thirteenth century, but the point clearly applies more generally.

is finishing the work of sanctification. It is about purifying our hearts completely so we fully achieve that holiness without which no man can see the Lord.

When the doctrine of purgatory began to emerge and take shape, the primary emphasis was on sanctification. However, there was also another element present as well, and the Roman Catholic view of purgatory has always included this other dimension along with sanctification. This other element was the idea that purgatory is about satisfaction, which is the idea of undergoing punishment to satisfy the justice of God.[10]

So here is an important point for emphasis. The doctrine of purgatory can be understood in terms of (1) sanctification, (2) satisfaction, or (3) some combination of the two. It is also important to understand that by the time of the Reformation, the emphasis on satisfaction had come to predominate almost entirely over sanctification, and in much later Roman Catholic theology, the emphasis on satisfying the justice of God was the exclusive emphasis. So let's look at the satisfaction view of purgatory a little more carefully, since that is the view most Protestants probably think of when the doctrine is mentioned.

The whole notion of satisfaction is integral to the Roman Catholic doctrine of penance, which has three parts. When sin has been committed, three things are required for the person to be made fully right according to the Roman Catholic view. The first is contrition, which simply means the guilty person must be truly sorry and sincerely repent of what he has done. The second is confession, which is the requirement that the sin must be confessed to a priest.

The third part of penance is what is most crucial to understand, however, for our purposes. In addition to truly being sorry and confessing one's sin, the person must make satisfaction by accepting whatever punishment is imposed by the priest. That is necessary to satisfy the justice of God. Now if a person fails to make satisfaction, he must undergo the appropriate punishment in purgatory until God's justice is satisfied.

---

10. For a recent defense of the Roman Catholic view of purgatory that attempts to show biblical support for the doctrine, see Gary A. Anderson, "Is Purgatory Biblical?" *First Things* (November 2011), 39–44.

Crystalizing the Differences

Now the differences between these two ways of conceiving of the nature and purpose of purgatory are profound indeed.[11] Whereas the sanctification model is about moral and spiritual transformation, the satisfaction model is about exacting punishment to pay a debt of justice. Whereas the sanctification model looks forward to the goal of achieving spiritual perfection and holiness, the satisfaction model looks backward to a "liquidation of the past."

But perhaps the difference between the two models can be seen most clearly in the reason why each believes purgatory requires a measure of time. Whereas the sanctification model believes achieving the goal of holiness is a pursuit that takes time to fully accomplish, the satisfaction model holds that the punishment of purgatory must be exactly as long, and as intense, as necessary to satisfy the demands of justice. Dorothy Sayers draws the contrast like this: "Purgatory is not a system of Divine book-keeping—so many years for so much sin—but a process of spiritual improvement which is completed precisely when it is complete."[12]

While Sayers's account of purgatory focuses primarily on sanctification, she does include a component of satisfaction as well, as noted above. So her view represents a blend of sanctification and satisfaction, with the accent on the former.

Now I reiterate, the satisfaction model of purgatory that had little or no concern for sanctification was in full force at the time of the Reformation and remained so for centuries after that, and it was this account of the doctrine the Reformers rejected so forcefully. Consider, for instance these words of Calvin.

> Therefore, we must cry out with the shout not only of our voices but of our throats and lungs that purgatory is a deadly fiction of Satan, which nullifies the cross of Christ, inflicts unbearable contempt upon God's mercy, and overturns and destroys our faith. For what means this purgatory of theirs but that satisfaction for sins is paid by the souls of the dead after their death?[13]

---

11. For a detailed discussion of these different models of purgatory, see chapter 3 of my *Purgatory: The Logic of Total Transformation*.

12. Dorothy L. Sayers, "Introduction" to Dante, *The Divine Comedy II: Purgatory*, 58.

13. John Calvin, *Institutes of the Christian Religion*, ed. John T. McNeill, trans. Ford Lewis Battles (Philadelphia: Westminster, 1960), 3.5.6.

Notice particularly the last sentence above. For the Reformers, purgatory represented nothing less than a denial that the death of Christ was sufficient to save us from the guilt of our sins and the punishment we deserve. Purgatory means we have to suffer to satisfy the justice of God. And it was this view of purgatory that fueled the indulgence business to such spectacular heights and generated the corruption Luther so passionately protested.

But here is the point I want to emphasize for now. To reject the satisfaction model of purgatory is not necessarily to reject the sanctification model. The sanctification model of purgatory offers a fundamentally different account of why we need purgatory. Indeed, the sanctification model of purgatory is entirely compatible with Protestant theology, and moreover, is an altogether natural fit in some versions of Protestant theology.[14]

But Is It in the Bible?

Before turning to look in detail at a model of purgatory that is fully compatible with Protestant theology, let us consider the question that will be asked by evangelicals and other Protestants, namely, where is the biblical support for the doctrine? The forthright answer to this question, one that is often conceded by Roman Catholics as well, is that there is little explicit biblical support for the doctrine. However, the doctrine of purgatory can rightly be considered biblical in the broader sense that it is a natural implication of things that are clearly taught in Scripture.

For some evangelicals, this will be the end of the discussion, and they will dismiss the doctrine as unworthy of serious consideration if it cannot be directly supported by sound exegesis. Such a response, however, is premature. For the reality is that Scripture does not settle the matter directly one way or the other, and this is true of many issues in eschatology. So unless we are simply going to take an agnostic position on all these issues, some degree of disciplined speculation is inevitable.

Moreover, it is important to recognize that the status of purgatory as a theological inference is similar in this regard to other doctrines that are a matter of broad consensus. Most notably, the doctrine of the Trinity is not directly taught in Scripture, but is an inference from things that are.

---

14. For a detailed discussion of these two models and the differences between them, see chapter 3 of my *Purgatory: The Logic of Total Transformation*.

The Trinity, however, is a central doctrine agreed upon by all orthodox Christians, so perhaps a better parallel here is another doctrine that has much broad support among evangelicals, namely, the doctrine that Satan is a fallen angel.

Now, despite the fact that many traditional interpreters cited biblical support for this claim, most contemporary exegetes do not think the texts cited (particularly Isaiah 14 and Ezekiel 28) refer to the fall of Satan. But the doctrine can still be defended as a reasonable inference from what is clearly taught in Scripture, namely, that beside God himself, everything else that exists was created by God. Furthermore, everything he created was originally good as it came from his hand. Thus, Satan must be a being who was originally good, but has gone bad, so he must have fallen.

Still, without overstating the case, I do think there are a few key texts that suggest purgatory a little more directly. Here is one of them, which was the text most commented upon during the period when the doctrine was being formulated and officially adopted.

> For no one can lay any foundation other than the one already laid, which is Jesus Christ. If anyone builds on this foundation using gold, silver, costly stones, wood, hay or straw, their work will be shown for what it is, because the Day will bring it to light. It will be revealed with fire, and the fire will test the quality of each person's work. If what has been built survives, the builder will receive a reward. If it is burned up, the builder will suffer loss but yet will be saved—even though only as one escaping through the flames. (1 Cor. 3:11–15)

The main thrust of this text pertains to rewards for good works, not to sanctification or its role in our salvation. Paul's main point is about the eternal value of our work, and which of it will survive the fire of judgment when its true quality is revealed. But what is particularly interesting for our purposes here is his description of those whose work is burned up, but are still saved "as one escaping through the flames" (v. 15).

The question is what is involved in being saved this way. I would suggest that this experience of escaping through the flames will be a sanctifying experience for all who undergo it. Recall Jesus' prayer to the Father, when he says "sanctify them by the truth; your word is truth"

(John 17:17). Here is what I am driving at. God's act of judgment in which the true quality of our works will be revealed will no doubt be a powerful and penetrating experience of facing the truth, truth that may be painful. We will see the true character of our choices, our values, what we have cared about, how we have invested our time, money and so on. Insofar as we have built with hay and stubble, we will see how misguided and shortsighted we were. We will see how our choices were motivated by love of self and superficial goals rather than eternal ones. Watching the fire burn would bring the truth home to us, and as we accepted and came to terms with it, our sanctification would go forward.

Now consider in this light Jesus' teaching that judgment is a matter of coming into the light and having our deeds exposed (John 3:19–21). John Polkinghorne comments on the implications of this judgment as follows.

> In the face of reality ('the light'), we reveal by our actions who we really are. If we can accept this revelation, we are enabled to know ourselves and to recognize our needs. The positive side of this image is expressed in the first epistle of John: 'when he is revealed, we will be like him, for we shall see him as he is' (I John 3:2). Once again there is a hint of a salvific process, for we can scarcely suppose that Christ will be taken in at a glance.[15]

Notice again the sanctifying nature of God's judgment as we come to see the reality both about ourselves and about Christ, God's ultimate Word of Truth.[16] Notice particularly Polkinghorne's suggestion that taking in the light of Christ will likely require a process rather than a single glance, and that will take some time.

Purgatory and Mere Christianity

To see this more fully, let us look at a very influential Protestant writer who embraced the doctrine of purgatory, namely, C. S. Lewis, who is as much an evangelical icon as any modern writer.

---

15. John Polkinghorne, *The God of Hope and the End of the World* (New Haven, CT: Yale University Press, 2003), 130–31.

16. My colleague Tim Brookins suggested to me that a similar point is made in 2 Corinthians 5:10, where we have the same metaphor, and perhaps even more clearly with reference to exposure at the final judgment: "It is necessary that all of us be *revealed* [φανερωθῆναι] before the judgment seat of Christ."

Lewis is a particularly interesting case because he is famous for espousing and articulating those core doctrines that are common to Christians of all traditions, whether Eastern Orthodox, Roman Catholic, or Protestant. And what is perhaps particularly noteworthy is that the doctrine of purgatory is integral to Lewis's account of that body of core doctrine that he called "mere Christianity," although his avowed intention in the book of that name was to avoid controversial issues that divided Christians. So the point of using Lewis here is not to appeal to him as some sort of authority, but rather because he provides for us a very interesting model of the doctrine of purgatory that is Protestant friendly.

While Lewis never explicitly affirmed purgatory in his most famous book of Christian apologetics, he did so in a number of other places, and there is no doubt he believed the doctrine. But what can be shown is that purgatory flows naturally from what he argues in that book, particularly from his account of salvation. In what follows, I want to look at three key issues and show how Lewis's stance on these issues leads to the doctrine of purgatory. But first, I want to sketch Lewis's account of salvation because it is essential to understanding why purgatory was a natural doctrine for him to affirm.

Here is a passage that expresses not only the heart of Lewis's view of salvation, but also his summary of the very essence of Christianity.

> Now the whole offer which Christianity makes is this: that we can, if we let God have His way, come to share in the life of Christ.... If we share in this life we shall also be sons of God. We shall love the Father as He does and the Holy Ghost will arise in us.... Every Christian is to become a little Christ. The whole purpose of becoming a Christian is simply nothing else.[17]

What we can see from this passage right away is that the central thrust of Lewis's account of salvation is relational and transformational. Christianity is about sharing in the life of Christ, and this means coming to love the Father as Jesus does. The whole purpose of becoming a Christian is to "become a little Christ." Notice: the point of emphasis here is not on being *forgiven by Christ*, but rather, *becoming like Christ*. Indeed, the emphases that are central in much contemporary Christianity are

---

17. C. S. Lewis, *Mere Christianity* (San Francisco: HarperSanFrancisco, 2001), 177.

not present in Lewis's theology of salvation. For instance, the word "justification" never even appears in *Mere Christianity*, let alone receives the sort of attention it does in much popular theology. Of course, Lewis avoided technical theological language in his book, so not much should be made of the absence of the word. And I certainly do not mean to suggest that Lewis did not affirm justification or that he denied that we are saved by grace through faith alone.

But the point is that he understood these things differently than they are understood in much contemporary Christian thought. There is nothing like "imputed righteousness" in his thought, nor did he believe that when we are justified, all our sins, past, present and future, are "under the blood."

Yet, whereas Lewis does not emphasize justification by faith as it is often understood today, he did place heavy emphasis on repentance as absolutely essential for salvation. What this points up is that Lewis saw our predicament as a much deeper problem than the fact that we have committed sinful acts for which we are guilty and require forgiveness. The deeper problem is our sinful tendencies that lead to those acts in the first place. It is our sinful tendencies, habits, and dispositions that keep us from loving God and each other as we should, and it is these that need to be healed in order for us to be fully restored to a right relationship to God and other persons.

Indeed, he described the theological significance of the incarnation and atonement in precisely those terms. That is to say, he described Christ as the "perfect penitent" whose perfect obedience to God throughout his life, and climaxing in the cross, enables and empowers us to repent and return to God.[18] So faith in the atonement for Lewis was not merely a matter of claiming forgiveness for past sins, but rather, it was an ongoing trust in Christ to transform us and remake us like himself, so we come truly to love and obey the Father from our hearts.

Now, with this sketch in mind, let us turn to consider three issues and how Lewis's stance on these issues naturally leads to the doctrine of purgatory.[19]

---

18. Lewis, *Mere Christianity*, ch. 4.

19. For a detailed account of Lewis's views on this matter, see chapter 6 of my *Purgatory: The Logic of Total Transformation*.

Is Our Free Cooperation Required Throughout the Sanctification Process?

Notice in the passage I quoted above our sharing in the life of Christ hinges on a very important condition: "if we let God have His way." This condition highlights the fact that Lewis's theology is thoroughly Arminian and emphasizes the importance of our free cooperation for our salvation. There is no suggestion that grace is irresistible or sovereignly bestowed on certain persons who are thereby determined to persevere and be saved. No, for Lewis, it is essential that "we let God have His way" if his saving purposes are to be achieved in our lives. While Lewis seldom cites Scripture in *Mere Christianity*, there are numerous New Testament texts that show the importance of our cooperation in our sanctification.[20]

This raises the more fundamental issue of why God created human beings with freedom in the first place. In Lewis's view, freedom is essential because of the good things it makes possible. He was clear, moreover, that genuine freedom for finite persons meant that those who have it could go either right or wrong. The price of such freedom is that it makes evil possible. Why was God willing to pay that price? "Because free will, though it makes evil possible, is also the only thing that makes possible any love or goodness or joy worth having." Lewis goes on to say that the happiness God wishes for us requires us to be freely united with him and with each other "in an ecstasy of love and delight.... And for that they must be free."[21]

It is important to emphasize here that Lewis places such a premium on freedom not because freedom is inherently so valuable, but rather because of the good things it makes possible, and those goods in his view are nothing less than "any love or goodness or joy worth having." And it is also important to recognize that the value of these goods is what makes the evil that results from freedom worth the price.

Now this suggests another crucial point. If the goods that freedom makes possible are worth the price of evil, God takes that freedom very

---

20. See Romans 6:11–14, 19; 8:12–14; 12:1–2; Ephesians 4:22–25; Colossians 3:1–14; 1 Thessalonians 4:3–8; Hebrews 12:1–3, 14; 2 Peter 1:5–11; 1 John 1:6–7; 3:3, 7–10. Several of these texts are also relevant to the second issue I will discuss, that moral and spiritual transformation is an essentially temporal, incremental process.

21. Lewis, *Mere Christianity*, 48.

seriously. And if we have good reason to think God takes our freedom seriously in this life because of the goods it makes possible, there is good reason to think he will continue to do so in the life to come until the goods that freedom makes possible are fully achieved. To put the point another way, if God can give us the goods of love, goodness, and joy unilaterally at the moment of death without our free cooperation, it is hard to see why freedom is necessary in this life to achieve these goods, particularly given all the evil that results from the misuse of freedom.

Now let us look more closely at how Lewis develops this point. First, he emphasizes that it is our choices over our whole life that save us, not a single, one-time choice that settles the matter once and for all. Indeed, it is this series of choices, Lewis says, which transforms the "central part of you, the part of you that chooses, into something a little different than it was before." Lewis goes on to elaborate how this long series of choices, each one of which alters our characters a little more, finally leads us to heaven or to hell.

> And taking your life as a whole, with all your innumerable choices, all your life long you are slowly turning this central thing either into a heavenly creature or a hellish creature; either into one that is in harmony with God, and with other creatures, and with itself, or else into one that is in a state of war and hatred with God, and with its fellow creatures, and with itself.... Each of us at each moment is progressing to the one state or the other.[22]

The fact that it is our life "as a whole" with our "innumerable choices" that "slowly" change us into creatures fit for heaven (or hell) underscores that our sanctification and moral transformation is very much a process. While Lewis strongly emphasized our freedom throughout this whole process of sanctification, it is vital to make clear that it is Christ himself who is doing the actual work of making us holy, albeit with our cooperation.

> You have free will, and if you choose, you can push Me away. But if you do not push Me away, understand that I am going to see this job through. Whatever suffering it may cost you in your earthly life, whatever inconceivable purification it may cost you after death,

---

22. Ibid., 92.

whatever it costs Me, I will never rest, nor let you rest, until you are literally perfect—until my Father can say without reservation that He is well pleased with you, as He said He was well pleased with me. This I can do and will do. But I will not do anything less.[23]

This passage is telling, not only because it stresses that the sanctification process continues throughout our life, but may also involve "inconceivable purification" after death. Again, if our cooperation is required in this process throughout our lives, if we always have the freedom to "push him away," then it only makes sense that our free cooperation will be necessary in whatever "inconceivable purification" we may face after death.

Is Moral and Spiritual Growth and Transformation an Essentially Temporal, Incremental Process?

This issue is closely connected to the first, and is perhaps implicit within it. In any case, it makes explicit the matters of temporality and the related notion of incremental growth and progress. Lewis highlighted these aspects of our sanctification when he noted that achieving moral and spiritual transformation is like a journey, and we must realize that we cannot reach our destination without going through the various stages along the way. "But there are a great many things that cannot be understood until after you have gone a certain distance along the Christian road."[24]

Lewis makes this observation at the beginning of the second of two chapters entitled "Faith" in *Mere Christianity*. In his previous chapter, he explored the first sense of faith, which is essentially a matter of believing the doctrines of Christianity are true and holding to this conviction even through shifting moods and circumstances. But in this second chapter, he explores a higher kind of faith that is necessary for us to achieve final salvation. Here are some of the discoveries on the journey of faith that we must make in order to exercise this higher kind of faith.

First, he says we must come to see the true depths of our sin. While our initial repentance and conversion reveals this to some extent, it is not fully apparent to us how deep our need truly is. And ironically, we

---

23. Ibid., 202.
24. Ibid., 144.

can only really understand this by trying really hard to be good, over an extended period of time. "No man knows how bad he is till he has tried very hard to be good.... Only those who try to resist temptation know how strong it is."[25]

By definition, this discovery is temporal in nature, for we cannot really understand how bad we are, Lewis insists, without a prolonged effort to be good, and repeatedly failing on our own. It takes time and experience walking the road of faith to see how deeply and thoroughly we need to be transformed and healed. The irony here is that one measure of progress down the road of faith is precisely that it enables us to see that our problem is even worse than we realized. "When a man is getting better he understands more and more clearly the evil that is left in him."[26]

Next Lewis says we must make another discovery. "Every faculty you have, your power of thinking or of moving your limbs from moment to moment, is given you by God."[27] The notion that we are utterly dependent on the goodness and power of God is not one we instinctively feel and believe. Rather, in our misguided sense of autonomy, we imagine that we have abilities and control that we do not. Even as we go our own way and dishonor God, we do so with power and faculties he supplies. This is not an easy thing truly to internalize.

Lewis made a similar point elsewhere when he described how grace enables us joyfully to acknowledge just how needy we are and to embrace the reality of what he calls our "need love" of God. Although we are utterly dependent upon God, his love for us is not in any way motivated by a need for us. Arriving at this insight, however, is not easy.

> Thus, depth beneath depth and subtlety within subtlety, there remains some lingering idea of our own, our very own, attractiveness. It is easy to acknowledge, but almost impossible to realize for long, that we are mirrors whose brightness, if we are bright, is wholly derived from the sun that shines upon us. Surely we must have a little—however little—native luminosity? Surely we can't be *quite* creatures?[28]

---

25. Ibid., 142.
26. Ibid., 93.
27. Ibid., 143.
28. C. S. Lewis, *The Four Loves* (New York: Harcourt Brace Jovanovich, 1960), 130–131.

Particularly interesting here is Lewis's phrase "depth beneath depth and subtlety within subtlety." What this phrase captures is the complicated, tangled nature of our sin and self-deception, and that it is no simple matter to get to the bottom of it. As the truth penetrates one layer of our evil, it may bring into focus another layer or another subtlety that we had no idea was even there. Only by working through these layers successively and allowing the truth to illumine and untie these various tangled knots can we embrace the grace that fully transforms.

These are the sorts of things we can only understand by pursuing the journey of faith and doing so for a considerable time. And Lewis emphasizes that the kind of understanding he is talking about is far more than a matter of having the right concepts or knowing the right words to say. "When I say 'discovered', I mean really discovered: not simply said it parrot-fashion."[29]

And again, discovering these things by experience and internalizing them is far more difficult than reading about them in a book and mentally assenting to them. It takes far more time and personal engagement. Only when we have made these discoveries can we exercise the higher kind of faith in which we can trust Christ to share with us his perfect obedience, and "make us, like Himself, Sons of God."[30] It is when we exercise this higher faith that he can make real progress in his ultimate project to make each of us a "little Christ."

Is Pain Integral to Moral and Spiritual Transformation?

Recall Dorothy Sayers's fourth point in her summary of the doctrine of purgatory cited above (p. 148). There she made the point that although God in his mercy will accept repentance right up to the very end of our lives, this does not mean that the procrastinating penitent "'gets away with it' scot-free." To the contrary, "the soul is now obliged, with prolonged labour and pains ... to accomplish in Purgatory the entire process of satisfaction and purification."

As we have noted, the "satisfaction" model of purgatory was in full force at the time of the Reformation, and it was that version of the doctrine the Reformers rejected so vehemently. Protestant theology

---

29. Lewis, *Mere Christianity*, 145.
30. Ibid., 128.

recoils from the suggestion that the death of Christ was not sufficient to provide satisfaction and that we must suffer in order to satisfy the justice of God. I have been exploring an account of purgatory that I contend is fully compatible with Protestant theology, an account that focuses entirely on sanctification and purification. But what about this notion of suffering and pain as part of purgatory? Is it essential to the doctrine, and if so, does not this introduce an element of satisfaction that will be at odds with Protestant theology?[31]

So here is the question: Can we recognize pain as integral to purgatory even if we understand purgatory entirely in terms of sanctification and purification? I think the answer is yes, and again, Lewis points the way.[32]

Recall the passage cited above where Lewis says that whatever suffering it may cost us in this life, whatever "inconceivable purification" it may cost us after death, whatever it costs Christ, he will never rest, nor let us rest until we are absolutely perfect. Lewis goes on later in that chapter to remark: "The job will not be completed in this life; but he means to get us as far as possible before death." Again, note the allusion to postmortem purification. But the next sentence is also telling: "That is why we must not be surprised if we are in for a rough time."[33]

The reason we are in for a rough time is that God's plan to transform us is far more radical than we have any idea. He is determined to change us in ways we cannot conceive and take us way out of our current comfort zone. And that, Lewis contends, will be a painful experience for us.

Lewis elaborates on this by recalling a parable from George MacDonald in which you are invited to imagine yourself as a living house, which God enters for the purpose of rebuilding it. Initially we understand what he is up to and concur with his plans as he patches holes in the roof, repairs the plumbing, and the like. "But presently he starts knocking the house about in a way that hurts abominably and does not seem to make sense." You completely fail to understand how thoroughly the house must be renovated because you do not grasp the

---

31. For Sayers's account of pain in purgatory, which includes some element of satisfaction, see "Introduction" to Dante, *The Divine Comedy II: Purgatory*, 57.

32. In addition to the texts I discussed in an earlier section, namely 1 Corinthians 3 and 1 John 3, other texts that suggest the way of sanctification and transformation involve pain are 1 Corinthians 5:4–5; 2 Corinthians 2:5–8; 7:8–12; Colossians 3:5; Hebrews 12:4–11.

33. Lewis, *Mere Christianity*, 204.

scale of his project. "You thought you were going to be made into a decent little cottage: but he is building a palace. He intends to come and live in it himself."[34]

Now the point I want to emphasize here is that the pain that Lewis says we should expect does not in any way appear to be necessary in order to satisfy the justice of God or offer him any sort of satisfaction. Rather, the pain is due essentially to the radical transformation we must undergo in order to become the sort of persons who could truly welcome a God of perfect holiness to take up permanent residence in every part of our lives.

How this relates to purgatory is demonstrated most vividly in *The Great Divorce*, where Lewis depicts a number of persons from the "grey town" who take a bus ride to heaven and are invited to stay as long as they want. In one of the most fascinating passages in the book, the narrator asks George MacDonald, whom he has encountered in heaven, whether the visitors from the grey town can really stay, whether there is actually a way out of hell into heaven. MacDonald's answer makes a fascinating point about the identity of the grey town: "It depends on the way ye'er using the words. If they leave that grey town behind it will not have been Hell. To any that leaves it, it is Purgatory."[35]

The grey town is a place of shadowy illusions, and its inhabitants are likewise insubstantial figures, mere ghosts. What Lewis skillfully depicts in his narrative is how these ghosts who arrive at the outskirts of heaven find it to be not only unpleasant, but profoundly painful to them. The superficial assumption we often make is that anyone in hell would enthusiastically jump at the chance to leave it behind and go to heaven. What Lewis shows is that heaven is not appealing to those who are not fitted for it.

One of the most revealing lines in the book is a concise definition of heaven in response to the suggestion that heaven and hell are merely states of mind. MacDonald "sternly" replies that while hell may be a state of mind, it is blasphemy to say that about heaven. "Heaven is reality itself. All that is fully real is Heavenly."[36]

Now consider this passage in light of an earlier one in which one of the shadowy figures from the grey town is being entreated to stay in

---

34. Ibid., 205.
35. C. S. Lewis, *The Great Divorce* (San Francisco: HarperSanFrancisco, 2001), 68.
36. Ibid., 70.

heaven and to advance to the mountains, despite his discomfort there. His guide issues the invitation as follows: "It will hurt at first, until your feet are hardened. Reality is harsh to the feet of shadows. But will you come?"[37] Notice: heaven is reality, and reality is painful to shadows until they become accustomed to it. But the promise is that if they endure the pain, their feet will harden, and they will come to love being in heaven.

Let us return now to the passage where MacDonald insists, "Heaven is reality itself." A few paragraphs later we come to one of the most quoted passages in the whole book. This passage is MacDonald's answer when the narrator asks what it is they choose who refuse to stay in heaven and return to the grey town.

> 'Milton was right,' said my Teacher. 'The choice of every lost soul can be expressed in the words "Better to reign in Hell than serve in Heaven." There is always something they insist on keeping even at the price of misery. There is always something they prefer to joy—that is to reality.'[38]

Notice the equation: heaven is reality; reality is joy. And this passage tells us something important about both hell and purgatory. Those who choose to remain in hell are persons who prefer something to joy and refuse to come to terms with reality, whereas those who choose to undergo purgatory are those who are willing to come to terms with reality in order to achieve joy.

But to understand this more fully, we need to see the deepest reason why heaven is reality and reality is joy. Let us recall the passage quoted above in which Lewis tells us "we can, if we let God have his way, come to share in the life of Christ. ... Every Christian is to become a little Christ." Earlier in this chapter, Lewis points out how the fact that God is a Trinity explains that he is love in his very nature because the Persons of the Trinity have loved and delighted in each other from all eternity, before there were any creatures who were objects of that love. Lewis goes on to comment on what is distinctive about the Christian view of God. There, he observes, "God is not a static thing—not even

---

37. Ibid., 39.
38. Ibid., 71.

a person—but a dynamic pulsating activity, a life, almost a kind of drama. Almost, if you will not think me irreverent, a kind of dance."[39]

This is the context for understanding God's purpose to make each of us into a "little Christ." And this is the context for understanding the pain that he may require us to undergo. Here is what I am driving at. The pain of moral and spiritual transformation, including the pains of purgatory, take on an altogether different hue if that pain has nothing to do with satisfying the justice of God, but is rather simply an integral component of becoming acclimated to joy.

In other words, our self-centered attitudes badly skew our perspective on reality and put us out of joint with it. Our disordered loves close our hearts to Love himself. Our sinful dispositions keep us out of step with the Trinitarian dance of joy. So long as we remain in this condition, we cannot know either true love or joy. So long as we resist coming to terms with reality, so long shall we disqualify ourselves from joining the Trinitarian dance.

The pain that we may have to face is the pain of following the "perfect penitent" as he leads us in the way of radical repentance on the way back to the Father. And if we do not "push him away" he will take us all the way there, and when we arrive, we shall be like him, and our joy will be complete.

But Isn't This Still Salvation by Works?

The three issues we have been discussing are at the heart of the doctrine of purgatory, and anyone inclined to return a positive answer to them, as Lewis did, will be inclined to accept the doctrine. I fully acknowledge that the case for a positive answer to these questions is far from decisive, though I do think there are good reasons, along the lines Lewis suggested, for a positive answer to each of them. I think, moreover, that the account of purgatory that is implied is fully compatible with Protestant theology. It is essentially in agreement with the account sketched by Sayers, cited above, with the revised account of why pain may be integral to moral and spiritual transformation.

Recall Sayers's point that the doctrine of purgatory, while providing a more expansive hope of who may be saved, does not allow sinners to

---

39. Lewis, *Mere Christianity*, 175.

"'get away with it' scot-free" and simply bypass the whole process of purification and satisfaction. Now I have defended purgatory solely in terms of purification and sanctification, with no element of satisfaction, but the basic point that sinners "do not get away with it" remains intact.

Here is what I mean. The doctrine of purgatory underscores in emphatic terms not only that sanctification is essential to our final salvation, but so is our cooperation throughout the process. So this point applies not only to deathbed penitents, but to all of us. We should be under no illusion that our entrance to heaven is fully assured by justification or having the righteousness of Christ imputed to us. Sanctification is not an optional matter to be chosen only by the super spiritual, but rather, it is simply a necessary condition for all of us who want to experience joy in the presence of a holy God.

Moreover, our sanctification requires our cooperation and does not go forward unless we seriously pursue that "holiness without which no one will see the Lord" (Heb. 12:14 ESV).

On this point, it is significant that the Reformed tradition largely agrees. One issue of *Credo* magazine that was devoted to purgatory roundly rejected the doctrine. One of the authors, Chris Castaldo, made it clear that to reject purgatory was not to reject the importance of sanctification or of the need for our cooperation. "Sanctification is a gift for which God is ultimately responsible, but this does not preclude human cooperation. It is precisely because God is at work in us, both to will and to work his good pleasure, that we continue to work out our salvation with fear and trembling (Phil. 2:12–13)."[40]

It is noteworthy that one of the few passages of Scripture Lewis quotes in *Mere Christianity* is this passage from Philippians, and he does so in his second of two chapters called "Faith," from which I have been quoting. Lewis cites this Scripture text in the context of noting that Christians have often disputed whether it is good actions or faith in Christ that leads them to heaven. Lewis says this is like asking which blade in a pair of scissors is most necessary. As we exercise true faith in cooperation with God's grace, it will certainly issue in good actions, in his view.

---

40. Chris Castaldo, "Purgatory's Logic, History and Meaning," *Credo* 3 (January 2013): 41; cf. 49.

Still, when purgatory comes into the picture, the charge of works righteousness is often leveled by Protestant critics of the doctrine. The question is why this is so if it is truly recognized that our cooperation is required for our sanctification.

The answer, I suspect, involves a couple of factors. First, Protestants often instinctively, and understandably, still react to purgatory in terms of satisfaction and fail to understand it in terms of sanctification, even when it is defended in those terms. Second, and perhaps more fundamentally, many Protestants think of grace primarily, if not exclusively, in terms of justification.

Consider a recent editorial by *Christianity Today* editor Mark Galli, entitled "Whatever Happened to Grace?" in which he tells three stories of his recent experiences in which he saw the message of grace distorted into a message about works. It is, he notes, "understandable why we're tempted to shift the message of grace to a form of works. The radical grace outlined in Romans and Galatians seems too good to be true." And while Galli's editorial is in many ways a salutary warning and a call to be true to the heart of the gospel, it also gives a rather one-dimensional view of grace. Consider the conclusion of his editorial, where he describes the message of grace that he believes has been lost in too many churches. "There was once miraculous talk of the impossible possibility that a way had been made to return to Eden. And the angel standing at the entrance did not demand intellectual or emotional or moral visas to get in. The only passport required was one with a full list of all our sins, each stamped over, blotted out really, with the red ink of grace."[41]

Notice that all that is required to enter heaven is to have our sins blotted out with the red ink of grace. There is no sense here at all, as Lewis emphasized so strongly, that heaven simply would not be heaven to a person who was not appropriately transformed to enjoy it. To truly find pleasure in the presence of a holy God requires that we love him with all our heart, soul, mind and strength, and that we love our neighbors as ourselves. And that requires that our intellects be ordered to truth; that our emotions respond rightly to reality, and that our moral dispositions are rightly ordered, the very things that Galli suggests are legalistic "visas" that are not necessary for final salvation.

---

41. Mark Galli, "Whatever Happened to Grace?" *ChristianityToday.com* (October 2013), 24.

Worse, not only do Galli's comments suggest that thorough transformation is not necessary to enter and enjoy heaven, but they also imply a one-dimensional view of grace, as noted above. There is no suggestion here at all that sanctification is as much a work of grace as justification is, and indeed that sanctification is the very grace that deals with a problem that goes deeper than our guilt and acts of sin. Again, grace seems to be reduced essentially to justification and forgiveness, and sanctification is trivialized as some sort of legalistic "visa."

Now, consider these lines from William Crockett's critique of purgatory in the 1992 *Four Views of Hell* volume. In particular, Crockett is responding to Zachary Hayes's argument that purgatory is needed because many believers are far from perfect when they die and are accordingly not ready to meet God.

> The point is that in solidarity with Christ, believers *already* have forgiveness of sins (Rom. 8:31–39; Col. 1:14). As Paul said: 'If righteousness could be gained through the law [through our good deeds], Christ died for nothing' (Gal. 2:21). To suggest, as Hayes does, that most believers are not ready for heaven, smacks of the kind of works theology Paul so strongly opposed.[42]

Now what is telling here is that Hayes defended an account of purgatory that emphasizes sanctification, but Crockett responded in terms of forgiveness and justification (i.e., the *satisfaction* model). To appeal to the fact that we are forgiven, that our sins are under the blood, that there is no condemnation to those who are in Christ, simply misses the point. Having our sins forgiven, even being in solidarity with Christ, does not automatically transform our character and make us fully perfect in such a way that we are "little Christs." That requires a different sort of operation than justification.

In short then, the doctrine of purgatory will be plausible insofar as we take sanctification seriously and believe that our cooperation is essential to achieving it. It will be a theologically viable option for Protestants to the degree that they have a holistic view of salvation by faith that emphasizes that sanctification is a work of grace just as much as justification is. On the other hand, insofar as sanctification is

---

42. William V. Crockett, "Response to Zachary J. Hayes" in *Four Views of Hell*, 125.

trivialized, or the necessity of our cooperation in our sanctification is construed as "works theology," the doctrine of purgatory will be viewed as a dubious one that is at odds with biblical faith.

Expanding Purgatory Hope Even Further?

Before concluding, I want briefly to suggest another revision in the traditional doctrine of purgatory that I think is fully in accord with the rationale that motivates the doctrine. Recall the quote from P. T. Forsyth with which I began this essay in which he claims that Protestants threw out too much when they rejected the doctrine of purgatory. Forsyth made that comment in the aftermath of World War I when he was dealing with families who had lost loved ones in that terrible conflict. The piety and faith of many of these men was uncertain, and many of their families struggled with fears that they might be eternally lost. In a pastoral role, Forsyth appealed to the doctrine of purgatory to provide hope to grieving families. Here is the larger context of that quote.

> It [a heroic death] does not save. Yet it may be the moment of his conversion. It may open his moral eyes. It may begin his godly sorrow. It may be the first step in a new life, the beginning of repentance in a new life which advances faster there than here. We threw away too much when we threw purgatory clean out of doors. We threw out the baby with the dirty water of its bath. There are more conversions on the other side than on this, if the crisis of death opens the eyes as I have said.... If a man does not at once receive the prodigal's robe, at least he has entrée to the father's domain.[43]

Now there is an ambiguity in this passage with respect to when Forsyth thinks conversion may take place for these heroic soldiers who died in the war. On the one hand he suggests the moment of death may be the moment of conversion. On the other hand, he suggests it may be the beginning of conversion, and that conversion proper may take place "on the other side."

It is this last suggestion I find particularly interesting. Recall that on the traditional view of purgatory, it is not a second chance to repent.

---

43. Forsyth, *This Life and the Next*, 37.

Any who do not repent in this life, even as late as the moment of death, are forever lost.

But here is the question I want to press for the traditional view. Why is repentance at the very last moment of death always accepted, but repentance a moment after death too late? Indeed, what is objectionable about the idea of a "second chance," especially since many people have countless chances in this life? By contrast, many other people have few if any chances to hear the gospel and respond to it. Now if God truly loves all persons and desires the salvation of all, would he not make certain that all persons have ample opportunity to receive his grace, even if that entails chances to receive the gospel after death?

It is most interesting in this connection that some Protestant theologians who have recently expressed sympathy for the doctrine of purgatory have done so in the same vein as Forsyth's suggestion. That is, they have appealed to the notion of purgatory to make theological sense of the idea of postmortem repentance. A notable example is Donald Bloesch, who suggests that Scripture gives us reason to believe postmortem repentance is possible.

> The unbridgeable gap spoken of in Luke 16:26 is between hades and paradise, and it is a gap only in the sense that unrepentant sin constitutes a formidable barrier to salvation. The gates of the holy city are depicted as being open day and night (Is 60:11; Rev 21:25), which means that access to the throne of grace is a continuing possibility.... Even when we find ourselves prisoners in the inner darkness that we have created, Jesus has the keys to this hell and can reach out to us by his grace (Rev 1:18). Even when one is in hell, one can be forgiven.[44]

Again, this is a significant modification of the doctrine of purgatory as traditionally understood. However, it is one that I believe is completely consistent with the whole thrust of the traditional doctrine, which was to expand our hope of who might be finally saved, while insisting that final salvation requires thorough transformation.

---

44. Donald Bloesch, *The Last Things* (Grand Rapids: Eerdmans, 1992), 190–191. Bloesch cites a number of other texts that he thinks support the idea of postmortem conversion including: Psalm 49:15; Isaiah 26:19; Matthew 12:31–32; 27:51–54; John 5:29; 1 Corinthians 15:29; 1 Peter 3:19–20; 4:6.

Indeed, one objection to postmortem repentance is an objection that can also be leveled at deathbed repentance, namely that it trivializes our choices in this life and lets sinners off the hook too easily. But if grace can be extended to deathbed penitents, it is hard to see a good reason why it should not be extended to postmortem penitents on the same terms.

The fundamental question here, as always in theological disputes, is how we understand God. Do we really believe God truly and deeply loves all persons and desires the salvation of all? If so, what does this imply for this issue?

I have argued elsewhere in defending the doctrine of eternal hell that what damns a person is a decisive choice of evil. Such a choice of evil depends on what I have called "optimal grace." It is precisely the rejection of optimal grace that constitutes the decisive choice of evil that leads to eternal damnation. So let us consider optimal grace for a moment.

The notion of optimal grace, roughly speaking, is the measure of grace that is best suited to elicit a positive-free response to God and his offer of love and salvation. Such grace will not causally determine a positive response or be "irresistible," but it will be an offer of grace such that the person receiving it is presented with an accurate account of the gospel that is also true to its beauty and goodness. Such grace, however, will also vary in certain respects from person to person because we are individuals, and what might best elicit a positive response from Mackenzie might not do the same for Madelyn. But the main point is that optimal grace means God will do everything he can, short of overriding our freedom to communicate the gospel to us and elicit a positive response from each of us.

Optimal grace is thus very much at odds with what we might call "minimal grace," which is the notion that God takes care only to give all persons at least some chance to be saved, so that he will be just in damning all who are not. Optimal grace is not motivated merely by a concern to maintain God's justice in damning the lost, but rather is a reflection of his heart of genuine love for all his fallen children and his willingness to save all of them. Those who are lost are only lost because of their own free choice to persist in rejecting God's lavish grace bestowed upon them.[45]

---

45. For more on optimal grace, see Jerry L. Walls, *Hell: The Logic of Damnation* (Notre Dame: The University of Notre Dame Press, 1992), 88–91, 93–104, 131.

Now here is the connection between the idea of optimal grace and postmortem repentance. It seems unlikely that all persons have the best opportunity to receive salvation in this life, so if God is going to supply such grace, it will have to happen in the life to come for many people. If we believe God truly and deeply loves all persons, we have a good reason to modify the traditional doctrine of purgatory to include postmortem repentance.[46]

Conclusion: Purgatory As Grace

One of the most poignant and memorable scenes in *The Great Divorce* vividly illustrates many of the central points of this essay. The scene involves a man from the grey town whose wife is in heaven, and she is the one who greets him and tries to persuade him to stay. The man was a highly manipulative person who pouted and sulked as a child in order to get his way, and he carried this tendency into his marriage, where he often used "love" to control his wife. While she was hardly perfect, she was nevertheless a deeply loving person, who generously gave of herself to many people throughout her life, and now she has been perfected in heaven, and is gloriously radiant and beautiful.

When the husband meets her, he resorts to old habits, trying to play on her pity, assuming she cannot be happy as long as he is in hell. She explains that she is now in perfect love and can no longer be manipulated by such ploys and he cannot hurt her by sulking in hell. She then urges him to let go of the attitudes that are keeping him in hell, and to embrace true love and all the joys that go with it.

The narrator goes on to describe how the brightness of her beauty and the sincerity of her love touched his heart, at least to some degree.

> And really, for a moment, I thought the Dwarf [her husband] was going to obey: partly because the outlines of his face became a little clearer, and partly because the invitation to all joy, singing out of her whole being like a bird's song on an April evening, seemed to me such that no creature could resist it.[47]

---

46. For a further defense of these claims see Jerry L. Walls, *Heaven: The Logic of Eternal Joy* (New York: Oxford University Press, 2002), 63–91; *Purgatory: The Logic of Total Transformation*, 123–52; *Heaven, Hell, and Purgatory: Rethinking the Things That Matter Most* (Grand Rapids: Brazos, 2015), 187–211.

47. Lewis, *The Great Divorce*, 123–24.

And yet, he does resist, clinging to the illusion that by returning to hell, he can inflict emotional pain on her. The narrator later comments: "I do not know that I ever saw anything more terrible than the struggle of that Dwarf Ghost against joy."[48]

Notice, this ghost was given optimal grace. He was presented with a beautifully gracious invitation to love and happiness, one that moved him to feel the attraction of it. But to accept it, he had to come to terms with reality. He had to acknowledge the truth about himself, painful though it was, in order to open his heart to true joy. He had to be willing to walk on the grass, harsh though it was, until he became more solid and could positively relish its pleasures.

To fully appreciate and assess purgatory, we must understand it as a work of grace that finishes our sanctification in order to make us fit to enjoy the glories of heaven. To invoke Lewis's delightful imagery of the Trinity once more, it is like training our muscles so that our clumsy missteps keep perfect time with the music. It is like internalizing the Trinitarian dance steps so fully that we can take our place in the dance with joyful abandon.

The problem with the popular view of grace is not that it is too good to be true. The problem is that it is not true to Reality and what is required to come to terms with it. And for that reason it is not true to Heaven.

---

48. Ibid., 129.

DENNY BURK

The author begins his essay by expressing hope that evangelicals might reconsider their rejection of the doctrine of purgatory. Even though Clark Pinnock may have expressed some sympathy for the doctrine in the 1992 edition of *Four Views of Hell*, Pinnock has not proven to be a reliable bellwether of evangelical belief. In fact, there is little evidence that evangelicals have moved much on this question. Yes, Walls's revision removes some of the more problematic elements of the Roman Catholic version of purgatory, but several serious flaws still remain. For this reason, Walls's Protestant reconstruction of purgatory is unlikely to move the needle in favor of purgatory among evangelicals. Here is why.

1. Walls's argument has very little engagement with Scripture.

Evangelicals are a people of the book. We are a tradition still animated by the Reformation slogan *sola scriptura*. When the Bible speaks, God speaks. This means that the final authority for faith and practice is the Bible. Our consciences are to be bound by that revelation as the very word of God. In this way, the Bible defines reality for us. It tells us everything we need for life and godliness, and it equips us for every good work (2 Tim. 3:16–17; 2 Pet. 1:3). If a doctrine has no basis in the clear teaching of Scripture — or at the very least a clear implication of Scripture — then it can have no binding authority over the conscience. It can only be accorded the status of speculation. It cannot be accorded the status of divine truth.

The Bible's message has very little role in Wells's argument for purgatory. In the main text of his essay (excluding footnotes and quotations), I counted about eight passing references to Scripture. None of those eight references to Scripture are accompanied by serious exposition of the text in question. The majority of the essay is taken up with a history of the doctrine of purgatory and a special emphasis on C. S. Lewis's contribution to the concept. Walls explains why he believes the doctrine of purgatory need not contradict the central insights of the Reformation, but he gives the reader no reason to believe that the doctrine emerges from Scripture. This lack of attention to Scripture is unlikely to persuade evangelicals who still take *sola scriptura* seriously.

2. Walls misinterprets a "key" text that he believes teaches purgatory.

Walls's most extensive interaction with Scripture is a couple of paragraphs commenting on 1 Corinthians 3:11–15. Walls argues that this is one of "a few key texts that suggest purgatory a little more directly." After quoting these five verses, he concludes that "the main thrust of this text pertains to rewards for good works.... Paul's main point is about the eternal value of our work, and which of it will survive the fire of judgment when its true quality is revealed." For Walls, this text teaches that "escaping through flames" indicates a process of sanctification that unfolds in the life of some believers after death. Paul's imagery in this text, therefore, is very amenable to the model of purgatory that he is arguing for.

The main problem with this section of the essay is that Walls has completely misunderstood the meaning of this passage. The passage is not about the flames of purgatorial judgment that believers face after death. It is about the integrity of gospel preaching and the fruit that flows from it. In this text Paul is using building imagery to describe the "building" of Christ's church. As an apostle, Paul is the "wise master builder" who "laid a foundation" when he originally preached Christ in Corinth (v. 10 NASB). Other preachers have come along behind Paul and are "building" on the foundation that he laid. In other words, these other preachers have continued to build the community through the preaching of Christ.

Paul says that his original foundation cannot be added to: "For no man can lay a foundation other than the one which is laid, which is Jesus Christ" (v. 11 NASB). This means that if other teachers try to build the church through human wisdom or persuasive rhetoric, they are building with materials that do not match Paul's foundation and their work will be burned up in the judgment—even though the teacher himself may escape judgment, "yet so as through fire" (v. 15 NASB). As Richard Hays observes in his comments on this text, "Paul is not talking about the fate of individual souls at the final judgment, but about God's scrutiny of the building work of different preachers and leaders."[49] Hays makes clear the implications for the doctrine of purgatory:

> [Paul] is applying the image of judgment by fire not to the fate of individuals but to the ecclesiological construction work done by different church leaders ... there is not "the remotest reference to the state of the soul between death and judgment." Nor is there any reflection here on the purifying effect of fire. Paul is talking not about purgatory for individual souls but about the final divine testing of the solidity of the church as constructed by various apostolic laborers.[50]

In short, the idea that this text has anything to do with the individual disposition of souls after death is mistaken. Nothing like purgatory is in view here. Rather, it is a statement about the integrity of gospel ministry in the wake of Paul's mission to Corinth. Thus the central text brought forth by Walls to support purgatory is no support at all. Far from it.

3. Walls cannot recover purgatory by removing "satisfaction."

Walls argues that the traditional Roman Catholic doctrine of purgatory has two parts: *satisfaction* and *sanctification*. Satisfaction refers to the punitive aspect of purgatory. Sanctification refers to the restorative aspect of purgatory. Walls contends that purgatory offends Protestant sensibilities because of *satisfaction*, not because of *sanctification*. He agrees that we should not regard purgatory as a place where people go in order to pay for their own sins (satisfaction). Walls simply contends that a postmortem work of sanctification in a place like purgatory can be reconciled with biblical doctrine. He writes, "To reject the satisfaction model of purgatory is not necessarily to reject the sanctification model.... The sanctification model of purgatory is entirely compatible with Protestant theology, and moreover, is an altogether natural fit in some versions of Protestant theology."

Walls does indeed remove some of the more serious errors involved with the traditional doctrine of purgatory. His version does not make purgatory into a place where people pay the penalty for their own sins.

---

49. Richard B. Hays, *First Corinthians*, Interpretation (Louisville, KY: John Knox, 1997), 56.
50. Ibid., 55.

In other words, Walls's purgatory is not punitive. Having said that, Walls's case for purgatory still falters. It is not merely the idea of "satisfaction" that is unbiblical. The doctrine of progressive sanctification after death is deeply unbiblical too. Walls argues that sanctification in purgatory "will likely require a process rather than a single glance, and that will take some time." But the Scripture presents glorification, not as a process, but as an event that happens "in the twinkling of an eye" (1 Cor. 15:52). The Bible says that when we see Jesus in the age to come, we will be made like him for we shall see him as he is (1 John 3:2).

There is no hint in any of these texts of a long postmortem process. Rather, the texts indicate an instantaneous transformation at the time of resurrection. Again, Walls's purgatory has no explicit support in Scripture.

4. Walls's version of purgatory is tailor-made for Arminians and will have little appeal to Reformed Christians.

Walls explains that the sinner's free cooperation is required throughout the sanctification of process, and he defines this "free cooperation" on Arminian terms. Any "love or goodness or joy worth having" must emerge from free choices. He writes that "the doctrine of purgatory will be plausible insofar as we take sanctification seriously and believe that our cooperation is essential to achieving it."

On these terms, then, Walls's version of purgatory relies on a libertarian view of free will. If God acts to sanctify the sinner apart from the sinner's free will, there can be no love. Our love for God and God's love for us would be diminished if God were to act unilaterally to transform the body of our sinful state into conformity with the body of his glory. Never mind that Philippians 3:21 says that God will do precisely that. Walls rejects this possibility out of hand because it does not comport with libertarian free will. This is not the place to debate the merits of libertarian free will, but it is the place to say that anyone with a Reformed understanding of the will shall find this piece of Walls's argument to be singularly unpersuasive.

5. Walls opens the possibility of postmortem opportunities for salvation.

Although not an emphasis of his essay, Walls does in fact open the door to postmortem opportunities for repentance and faith. He writes,

Why is repentance at the very last moment of death always accepted, but repentance a moment after death too late?... If God truly loves all persons and desires the salvation of all, would he not make certain that all persons have ample opportunity to receive his grace, even if that entails chances to receive the gospel after death?

Again, Walls offers no biblical warrant for this argument. He simply argues from the premise that God's love for all persons implies postmortem chances for conversion. Yet, as observed in my response to the universalist essay, this premise runs contrary to clear statements of Scripture that teach of the finality and irreversibility of divine judgment (e.g., see discussion of Heb. 9:27 above).

At the end of the day, the doctrine of purgatory seems to have more grounding in human speculation than in divine revelation. To put the matter in Walls's own words: "There is little explicit biblical support for the doctrine [of purgatory].... Some degree of disciplined speculation is inevitable." No dispute there. The doctrine of purgatory does not appear in Scripture, nor is it a necessary implication of what is taught in Scripture.

A TERMINAL PUNISHMENT RESPONSE

JOHN G. STACKHOUSE JR.

While I recognize that there are good reasons to include a discussion of purgatory in a discussion of heaven, I remain unconvinced that such a discussion belongs in a discussion of hell. Properly understood—and Jerry Walls has helped us understand it properly—purgatory is only and ever an "anteroom to heaven," and neither an "anteroom to hell" nor an alternative description of hell.

C. S. Lewis's oft-quoted *The Great Divorce* has many virtues, but not all readers have understood its symbolism. So let's be clear, as I am sure Lewis intended we should be, that hell is not merely a kind of drab, shadowy sheol or hades, a place of almost metaphysical ambiguity—not according to the increasingly frightening depictions of the New Testament that culminate in the book of Revelation. Whatever intermediate experiences lie between our deaths and our final destiny, hell itself is one thing only: The furnace of God's righteousness burning against, and burning up, all that is evil, such that the new cosmos of the age to come is only and ever purely good.

As Walls rightly avers, then, "the doctrine of purgatory provides an answer to a question that every viable Christian theology must answer, namely, how is it that persons who die in a state of grace, but are less than fully perfect, are made fit for heaven?" I should like not so much to critique Walls's exposition as to clarify what a Protestant—indeed, an evangelical—understanding of purgatory might be.

Believing that Christ's suffering and death made entire satisfaction for the eternal consequences of sin, Protestants are repelled by the notion that any further atonement of any sort is needed for those justified before God through faith. Walls is quite right to separate purgatory-as-satisfaction from purgatory-as-sanctification.

But what happens to Christians after being justified? For both Protestants and Catholics, the next stage is one of *sanctification*, the process by which we shed our remaining inclinations to sin and acquire a Christlike goodness that hungers and thirsts after righteousness. No one can enter into the presence of God without "clean hands and a pure heart" (Ps. 24:4). So between the time of our initial conversion and justification and the time of our final entrance into the life to come (glorification) occurs the process of sanctification. Indeed, the Reformers themselves never confused the state of being reckoned (officially) righteous with the process of being made (actually) righteous.

Here, therefore, Protestants have a problem: What happens to Christians who are not entirely sanctified by the end of their lives? How can such imperfect people transit into the perfect state of the world to come? Catholics would say, "We are made ready via the purging of purgatory."

Purgatory understood in terms of sanctification is simply the extension in the life to come of what we clearly see in our present life. Sanctification is a long, painful process that is nonetheless necessary. Christians who have died and who need to be purged of remaining evil would undergo purgation in the interim before the Lord's return. Christians who happen to be alive at the time of Christ's second coming presumably would enter into their own intermediate state. (I say presumably because there is no Scripture that explicitly teaches this idea—it is merely a speculative extension of the logic we are following here.)

Some might worry that such a concept contradicts scriptural texts that promise immediate communion with Christ after death. But there is no reason to fear that Christians in purgatory will not be truly "with the Lord" (2 Cor. 5:8). First, we are "with the Lord" as soon as we are regenerated and are indwelt by the Holy Spirit. Second, the believer would be fully engaged with God in the process of sanctification in purgatory, and thus after death they would be immediately enjoying a communion with the Lord that would only increase moment by moment. (Indeed, Thomas Aquinas, among others, assures us of the constant and consoling presence of the Holy Spirit in purgatory.)

The typical Protestant response to all this talk of purgatory is a simple one: Purgatory isn't taught in the Bible. It certainly is not ever mentioned as such in canonical scriptures, and only enigmatically and implicitly even in the Apocrypha. The Protestant hope typically is that humans will be instantly sanctified of our remaining sinfulness either at the point of death or immediately afterward. Luther's lieutenant Philip

Melanchthon felt that the horrors of death suffice to provide the soul with its final purgation. John Wesley taught that entire sanctification is possible in this life, but he allowed that such a blessing is extremely rare, and his general approach to sanctification was the typical Protestant one: It is a gradual, difficult process extending over one's whole life that is finalized in the traumatic moments surrounding death. As Walls indicates in his essay, Charles Hodge was among those who believed that God could sanctify one instantly at the point of death by sheer divine power, just as Christ healed a man of leprosy even though normally a cure would require extended medical process.

This Protestant hope of more-or-less instant sanctification, however, poses two questions: (1) If sanctification can be given in an instant at the end of life, then why does God not give it to us now? (2) If sanctification is only gradual and difficult in this life, why do we expect that it will be different in the life to come? Ironically enough, one of the main Christian responses to the problem of evil and particularly for the persistence of suffering in the world is that the experience of suffering can promote the process of sanctification. But if sanctification can be granted instantly, then why would God instead compel so many people to endure so much suffering? A more coherent view would be that suffering is sometimes a long process precisely because sanctification itself is necessarily a long process. Even God cannot shorten it to an instant.

We Protestants might still say that purgatory is not explicitly taught in Scripture. But we would have to acknowledge the inconvenient fact that the model of an "express elevator to holiness at death" is *also* not explicitly taught in Scripture. Quite the contrary: this model of instantaneous sanctification seems out of keeping with what *is* explicitly taught in Scripture about the nature of sanctification *and* everything we know about sanctification from experience.

Whatever one makes of this understanding of purgatory, it needs to be kept separate from at least three other questions that tend to arise alongside it. First, purgatory is separate from the possibility of postmortem evangelization. Purgatory is about the sanctification of people who are Christians, whereas postmortem evangelization has to do with the gospel coming to those who did not receive it, or did not receive it in an adequate way, in this life. We have enough to debate in this volume already without opening up other controversies such as the destiny of the un- or inadequately evangelized, so I will leave alone Walls's speculations about postmortem evangelism.

Second, purgatory is separate from a universalism that would transform hell into purgatory—a place in which those who are definitely not believers suffer for their sins (since they do not have Jesus to suffer on their behalf), but then eventually are transformed by the patient ministrations of God, succumb to God's beautiful winsomeness, and eventually find the back door to hell and arrive in heaven. Again, purgatory is the place for the purification of people who already are covered by the blood of Christ, who enjoy a full atonement for their sins, who have already cooperated with the Holy Spirit in the earlier stages of sanctification, and who are now simply undergoing willingly the final readying for full enjoyment of the life to come. One can certainly hold to a Protestant view of purgatory—and, indeed, to a Roman Catholic one—without surrendering a traditional understanding of hell as a place of final judgment. Indeed, Roman Catholics have been keeping a very clear distinction between purgatory and hell for a very long time.

Third, purgatory is separate from the notion that human beings have the capacity to cooperate with God in the processes of salvation. Such views are known by the technical term *synergism*. In this view, purgatory has two exit doors, not just one: A person can choose either to continue in the process until one is finally ready to open the door to heaven, or one can take the other exit and go to hell. (*The Great Divorce* can be read this way.) The perennial question of whether one can finally desert the Lord during the process of sanctification—whether in this life or even in the next—is an argument that I here leave to intramural Protestant theological disputes. The main point for our purposes now is that orthodox monergists can believe in an evangelical version of purgatory as easily as synergists can, since both kinds of Christians believe that sanctification is gradual and difficult and almost never complete at the time of death.

We must never lose sight of the fundamental dynamic in salvation: the grace of God, God's loving power exercised for our salvation. Yet, sinners that we are, we corrupt even the best of teachings, and we easily distort an emphasis on grace and turn it into a free pass to sin, as Paul warned we might (Rom. 6:1). Robust defenses of justification must not occlude equally strong teaching about sanctification. A Protestant understanding of purgatory confirms the inescapable importance of serious and sustained cooperation with God in the difficult but necessary and ultimately joyful discipline of becoming holy.

Sanctification remains a demanding, incremental regimen that cannot be short-circuited in this life. Why should we think there are shortcuts in the next? We might ponder, instead, at least the *prospect* of purgatory and then work out our salvation today in cooperation with the will and work of God as diligently as we can.

ROBIN A. PARRY

Yes ...

Jerry Walls sets out to propose and defend a Protestant-friendly account of purgatory.[51] I think that he has largely succeeded. When understood in terms of sanctification, rather than satisfaction, I see no reason for an evangelical to get overly steamed up about the idea.

Sure, Scripture itself does not directly teach purgatory, so the proposal is of necessity speculative. Nevertheless, it can still claim to be biblical in an extended sense. It is an inference from and extension of ideas taught in Scripture (e.g., the eschatological trial by fire for believers in Malachi 3:3 and 1 Corinthians 3:11–15) and a way of answering a question that naturally arises from what the Bible explicitly teaches (i.e., the need for holiness if we are to see God, and the difficult journey of sanctification that God leads believers on to conform them to the image of Christ). Walls asks, "How is it that persons who die in a state of grace, but are less than fully perfect, are made fit for heaven?" That is a completely legitimate question, and Walls's purgatory is a plausible candidate for an answer.

But ...

The traditional evangelical answer is that God finishes his work of sanctification instantaneously. This idea is typically based on texts such as 1 Corinthians 15:51–52, which says that believers alive at the final resurrection of the dead "shall all be changed, *in a moment, in the twinkling of an eye*, at the last trumpet" (NASB), and 1 John 3:2, which says, "when Christ appears, we shall be like him, for we shall see him as he is." These texts, combined with the lack of an explicit doctrine of purgatory in the Bible, provide the basis for thinking that God finishes

---

51. I would like to thank Brad Jersak for helpful reflections on an earlier draft.

the transformation process in a flash. I would have liked to see Walls engage these passages.

Admittedly, 1 John 3 does not say that we become *instantly* like Jesus; it allows the space for a process. However, 1 Corinthians 15 is somewhat trickier. True, it is speaking of the resurrection body rather than sanctification, but given that Paul sees sin as very much tied in with our fallen humanity—"the flesh"—it is hard to imagine folk with glorified bodies, unaffected by sin and death, needing to be purified from sin. That is not to say that purgatory is incompatible with 1 Corinthians 15. Speculating, we could imagine that God compresses the process into a tiny amount of clock-time (a moment, the twinkling of an eye), but that the believer subjectively experiences it as a protracted process of purification.

If you watch sci-fi movies, you will be familiar with the idea of time passing at different speeds for different people. And it is not simply fiction, as Albert Einstein would tell you. Or we may think of it in the manner that people speak of time slowing down just prior to a car crash. The brain goes into hyperdrive, as it were, and people experience this as time running in slow motion—perhaps their whole life will "flash before their eyes." So God could certainly compress the process of purgatory into a tiny amount of clock time.[52] Maybe, but I would still value a careful exegetical and theological discussion of such texts from defenders of purgatory.

In defense of Walls, the process of transformation itself is important, as he explains so well. Some tricky issues of identity can be raised if someone has been foul-hearted for a lifetime, then instantly becomes perfectly pure and loving. Is this the *same* person, given that there are no intermediate points connecting the journey from state A to state B? Or has the man been annihilated and replaced by someone else who inherits his memories? We would need to grapple with these issues if we desire to bypass purgatory.

---

52. "It is clear that we cannot calculate the 'duration' of this transforming burning in terms of the chronological measurements of this world. The transforming 'moment' of this encounter eludes earthly time-reckoning—it is the heart's time, it is the time of 'passage' to communion with God in the Body of Christ." Benedict XVI, *Spe Salvi* (2007), 47.

Musings on Fire

I am not infrequently asked whether my view of hell is identical to purgatory. Clearly, affirming purgatory is not to affirm universalism! The classical doctrine in all its forms made a sharp distinction between those who go to hell (for whom exit is impossible) and those who go to purgatory (for whom exit is inevitable). Walls, too, makes a distinction between hell and purgatory, albeit one with somewhat fuzzier boundaries. Walls — and for this I commend him — allows for the possibility that one can be saved from hell. He is a cat's whisker (or a freewill theodicy) away from being a universalist. Still, it's a pretty stubborn whisker!

I would like to offer some brief off-the-top-of-my-head theological musings about hell and purgatory inspired by insights offered by Burk, Stackhouse, and Walls. Currently, theologically speaking, I only see men who look to me like trees walking, so please take this as it is intended — mere thinking aloud. (Thinking is allowed.)

Fire as Divine Presence

Consider the image of fire in Scripture. In the first instance, fire is a symbol *of the divine presence*. In divine manifestations, God appears as a blazing torch passing through Abram's sacrifice (Gen. 15:17), in a burning bush (Exod. 3:1–6), in flame atop Mount Sinai (Exod. 19:18; 24:17; Deut. 4:11), as a guiding and protecting pillar of fire (Exod. 14:24), and in flames settling on the heads of the disciples at Pentecost (Acts 2:3). Examples could easily be multiplied. As Burk notes, fire is "an image of God's holy presence." This is not a cuddly image of God, but of God as *mysterium tremendum et fascinans* — the mystery that strikes awe, even dread, into one's heart and yet at the same time is profoundly beautiful and attractive.

Fire as Divine Punishment

Fire is also a symbol of *divine punishment:* the consuming fire destroyed Sodom and Gomorrah for its sin (Gen. 19:24) and burned up Nadab and Abihu (Lev. 10:1–2) and the followers of rebellious Korah (Num. 16:35; 26:10) for their unauthorized cultic activity. All the hell-as-fire texts fit here, too, as Burk and Stackhouse show. Consider also the fearsome warning in Hebrews 10:26ff.

If we deliberately keep on sinning after we have received the knowledge of the truth, no sacrifice for sins is left, but only a fearful expectation of judgment and of *raging fire that will consume the enemies of God....* It is a dreadful thing to fall into the hands of the living God.

Sober words indeed. Hebrews picks up the theme of consuming fire again in 12:28–29. We should worship God "acceptably with reverence and awe, for our God 'is a consuming fire'" (quoting Deut. 4:24). Note: *God himself* is a consuming fire. The fire that burns sinners is the holy divine presence itself. This reminds me of that biblical image in which none can look at God's face (a symbol of direct divine presence) and live (Exod. 33:20).

Hell is something that can only be adequately expressed through contrasting images. It is alienation from God; it is being thrown out of the house in which the divine feast is being celebrated "into outer darkness" (Matt 8:12; 22:13; 25:30); it is being cast into the valley of Gehenna outside the holy city in which God dwells. So on the one hand, hell is where God is *absent*. But this is an image. Divine absence is always paradoxical: an absence-in-presence. So on the other hand, "hell" is not where God is absent, but where he is *all-too-present*. Revelation pictures those who worship the beast being "tormented with burning sulfur *in the presence of ... the Lamb*" (14:10). As we have seen, God himself is holy fire, and when sinners are exposed to that presence, it burns with "fierce holiness."

Fire as Purification

Fire, as Stackhouse observes, is also a symbol of *divine testing and purification*. It can symbolize trials that the saints must undergo, which have the effect of burning away impure elements, leaving only the pure (e.g., 1 Pet. 4:12). Such fire hurts, but is intended for the good of those who undergo it. As Gregory of Nyssa puts it,

> Just as those who refine gold from the dross which it contains not only get this base alloy to melt in the fire, but are obliged to melt the pure gold along with the alloy, and then while this last is being consumed the gold remains, so, while evil is being consumed in the purgatorial fire, the soul that is welded to this evil must inevitably

be in the fire too, until the spurious material alloy is consumed and annihilated by this fire.[53]

What if we take all of these pictures as images of the way that humans encounter the holy presence of God? God's presence is a holy flame, pure and beautiful, but the human experience with that presence will vary depending on the state that one is in when one encounters it. (Think of the contrasting encounters of the Israelites and the Egyptians with the presence of God in the pillar of fire.) Speaking theologically, if one is "in Adam" — sold in slavery to sin and death — then God's presence can be experienced as like burning wrath, retributive punishment, and consuming fire — a great and terrible day of judgment.[54] The corruption in us is utterly incompatible with divine purity, and their meeting creates torment and feels like being cast out, away from life into death and darkness. And it can generate a range of emotional responses in us — weeping and angry gnashing of teeth, despair, and growing realization of the true depths of our brokenness. "Hell," as Stackhouse observes, is "the natural result of a moral agent choosing to separate from God, the source of life."

To speak of God's wrath is to speak of God handing us over to the consequences of our sin (Rom. 1:18–28). However, if we are united to Christ, sharing in his resurrection life, then the *same* holy presence and the *same* divine fire are experienced by us as a purifying fire, as flames of love fitting us for the new creation. I find suggestive the scene Walls quotes from Lewis's *The Great Divorce*, in which those who leave

---

53. Gregory of Nyssa, *On the Soul and the Resurrection* 7 (Crestwood, NY: St. Vladimir Seminary Press, 1993).

54. The early church had to wrestle with the very earthy biblical language about God. The Bible speaks of God's hands, feet, face, ears, eyes, and so on. Did God literally have a body that was located somewhere in the cosmos? Sometimes the Bible pictures God like that, but the language was rightly interpreted symbolically and metaphorically. But what about when Scripture presents God as changing his mind or regretting having done something or being shocked to see something? Again, such language was not seen as true *in a literal way*. God knows all things, sees the end from the beginning, and is Wisdom itself. Now, one of the aspects of the biblical presentation of God the early church wrestled with was wrath. Anger was understood to be something of a vice, but God is perfect. One common proposal in the early church, though not the only one, was that language about God's anger was not to be understood as a *literal* description about God's "feelings" toward someone, but rather as a way of picturing *how it feels to us* when we sinners encounter God's holy presence, have our sins revealed, and are burned by it. We experience it like retributive anger, like our sins catching up with us. On divine anger in the early church, see Paul Gavrilyuk, *The Suffering of the Impassible God: The Dialectics of Patristic Thought* (Oxford: Oxford University Press, 2004), 51–60.

the grey town behind will find that the flames they experienced will not have been hell, but purgatory. The *same flames* can serve different purposes, depending on how we react to them.

We experience the divine presence as "hellfire" precisely when we begin to appreciate the true nature of our corruption in the light of God's purity, and it hurts like hell. It strips away all the illusions we create around ourselves about how sin is not all that bad. Some Orthodox theologians speak of the fires of hell as internal psychological fires as we see ourselves as we are. For this very reason it can serve to turn us away from sin and toward God, toward a new way of being human in Christ.

This self-revelation in light of God's presence can motivate us to abandon self-reliance and to seek the mercy and grace offered in Jesus. It may not do so immediately—humans are complex creatures, and God works with, not against, our free wills (in order to free our wills). But we are also creatures created in God's image, whose hearts are restless until they find rest in God. At the deepest level of our humanity we *all* desire the good, the beautiful, and the true; we *all* desire God, even if that desire is buried beneath layers of crud.

This is nothing to do with God torturing people to love him. God is simply manifesting his holy presence to people. That presence calls us to account and judges us. But in so doing, it points toward a better way. As people turn toward grace, they will find that their hell becomes purgatory, that the consuming fire becomes purifying fire; they experience "the furious love of God" as "everlasting kindness" and "forever-enduring mercy." Indeed, they see in hindsight that it always was this. And so, ultimately, they will be fitted for and welcomed into the New Jerusalem, through gates that never shut, where the tree of life bears healing leaves and the presence of God will be like a life-giving stream.

CONCLUSION

PRESTON M. SPRINKLE

The four essayists have accomplished what they were enlisted to do: lay out with clarity and depth the biblical and theological evidence for their views. As promised in the Introduction, none of the four authors deny the existence of hell. Denny Burk defends a traditional view of hell by examining ten scriptural passages in detail, interpreting them with depth and clarity. John Stackhouse agrees with Burk that hell is a place of irreversible punishment, but argues that its duration is limited. Unbelievers will be destroyed after they face judgment. Robin Parry believes that hell is real and that people will endure ongoing punishment; however, he argues that the biblical narrative looks forward to an ultimate reconciliation of all things, including everyone in hell. All people will ultimately be redeemed. Jerry Walls agrees with Burk's traditional view of hell, but argues that believers will undergo a time of postmortem sanctification whereby they will be made holy in preparation for eternal life.

While I have my own leanings, I will do my best to evaluate each view as fairly as I can.

Eternal Conscious Torment

Denny Burk opens his argument with a passionate plea that biblical interpreters should come to the hell question with a high view of God and a high view of sin. "We tend to have a diminished view of sin — and thus of the judgment due to sin — because we have a diminished view of God." Burk then suggests that "the question of eternal conscious torment really does come down to who God is." The implication is that an interpreter with a high view of God and a high view of sin will embrace — and celebrate — the eternal conscious view of hell, insofar as the exegetical evidence is clear.

Burk argues that it *is* clear based on ten passages: Isaiah 66:22–24; Daniel 12:2–3; Matthew 18:6–9; 25:31–46; Mark 9:42–48;

2 Thessalonians 1:6–10; Jude 7, 13; Revelation 14:9–11; 20:10, 14–15. Through rigorous exegesis, Burk contends that all of these passages teach that hell consists of final separation, unending experience, and just retribution. His case is both clear and compelling—a robust defense of the traditional view. Most of all, Burk engages the topic, not just as a scholar, but as a pastor, rounding off his discussion with several practical pleas.

I agree with Burk's essay at many points. In particular, the aspects of "final separation" and "just retribution" certainly appear to be present in the ten passages he cites. I wasn't as convinced, however, that the aspect of "unending experience" is as clearly taught by these passages as Burk thinks it is.

For instance, Burk argues that "the dead bodies" of Isaiah 66:24 are experiencing never-ending torment, since the text says "the worms that eat them will not die" and "the fire that burns them will not be quenched."[1] The text, he says, therefore offers "explicit support for the traditional view." If Isaiah was referring to eternal conscious torment, it's *anything* but explicit. Burk himself admits that "the dead bodies" must refer to resurrected bodies given to the wicked, capable of withstanding the destruction that would otherwise be wrought by the everlasting worm and the unquenchable fire: "Though not mentioned specifically in this text, this scene seems to assume that God's enemies have been given a body fit for an unending punishment." Not only is the resurrection of the wicked not mentioned in the text, but the "dead bodies" of Isaiah 66:24 are the same ones that are "slain by the LORD" in verse 16: "For with fire and with his sword the LORD will execute judgment on all people, and many will be *those slain by the LORD*." It's quite a stretch, then, to say that people on earth who have been "slain by the Lord" and whose "dead bodies" lay lifeless on the ground are actually being tormented in hell forever and ever. At least, it's far from being "explicit" as Burk promises. (The Isaiah 26:19 text Burk uses to support his argument only references the resurrection of the righteous and not the wicked.)

Moreover, the reference to the "unquenchable fire" does not clearly point to eternal conscious torment. In the Old Testament, the idea of an

---

1. All Scripture citations are from the NIV unless otherwise noted.

"unquenchable fire" in contexts of judgment communicates that God's wrath cannot be prevented or reversed, not that it is poured out unendingly. See, for instance, Ezekiel 20:47–48; Jeremiah 17:27; and Amos 5:6, all of which use the same Hebrew word *kabah* ("unquenchable") to refer to a fire so strong that it can't be extinguished before it completes its work. That is, *kabah* doesn't in itself mean that the fire literally never ends, forever consuming and consuming the living corpses without ever fully consuming them. *Kabah* highlights the strength of the fire (i.e., God's judgment) and not its duration — that it is incapable of being *put* out, not that it will never *die* out.

The reference to the worm that "will not die" is trickier. It should be noted that it is only the worm that "will not die," and not the "dead bodies" of people. In any case, does Isaiah promise that God will grant these worms an everlasting afterlife? Will they somehow be permitted to nibble from the Tree of Life? Surely Isaiah is using the image of an undying worm as a metaphor. And standing in parallel to the unquenchable fire, the worms probably underscore the strength and surety of God's judgment, not its duration, very much like the scavenging beasts and birds of Jeremiah 7:33 that won't be frightened away from the dead bodies upon which they feed.

When Isaiah's "explicit support for the traditional view" is reexamined, other texts prove to be less clear as well. Burk rightly points out that Mark 9:48 alludes to Isaiah 66:24 when it says, "their worm does not die and their fire is not quenched." Inasmuch as Jesus is rightly interpreting Isaiah, he probably doesn't have eternal conscious torment in mind. Again, Isaiah's images, interpreted in light of their use elsewhere in Scripture, probably don't mean eternal conscious torment.

Burk's use of Jude 7 is particularly curious. Jude offers the destruction of Sodom and Gomorrah — not their torment — as an example of what will happen to the ungodly. Citing this text, Burk argues that "the annihilation of Sodom and Gomorrah does not imply some kind of eschatological annihilation of the wicked in hell. Rather, the fire that rained down on the infamous cities was an example of 'eternal fire' or 'fire of the age.'" Yet, Jude says that in their earthly destruction, Sodom and Gomorrah "are exhibited as an example in undergoing the punishment of eternal fire" (Jude 7 NASB). You can read about this destruction in Genesis 19. There is no ongoing torment in that passage, and the cities of Sodom and Gomorrah aren't still burning in an "eternal fire." The phrase "eternal fire" (*puros aioniou*) is stock Old Testament imagery for the intensity of God's judgment and — again — not its duration.

This meaning of Jude 7 is confirmed by the parallel in 2 Peter 2. Jude and 2 Peter 2 show tremendous overlap in flow of thought, imagery, argumentation, and meaning. (And no one disputes this.) This is why 2 Peter 2:6, which parallels Jude 7, is an important cross-reference:

> [God] condemned the cities of Sodom and Gomorrah by burning them to ashes, and made them an example of what is going to happen to the ungodly.

Burk doesn't deal with this passage, so I don't know what he would say. But the text clearly says that in "burning ... to ashes" Sodom and Gomorrah are "an example of what is going to happen to the ungodly." The parallels in thought and terminology to Jude 7 are striking. It seems that 2 Peter 2:6 (and Jude 7, I would argue) cannot be interpreted with exegetical honesty to support the traditional view.

To my mind, the best text Burk enlists in his case for the traditional view is Matthew 25:46, in which Jesus says that the wicked "will go away to eternal punishment, but the righteous to eternal life." The parallel between "eternal punishment" and "eternal life" strongly suggests that the punishment of the lost will last forever, since the life given to the saved will last forever. Still, Burk doesn't entertain the possibility — some would say probability — that the adjective "eternal" (*aiōnios*) doesn't describe the *act* of punishing, but the *results* of that act, and that Jesus here warns not of eternal punish*ing*, but of an eternal punish*ment*, one described as death and destruction elsewhere in Scripture (Matt. 10:28; John 3:16; Rom. 6:23). After all, when Hebrews 9:12 refers to our "eternal redemption," it most probably doesn't refer to a never-ending act of redeem*ing*, but to the never-ending redemp*tion* that results from God's saving work.

Burk may be right in affirming the eternal conscious view of hell. This view certainly has the support of many towering theologians throughout history, and that tradition is nothing to sneeze at. Still, it doesn't appear that it's as clearly revealed in the texts Burk uses to support it.

Terminal Punishment

What I love about John Stackhouse's essay is that it brings a healthy blend of theology, philosophy, and biblical exegesis to bear on the question of hell. Debates on this topic often linger on philosophical arguments without sufficient exegesis, or expound exegetical details without addressing theological incongruences. Stackhouse, however, addresses various questions on all three levels—philosophy, theology, and exegesis—and brings them into interaction with one another. Nevertheless, Stackhouse prioritizes biblical exegesis as he argues for annihilationism, or what he calls "terminal punishment."

There are several elements of Stackhouse's case that I would like to reiterate and affirm. First, his discussion of the term "eternal" (Greek *aiônios*) needs to be re-read and seriously considered. Interpreters sometimes assume that when describing an action noun like "punishment," *aiônios* always means that the action carries on throughout eternity. Stackhouse shows, however, that this simply isn't true. "The crucial distinction here," he argues, "is between an event or an action that occurs for only a segment of time, on the one hand, and the *result* of that event or action that is indeed 'without end,' on the other. Thus the event or action itself can properly be called 'eternal' because of its everlasting *implication*." Again and likewise, it is the *result* of God's redeeming work that is without end in the phrase "eternal redemption."

In other words, the duration of hell must be argued from the context. It cannot be assumed from the word *aiônios* alone.

Second, Stackhouse points out that the dominant biblical language used to describe the fate of the wicked is language that suggests some sort of "terminal punishment." Words like "death," "destruction," "perish," and "extinction" are used more frequently than any others, and their natural (and lexical) meanings suggest finality rather than an ongoing conscious existence. The lexicon only gets us so far, however. Careful attention must be paid to the context of each relevant passage.

Third, Stackhouse draws attention to the scriptural theme that "the wages of sin is *death*" (Rom. 6:23). The punishment that fits the crime, according to the Bible, is that people would suffer death for their sin, not that they would be tortured forever and ever. Death—the cessation of life; *capital* punishment—is the consequence for sin.

Lastly, Stackhouse demonstrates that immortality is not intrinsic to the fallen human person, but is a gift given to believers through the death and resurrection of Jesus — hence the phrase "conditional immortality" is often used to describe John's position. If people are not immortal, then left to their natural state they would die at some point, and only those who believe in Jesus would go on living forever. All the other views of hell represented in this volume, however, maintain that *everyone* will live forever. Jerry Walls and Denny Burk believe that some will live forever in everlasting bliss, others in everlasting conscious torment. Robin Parry believes that everyone will live on in some sort of torment until they repent and then forever in eternal bliss. Stackhouse is the odd man out, since he believes that the wicked will not live forever; their life will be terminated at some point.

According to Stackhouse, the biblical witness is quite clear that living forever is contingent upon believing in Jesus Christ (2 Tim. 1:10; 1 Cor. 15:53–55; cf. Gen. 3:22). The other contributors must explain from Scripture how it is that those who do *not* believe in Jesus will be granted immortality. Parry has an easier time with this question, since he believes everyone *will* believe in Jesus and therefore experience never-ending life, but he must still explain how the mortal lost will be capable of enduring hell long enough to believe in the first place. They must, according to Parry's view, be granted some sort of immortality permit until they are given a full-fledged immortality license after they repent. But I digress.

This does lead, however, to some criticism I have of Stackhouse's case — criticism that actually overlaps with my agreement. When Stackhouse talks about human immortality, he argues that "eternal life is a *gift* of God to *believers* (John 3:16; 1 Cor. 15:50–54)." This is certainly true, but the biblical concept of "eternal life" isn't limited to its duration — i.e., living forever. It equally emphasizes a *quality* of life and not *just* its duration. Jesus says, "This is eternal life: that they know you, the only true God, and Jesus Christ, whom you have sent" (John 17:3). So John 3:16 and other passages that promise eternal life to believers may refer to the quality of life uniquely given to believers. They do not in themselves demand that only believers will live forever *at all*. The wicked and righteous both could theoretically live forever, while only believers experience *eternal* life — biblically conceived.

Additionally, by way of critique, I do not feel that Stackhouse has thoroughly addressed the passages typically pointed to as support for the traditional view that the wicked will suffer never-ending torment in hell. He argues that Matthew 25:46 is "utterly unambiguous" in speaking to the irreversible results of the punishment (thus confirming his view) and not its never-ending process. Maybe he is right, but I need to see further robust exegetical evidence to prove his point. At face value, the text seems to be capable of going either way.

I also found his treatment of Revelation 14:9–11 to be lacking, or at least a more difficult sell than the plainer reading offered by the traditional view. This text says that those who worship the beast "will be tormented," not just killed, and that "there will be no rest day or night for those who worship the beast and its image." Maybe this is symbolic; maybe it does not refer to the act of punishing. But these need to be proven through exegesis and not just assumed. "No rest day or night" is an odd way to describe someone who has died the death of a terminal punishment.

At the very least, any honest interpreter should not be shocked that so many Christians have historically affirmed what Revelation 14 seems on its face to affirm: The wicked will be punished forever and ever. We can quibble over finer points of exegesis, but the traditional view is not without at least some exegetical fodder.

Ultimate Reconciliation

I found Robin Parry's essay to be a fascinating read! And, if I can be quite honest, I think it is a game-changer. I do not say this because I agree with his ultimate conclusion (I don't), but because he has brought what is often assumed to be a heretical view into the arena of biblical exegesis and theology. Christians can no longer dismiss his view as unorthodox. We must now actually crack open our Bibles and, like the noble Bereans (Acts 17:11), see if these things are so.

Universalism—or ultimate reconciliation—is often dismissed in light of its association with pluralism, the view that all roads lead to heaven. Parry has shown that it's much more complicated than that. There are many biblical passages and themes that can be used to support ultimate reconciliation, as Parry has shown. Popular-level writers like Rob Bell have done universalists a disservice by relying on emotional appeals and rhetoric (and some rather torturous exegesis) in arguing that love will win out in the end. Unfortunately, Parry's view has been lumped in with such exegetically anemic arguments that win the crowd but cause biblical scholars to wince with embarrassment.

So what are we to make of Parry's case? I will say up front that if Stackhouse is right, then Parry is wrong. If the wicked receive terminal punishment (death) when Christ returns, then they will not be around thereafter to accept Christ. While the traditional view (including Walls's purgatorial view) logically makes room for Parry's contention that the lost will one day repent and be freed from hell, Stackhouse's terminal punishment view rules it out.

But if Stackhouse is wrong, then what are we to make of Parry's view of ultimate reconciliation?

First, I want to emphasize that Parry is advocating a view that is centered on the atoning work of Christ. He believes that the death of Jesus is so powerful, his blood so mighty, that it is able to overcome and reverse human unbelief. If anyone reads Parry's essay and concludes that he thinks "all roads lead to heaven," then they haven't thoughtfully read it. That's not what Parry believes. He believes that the death and resurrection of Christ are the only means of salvation and that God's free offer of forgiveness is available to those who will repent and believe, both in this life and in the next. After all, isn't the God of today the same God of tomorrow? Why would the forgiving God turn into an unforgiving God in the future?

Evangelicals must think deeply and critically—indeed, *biblically*—about Parry's argument. And if I can be completely honest, I hope that Parry is right.

However, I still find some exegetical questions unanswered. Again, all of the biblical evidence for terminal punishment rules out Parry's view, and I do not think he has successfully explained all of the many passages that appear to support annihilationism. Until he does, the jury is still out, in my mind, regarding the strength of ultimate reconciliation over against terminal punishment.

Parry also argues from the Old Testament that God's "punishment" of Israel is often conceived in terms of "refinement," and not bare, retributive torment or destruction. In other words, the exile—the ultimate punishment from an old covenant perspective—was never designed to terminate Israel's existence, nor to inflict an indefinite duration of torment. Rather, the exile was intended to refine Israel, burn off the dross, and shape a righteous people more fit for the kingdom. The Old Testament, Parry argues, holds out hope beyond the grave for those who are judged.

This argument seems, however, to beg a critical question: To the extent that punishment in the Old Testament was intended to refine *corporately*, was it equally and always intended to refine *individually*? Parry appears to assume that it was, but I am not as prepared to grant that premise. Remember, most of the Israelites were killed in the Babylonian invasion (Ezek. 5:1–12); only a remnant were exiled and even fewer returned. In other words, most Israelites did not find hope on the other side of judgment. Most were killed as a result of God's covenantal wrath toward sin. And as Stackhouse pointed out in his response to Parry, even the Old Testament, in all its talk of refinement, only holds out hope for the remnant of Israel (Hos. 1:9–10), and not the entire nation. (And the New Testament suggests that Jewish and Gentile believers of the New Covenant age constitute the remnant of Israel [Rom. 9–10].)

Corporate refinement doesn't burn off the dross of every individual. When God punished Israel by making her wander for forty years, prohibiting her from entering the Promised Land until the older generation had passed away (Num. 14:26–35), their punishment may have been intended (at least in part) to refine *the nation*, but there is no indication that it was designed to refine *those who died*. Likewise, in wiping out all but Noah's family, the flood may have been to purify *mankind* (Gen. 6:11–8:19), but I see no reason to believe it was to purify *those who were destroyed*. By pointing to these events as examples of what is to take place on the Last Day, Peter and Jude suggest (2 Pet. 2:5; Jude 5) that it will be humanity that is corporately refined, and not the wicked themselves, who will instead be burned away like so much dross.

If Parry is right to extrapolate from punishment that refines corporately in the Old Testament to punishment that refines individually, and if the New Testament shares this view of punishment as individual refinement (rather than as finality), then Parry may have a strong case. But it does not appear that the New Testament holds out the kind of "hope beyond the grave" for the wicked that Parry argues is expressed by the Old Testament.

From my vantage point, the irreversibility of God's judgment upon the wicked does appear to be a rather pervasive theme in the New Testament. We see this in a myriad of images that describe the final state of the wicked as burned up chaff, weeds, and branches (Matt. 3:12; 7:19; 13:40; John 15:6); a destroyed house, discarded fish, an uprooted plant, and a chopped down tree (Matt. 7:27; 13:48; 15:13; Luke 13:7); ground-up powder or chopped-up pieces (Matt. 21:41, 44; 24:51). Even though these are all images and probably not literal descriptions, they nevertheless all suggest that the judgment of the wicked is final.

God's irreversible judgment is seen most clearly in New Testament terms for destruction (*apollumi*, *oletheros*). While it's true that these terms sometimes mean only "ruin" and not "destruction" (e.g., Mark 3), whenever *apollumi* ("destroy, kill, ruin") is used in the Synoptic gospels in the active voice and describes a personal agent acting toward another personal agent, the meaning is always "kill" or "put to death" (e.g., Matt. 2:13; 10:28; 21:41; 27:20; Mark 3:6; 9:22; Luke 6:9).[2] This meaning appears to be intended in nearly every other use of *apollumi* in the New Testament where one agent is acting upon another agent, especially in contexts where future judgment is in view.

To these images and words we can add the destruction of Sodom and Gomorrah, which is often viewed as a template for the future judgment of the wicked (Luke 17:27, 29, 32; 2 Pet. 2:6; Jude 7). As we saw earlier, when Peter says that Sodom's "burning ... to ashes" is "an example of what is going to happen to the ungodly" (2 Pet. 2:6), Parry must interpret Peter as *really* meaning that "burning ... to ashes" is *not* "an example of what is going to happen to the ungodly."

Parry does raise an interesting question about the fate of Sodom in Ezekiel 16:53–58. There God says he "will restore the fortunes of Sodom and her daughters and of Samaria and her daughters" (v. 53). Does this mean that God will literally resurrect the citizens of Sodom and give them eternal life? While this reading is possible, I do not think it is likely. For instance, the prophet Ezekiel is notorious for his use of rhetorical moves that push theological (and logical) boundaries. In the same chapter, he describes God as adopting a child off the streets and

---

2. See Glen Peoples, "Introduction to Evangelical Conditionalism," in Christopher M. Date, Gregory G. Stump, and Joshua W. Anderson (eds.), *Rethinking Hell: Readings in Evangelical Conditionalism* (Eugene, OR: Cascade Books, 2014), 21–22.

then marrying her (vv. 1–14). Is YHWH an incestuous God? Take also chapter 23 which, according to a literal reading, says God has two wives: Oholah and Oholibah.

Surely Ezekiel's rhetoric should not be pressed into such a logical box. The rather positive evaluation of Sodom is designed to shame the southern kingdom of Judah: "be ashamed and bear your disgrace, *for you have made your sisters appear righteous*" (Ezek. 16:52). Ezekiel's focus is on the wickedness of Judah, not the future salvation of ancient Sodom. Jesus employs a similar rhetorical move when he describes Sodom as being better off than the Jewish cities of Chorazin, Bethsaida, and Capernaum (Matt. 12:20–24). And Jesus says that Sodom will be judged and not ultimately saved, as do both Peter and Jude.

Other passages appear to work against Parry's argument as well, passages in which the irreversible nature of God's judgment is explicitly stated. Take Luke 13, for instance, which goes unmentioned by Parry. Luke records Jesus' parable of the narrow door. "Once the owner of the house gets up and closes the door, you will stand outside knocking and pleading, 'Sir, open the door for us'" (13:25). According to Parry's view, the opportunity to repent and enter the door remains an everlasting option. But Jesus' parable is quite clear that there will be a time when the door will be shut and never reopened. The imagery of weeping and gnashing of teeth in verse 28 suggests that Jesus has the afterlife in view.

Although I think Parry's view faces many exegetical hurdles, I want to highlight two of his arguments that I found particularly strong. I won't offer my own response here; I want to commend these arguments to you, the reader, in hopes that you would consider their strength.

First, Paul says in Romans 5 that "just as one trespass resulted in condemnation for *all people*, so also one righteous act resulted in justification and life for *all people*" (5:18). If the first reference to "all people" means everyone — the most plausible meaning in light of the context — then what must the second reference to "all people" mean? The notion that the first means "all" while the second means only "some" appears to be exegetically suspect, to say the least.

Second, Revelation 15 says "*All nations will come and worship before you*, for your righteous acts have been revealed" (v. 4). As Parry points out, the phrase "the nations" in Revelation always refers to wicked people who "fail to heed a final call to repentance (14:6), and join in the final battle against the saints and the Lamb (20:8), thus becoming the objects of God's eschatological wrath (11:8; 12:5; 19:15)." Still, Revelation appears to hold out hope for "the nations" in the end, both in 15:4 and in 21:24–25, where the gates of New Jerusalem are open for the nations to enter. When I took Greek Exegesis in seminary, I was taught that one way to figure out what a word or phrase means is to look at how the biblical author uses the phrase elsewhere in the book. Since "the nations" always (according to Parry) refers to wicked people in Revelation, then according to the rules of my exegetical handbook, I ought to conclude that "all nations" means *everyone* in Revelation 15:4 and that *everyone* "will come and worship" God.

I will let you, the reader, chew on these arguments.

Purgatory

Jerry Walls's essay is different from the other three, since his focus is on the afterlife awaiting the righteous rather than the wicked. As he says both in his essay and in his response to Denny Burk, Walls is a traditionalist when it comes to the nature and duration of hell for the wicked. That is, unbelievers will suffer everlasting conscious torment in hell. However, Walls's focus is not on developing and defending this view; rather, he examines and defends what has traditionally been known as a Roman Catholic view of the afterlife for the righteous, bringing it back to the Protestant table for consideration.

Walls makes a crucial distinction between two different theological views of purgatory. One view says that purgatory is a means of *satisfaction*, while the other view says it is a means of *sanctification*. (Logically, of course, one could believe in both.) "Whereas the sanctification model is about moral and spiritual transformation, the satisfaction model is about exacting punishment to pay a debt of justice." Walls points out that when the Reformers rejected the doctrine of purgatory, they explicitly rejected the satisfaction model because they believed it was a denial of Christ's atoning work on the cross. However, as Walls points out:

> To reject the satisfaction model of purgatory is not necessarily to reject the sanctification model. The sanctification model of purgatory offers a fundamentally different account of why we need purgatory. Indeed, the sanctification model of purgatory is entirely

compatible with Protestant theology, and moreover, is an altogether natural fit in some versions of Protestant theology.

I draw attention to this point, since it opens the door for Protestants to reconsider, or consider for the first time, whether the "sanctification model" of purgatory has any biblical or theological merit. Indeed, Walls says it does.

Biblically, Walls points to passages such as Hebrews 12:14 and Revelation 21:27, which say that the righteous must be pure and holy if they are to enter the presence of the Lord. That is, believers must be *sanctified* even though the payment for their sin has been *satisfied*. These passages refer to the outcome of our sanctification, which, as Walls points out, involves both divine and human agency (e.g., Phil. 2:12–13). Because sanctification involves both divine and human agency in this life, then it logically—or theologically—follows that those who die before being fully sanctified will continue to undergo the process of sanctification in the afterlife.

Walls admits that the doctrine of purgatory is not explicitly taught in Scripture (though see 1 Cor. 3:10–16); rather, it is a theological inference from other biblical doctrines. Helpful here is his appeal to the Trinity as an analogy: The Bible never uses the word *Trinity* nor explicitly offers a Nicene formulation, but the plurality of divine persons combined with the singularity of God provide the scriptural basis for the doctrine of the Trinity.

I commend Walls for writing such a clear and engaging essay. He has definitely given me much to think about. My primary question, though, has to do with the aforementioned lack of biblical witness to the doctrine of purgatory—even the sanctification model. The New Testament talks a lot about sanctification. Hardly a page goes by on which believers are not encouraged to pursue holiness. Likewise, the New Testament often mentions the future resurrection of believers. It seems odd to me, therefore, that something so crucial to both of these themes—a time of sanctification before resurrection—would be left up to theological inference.

Furthermore, as Robin Parry points out in his response to Walls, the New Testament seemingly promises instant transformation when Jesus returns in passages like 1 Corinthians 15:51–52, which says that believers "will all be changed — in a flash, in the twinkling of an eye, at the last trumpet." Similarly, 1 John 3:2 says that "when Christ appears, we shall be like him, for we shall see him as he is." To Parry's texts I would add 1 Thessalonians 4:13–17, as well as Philippians 3:20–21, which says "the Lord Jesus Christ … will transform our lowly bodies so that they will be like his glorious body" (cf. Rom. 8:18–23). And while the New Testament does not explore in much detail the immediate afterlife of believers (i.e., their intermediate state between death and resurrection), the two passages that do mention this state (2 Cor. 5:1–5; Phil. 1:21–23) refer to being in the presence of Christ without any mention of a prior stage of purgatorial preparation.

So we find texts that appear to speak of instant transformation when Christ returns, accomplished by divine agency, yet no clear text speaks about a period of synergistic transformation between a person's death and resurrection. This leads me to be somewhat suspicious of the doctrine of purgatory, even if a Protestant theology of the cross might allow for it.

Where Do We Go from Here?

This book is designed to spur the reader into thinking more deeply about various Christian views on the afterlife, particularly the nature of hell. Again, every author affirms the existence of hell; they only disagree about its nature. And each provided solid scriptural and theological arguments for his view. As I said in the introduction: Bible-believing Christians must wrestle with these views and not just dismiss them out of hand.

Some conservative Christians will probably consider Parry's "Ultimate Reconciliation" and Walls's "Purgatory" to be outside the bounds of evangelical Christianity. However, I would only want to remind the reader, again, that Walls's version of purgatory does not conflict with a Protestant theology of the atonement, nor was it the brand of purgatory that was rejected by the Reformers. Walls's essay must be evaluated by its theological merit.

Parry's essay might have ruffled some evangelical feathers, but no one can deny that his essay is heavily driven by biblical exegesis. Any self-proclaimed evangelical will — or should — appreciate Parry's unashamed commitment to the authoritative word of God, to the rigorous exegesis of specific passages, and to the serious application of biblical theology. I have expressed my own disagreement with his essay, but this should not be seen as taking away from my utmost admiration of Parry's addiction to the Bible and love for its Author.

I expect much discussion to ensue from both Burk's and Stackhouse's essays. Burk has shown that the so-called "traditional" view is not just traditional; it aims to take seriously several biblical texts that seem to suggest it. While I find some passages stronger than others, it should not surprise readers that this view has been held by so many Christians throughout church history. Annihilationism is often thought to be a slippery step toward universalism, but as I pointed out, it is the only view of hell that logically rules out universalism. While some people have rejected the traditional view in favor of annihilationism for sentimental reasons—they just couldn't stomach eternal conscious torment—Stackhouse has shown that there is a wealth of biblical support for the view.

Again, Bible-believing Christians must examine the relevant passages (and there are a lot of them) to see if annihilationism carries more biblical weight than the other views. At the very least, any honest exegete should agree that annihilationism is a credible—indeed biblical—evangelical option.

As the discussion moves forward, here are four areas that deserve further exploration. These in no way exhaust the questions interpreters should pursue, and at least some of these questions have been addressed in scholarly articles and monographs. In any case, these are the four that came to mind as I reflected on the essays in this book.

First, while the Greek word *aiônios* ("everlasting") was briefly addressed, the complexity and variations of meaning need to be kept at the forefront of any discussion of hell.[3] Further research must also be done to test claims that *aiônios* either describes an action's results as everlasting, or that it doesn't mean everlasting to begin with. Unfortunately, merely quoting passages from an English translation of a text that uses *aiônios* will not get us very far.

Second, more exegetical work must be done on the Greek words for destruction (*apollumi*, *oletheros*, and others), which are the most common

---

3. See Ilaria Ramelli and David Konstan, *Terms for Eternity: Aiônios and Aïdios in Classical and Christian Texts* (Piscataway, NJ: Gorgias, 2013).

terms used to describe the fate of the wicked. Traditionalists will argue against annihilationism by pointing out that "destroy" can sometimes mean "ruin." Annihilationists will say that *apollumi* means "kill" or "put to death." Each group cites its favorite passages. What is needed is a more thorough examination of how these words are used in the New Testament and in cognate literature. When exactly, for example, does *apollumi* mean "ruin" (and not "kill"), and when does it mean "to put to death?"

Third, there is still too much fear-rhetoric surrounding this subject, and I was happy to see most of this avoided in this book. If someone expresses doubts about the traditional view—calling them a heretic, liberal, or soft on sin—it doesn't get anybody very far in understanding what the *Bible* actually says about the topic. Fear-driven exegesis rarely yields honest results. As the discussion moves forward, we must put to death (and not merely ruin) cowardly power-moves that demonize advocates of views sometimes considered unorthodox.

Fourth, the relevant passages must be examined in light of their Jewish and Greco-Roman background. How does the New Testament agree with or depart from its Jewish roots? Do we find evidence of ultimate reconciliation or purgatory in Judaism? How are images of hell understood by first-century Jews? And how do Greco-Roman views of the afterlife inform certain passages such as 2 Corinthians 5:1–5, as well as 2 Peter 2:4, which uses the mythological term *tartarus*?

Hopefully this book has opened the door for more fruitful discussions about this important topic.

SCRIPTURE INDEX

SUBJECT INDEX

AUTHOR INDEX

Counterpoints Biblical Studies Collection: 8-Volume Set

Resources for Understanding
Controversial Issues in the Bible

*Stanley N. Gundry, Series Editor; Matthew
Barrett, Kenneth Berding, Mike F. Bird, Ardel
B. Caneday, Charles Halton, Jonathan Lunde,
C. Marvin Pate, Alan P. Stanley, Wayne G.
Strickland, Editors*

The *Counterpoints Biblical Studies Collection: 8-Volume Set* is a value for readers (the total retail value of the individual books is over $155), covering topics in the area of biblical studies including volumes on the historical Adam, the genre of the early chapters of Genesis, the Canaanite genocide, the New Testament use of the Old Testament, the apostle Paul, and more.

With volumes featuring contributions from some of today's most respected scholars, these books represent the very best in Christian scholarship. Contributors include Michael F. Bird, Darrell L. Bock, James D. G. Dunn, Luke Timothy Johnson, Tremper Longman III, Douglas J. Moo, Thomas R. Schreiner, John H. Walton, Gordon J. Wenham, and many more.

The *Counterpoints Biblical Studies Collection: 8-Volume Set* includes the following volumes:

- *Five Views on Law and Gospel*
- *Four Views on the Apostle Paul*
- *Four Views on the Book of Revelation*
- *Four Views on the Historical Adam*
- *Four Views on the Role of Works at the Final Judgment*
- *Genesis: History, Fiction, or Neither?: Three Views on the Bible's Earliest Chapters*
- *Show Them No Mercy: Four Views on God and Canaanite Genocide*
- *Three Views on the New Testament Use of the Old Testament*

The Counterpoints series provides a forum for comparison and critique of different views on issues important to Christians.